WE WILL BE FREE

LIBRARY OF RELIGIOUS BIOGRAPHY

Mark A. Noll, Kathryn Gin Lum, and Heath W. Carter, series editors

Long overlooked by historians, religion has emerged in recent years as a key factor in understanding the past. From politics to popular culture, from social struggles to the rhythms of family life, religion shapes every story. Religious biographies open a window to the sometimes surprising influence of religion on the lives of influential people and the worlds they inhabited.

The Library of Religious Biography is a series that brings to life important figures in United States history and beyond. Grounded in careful research, these volumes link the lives of their subjects to the broader cultural contexts and religious issues that surrounded them. The authors are respected historians and recognized authorities in the historical period in which their subject lived and worked.

Marked by careful scholarship yet free of academic jargon, the books in this series are well-written narratives meant to be read and enjoyed as well as studied.

Titles include:

*A Heart Lost in Wonder: The Life and Faith of **Gerard Manley Hopkins***
by Catharine Randall

***Abraham Lincoln**: Redeemer President, 2nd edition*
by Allen C. Guelzo

*Strength for the Fight: The Life and Faith of **Jackie Robinson***
by Gary Scott Smith

***Harriet Beecher Stowe**: A Spiritual Life*
by Nancy Koester

***Howard Thurman** and the Disinherited: A Religious Biography*
by Paul Harvey

For a complete list of published volumes, see the back of this volume.

WE WILL BE FREE

The Life and Faith of Sojourner Truth

—

Nancy Koester

WILLIAM B. EERDMANS PUBLISHING COMPANY
GRAND RAPIDS, MICHIGAN

Wm. B. Eerdmans Publishing Co.
4035 Park East Court SE, Grand Rapids, Michigan 49546
www.eerdmans.com

Published 2023
Printed in the United States of America

29 28 27 26 25 24 23   1 2 3 4 5 6 7

ISBN 978-0-8028-7247-0

Library of Congress Cataloging-in-Publication Data

Names: Koester, Nancy, 1954– author.
Title: We will be free : the life and faith of Sojourner Truth / Nancy Koester.
Description: Grand Rapids, Michigan : William B. Eerdmans Publishing
    Company, [2023] | Series: Library of religious biography | Includes in-
    dex. | Summary: "An exploration of the ways faith animated the life and
    activism of Sojourner Truth, pathbreaking abolitionist and suffragette"–
    Provided by publisher.
Identifiers: LCCN 2022023808 | ISBN 9780802872470
Subjects: LCSH: Truth, Sojourner, 1799–1883. | Truth, Sojourner, 1799–1883–
    Religion. | African American abolitionists–Biography. | Abolitionists–
    United States–Biography. | Social reformers–United States–Biography.
Classification: LCC E185.97.T8 K64 2023 | DDC 326/.8092 [B]–dc23/
    eng/20220525
LC record available at https://lccn.loc.gov/2022023808

For Craig

I am pleading for my people, a poor downtrodden race
Who dwell in freedom's boasted land with no abiding place.

I am pleading that my people may have their rights restored
For they have long been toiling, and yet had no reward.

While I bear upon my body, the scars of many a gash,
I'm pleading for my people who groan beneath the lash.

Yet those oppressors steeped in guilt—I still would have them live
For I have learned of Jesus, to suffer and forgive!

I plead with you to sympathize with sighs and groans and scars,
And note how base the tyranny beneath the stripes and stars.

—Sojourner Truth

Contents

Foreword

Why Truth? Why now?

Sojourner Truth's name conveys the image of a towering woman of strength to many. In pictures, her height of five feet eleven seems apparent even when she is sitting. Born Isabella Baumfree (or Bomefree) in the waning years of the eighteenth century, Truth was known for her powerful oratory, which captivated many of her abolitionist hearers, and well over 150 years later, she continues to resonate with a new generation of readers with her familiar words, "Ain't I a woman?" Her life also captures both the process of grief and the powerful reclamation of personhood. While enslaved, she was separated from her parents and siblings and auctioned off, "along with a flock of sheep" (see below, 5–6). She gave birth to five children who, like their mother, were trapped by America's chattel slavery. Stripped of her humanity, she lived in what W. E. B. Du Bois called the "veil" of slavery and based her value on the commodification of her body and the number of children she could produce for her master (11). Yet, her self-image shifted from that of a victim to that of a survivor, and finally, to that of a challenger, and this shift in self-perception models the story of many formerly enslaved women who challenged their enslavement, whether through slowing their labor, running away, naming their children, or worshiping secretly and separately from white eyes. Formerly enslaved people found ways to chip away at America's chattel slavery when and where they could, and for Truth, that way was by directly emancipating herself and her son and by challenging not only the immorality of slavery but its dehumanizing impact on the nation as a whole.

Many Black Americans have identified the subtle but virulent trauma caused by their relationship to America's chattel slavery and embraced it as a motivator to publicly address inequalities that plague their communities. Ida B. Wells, Mamie Till-Mobley, and Fannie Lou Hamer are bright examples of this convergence, and in the twenty-first century, women of color have been central to movements for social justice. Alicia Garza, Patrisse Cullors, and Opel Tometi established the Black Lives Matter Movement (BLM) in 2013 as a direct response to the killing of Trayvon Martin and the acquittal of George Zimmerman for Martin's death. Their movement would gain national attention in 2014 with the deaths of Michael Brown in Ferguson, Missouri, and Eric Garner in New York City. Moreover, after the deaths of their sons, Trayvon Martin's mother, Sybrina Fulton; Michael Brown's mother, Lesley McSpadden; and Eric Garner's mother, Gwen Carr, all either ran for public office or became vocal advocates for reforms in legal and policing practices threatening the security of Black Americans. Their efforts were punctuated by eyewitness accounts and mobile phone videos that bear witness to their sons' trauma.

In many ways, Truth's witness to the horrors of America's chattel slavery mirrors the legacy of how trauma has motivated Black women toward social and political action. By identifying and calling out the brutality of slavery, she testified to its evils and served as an organizer of the abolitionist movement, which in Truth's time was often dominated by white men and women. Her presence and traumatic experience gave visible authenticity to America's chattel slavery, and her narrative and speeches testified to why the system should end. Similarly, Tarana Burke, a sexual assault survivor, determined to establish the MeToo movement in 2006 as a way for fellow survivors to find support, advocacy, and community. By the fall of 2017, as accusations of inappropriate sexual behavior made by several high-profile white women began to dominate the national news cycle, the movement shifted to #MeToo, and in that moment, advocates raised concerns about the absence of the experiences of women of color in a movement originally founded by a Black woman. Consequently, the lack of Black women recognized in the MeToo movement motivated Burke to write her 2021 memoir, *Unbounded*, in an effort to reclaim the voice of the movement's founder and to recognize the trauma of Black women. Her testimony mirrors that of Truth, who raised concerns over the equality of Black and white women with the simple question, "Ain't I a woman?"

Truth's faith tradition, as highlighted by Nancy Koester's important book, developed because of her interactions with a number of faith communities, and in this environment, she changed her name from Isabella Baumfree to Sojourner Truth. On July 4, 1854, during her speech at the annual picnic of the Massachusetts Anti-Slavery Society, she issued a direct challenge to the white Christian community by highlighting the contradiction of the Christian message and white Christian support for American chattel slavery and the undermining of the humanity of the enslaved. She testified that the selling of Black children spurred the spreading of the gospel, and she called out the hypocrisy of white Christians who supported any aspect of slavery (120). By challenging her overwhelmingly white audience, she called her listeners to reevaluate their affiliation with denominations and organizations that either actively or passively supported American chattel slavery. She called her hearers to consider the biblical story of Cain and Abel and God's judgment of Cain for the murder of his brother, and she warned of God's impending judgment for the wrong of slavery through her comparison of the murder of Abel and enslavement of Blacks. She challenged her white hearers to side with the justice demanded for Abel and to support the abolitionist movement, regardless of personal cost, as she wrote, "'White folks [who] don't suffer tribulation' will never know 'peace and joy in the kingdom'" (121). Since her personal experience of American chattel slavery could not be invalidated, opponents questioned her womanhood, and during one of her talks, a white male among her hearers, hoping to undermine her creditability, called for Truth to bare her breast in order to prove her womanhood.

By the time Truth was actively speaking publicly against American chattel slavery, Baptist, Methodist, and Presbyterian denominations in the United States had split over the issue of slavery and deepened regional divisions in the nation. Nancy Koester's book skillfully grounds the reader in understanding how Truth's faith served as the driving force in calling for the abolition of slavery. Like Truth, other Black leaders during her lifetime called out the inconsistency of the Christian message and American chattel slavery, and among them were Phillis Wheatley, David Walker, Richard Allen, Frederick Douglass, Linda Brent, and Martin Delany. Similarly, in the first decade of this current century, Black Christians have called out white evangelicals for their support of and complicity with politicians who implicitly question their humanity and systematically target predominantly

Black communities with unjust and often dangerous policies. Many Black and white Christians perceive that the Bible's condemnation of favoritism and its message of unity and equality are being replaced by a Christian nationalism that is centered on the supremacy of whiteness, and the result has been a deepening division between the faithful, illustrated in part by Black Christians leaving predominantly white denominations. By their exodus they ask, rephrasing Truth's original question, "Aren't I a Christian?" Similarly, as Black Americans fear the challenge to and abrogation of their political and voting power, they too are rephrasing her question by asking, "Aren't I an American?" Sojourner Truth's voice mattered in the nineteenth century, and quite possibly matters just as much today.

Alicia K. Jackson

Acknowledgments

I wish to thank all those at Wm. B. Eerdmans Publishing Company who have worked with me to bring this book into being. From acquisitions to review process, to working with images, cover design, copyediting and marketing, Eerdmans has been great to work with . . . especially after years of writing and researching in solitude. Thank you, Eerdmans!

This book could not have been written without the work of many historians. I am especially indebted to Carleton Mabee, Nell Irvin Painter, and Margaret Washington for their pathbreaking biographies of Truth. Many other scholars are mentioned in "A Note on the Sources" at the end of this book, but up front I must also thank Eric Foner, whose work on Reconstruction informed my understanding of Sojourner Truth's life after the Civil War. While I have learned much from these fine historians, any errors of fact or interpretation are my responsibility.

While writing this book I visited several places where Sojourner Truth lived, including Florence/Northampton, Massachusetts; Battle Creek, Michigan; Washington, DC; and Arlington, Virginia. But my work on the project began with a visit to New Paltz, New York, where Isabella (Sojourner Truth) grew up. There Anne Gordon, the historian for Ulster County, took my husband, Craig, and me on a tour of sites related to Sojourner's early life. She showed me several houses where Isabella was enslaved but which are not open to the public. Anne Gordon also took us on a drive through the hill country, tracing Isabella's probable escape route from slavery. She showed us the courthouse in Kingston where Isabella won custody of her son, Peter, after he was illegally sold south. There's nothing like being on location to make a story come alive.

Librarians and archivists helped me to find the print sources I needed. Peter Watters, of Luther Seminary Library in St. Paul, was my go-to person for interlibrary loan. Jody Owens at the Historical Society of Battle Creek Archive shared with me a wealth of material on Sojourner Truth. Corinne Nyquist, at State University of New York at New Paltz, welcomed me to the Sojourner Truth Library and shared helpful sources about Truth. A visit to the Library of Congress yielded some Sojourner Truth correspondence and newspaper clippings. The David Ruggles Center in Florence, Massachusetts, sent me copies of papers and articles about Truth and the Northampton Association. Staff at the University of Rochester Library helped me to locate correspondence relating to Sojourner Truth.

Several people have read drafts of chapters and offered their suggestions for improvement. Marty Levine (with CreativeNonfiction.org) teaches a course called "Historical Narratives" that helped me throughout the writing process. Brad Holt and Carol Lacey read and commented on several early drafts. Emily Koester, a fine writer and tactful editor, read several chapters and made valuable comments. Writers Randy Peterson and Gigi McGraw, whom I met in connection with the Center for Faith and Liberty in Philadelphia, were working on a play about Sojourner Truth and generously agreed to read and comment on several chapters. Two anonymous reviewers for Eerdmans made very helpful suggestions about bibliography to strengthen the historical context in some parts of the work.

Sojourner Truth is a grandmother to the civil rights movement. Getting closer to the civil rights movement helped me understand Truth better (despite the differences of generations and contexts). I therefore give special thanks to Mark Swiggum, who in 2018 led a group from St. Timothy Lutheran Church, St. Paul, Minnesota, on a civil rights trip to the Deep South. We went to Selma, Montgomery, Birmingham, and many lesser-known places where the movement unfolded. Most important, we spent hours listening to veterans of the civil rights movement, who told us of their experiences as foot soldiers for justice. Many of them spoke of their Christian faith, and how it empowered them to take a stand.

When the manuscript was in its final stages, my husband, Craig, listened as I read each chapter aloud. We both heard things that worked well and other things that did not. Craig was especially good at hearing what needed more explanation and what needed a haircut. Sojourner Truth used to say she could not read but she could hear; so it helped to step away from the computer screen and *hear* the story spoken aloud. The idea for this book began in conversation with Craig, and he always believed I would finish it, even when I had my doubts. This book is gratefully dedicated to my husband and best friend, Craig Koester.

She Belongs to Humanity

In the fall of 1865, Sojourner Truth stood on a busy street in Washington, DC, waiting for the horse-drawn streetcar. The Civil War was over, Lincoln was dead, and nobody knew what the future held for nearly four million freedpeople. Truth had come to town to work with these people, who crowded into the nation's capital. She was strong and vigorous for a woman in her late sixties, but she couldn't walk everywhere—especially not when she carried supplies to the Freedmen's Hospital.

Truth saw the streetcar coming. She raised her arm to signal for a stop. But the driver passed her by because, as far as he was concerned, the seats in this car were for whites only. This was the second time in one day a streetcar driver snubbed Sojourner Truth.

"I want to ride!" Truth shouted. "*I want to ride!!*" Her powerful voice rang out over the crowded street. All her years as a preacher, lecturer, and singer gave Truth vocal power. When she hollered, horses tossed their heads; they laid back their ears and balked. The streetcar stopped, blocked by other carriages and wagons. Sojourner strode forward and jumped onto the streetcar that had passed her by.

"Ha! Ha! Ha!" people on the street shouted in support of Truth. "She has beaten him."[1] The horses began to pull again, and traffic lurched forward.

The conductor was not amused. "Go ride up in the front, where the horses are," he barked. Blacks were not supposed to sit in the car, but they could ride standing up on a small platform just behind the horses. There was no seat, shade, or shelter. Those forced to ride that platform could easily be splattered with mud or covered with dust, and they always had a close-up view of the horses' backsides.

"I am a passenger," Sojourner said, settling into her seat inside the car.

"Go forward where the horses are," the conductor said, "or I will throw you out."

"I am from the Empire State of New York and know the laws as well as you do," Truth countered.

Truth had the law on her side. In March 1865 President Lincoln signed a new bill into law. It forbade "any exclusion from any car on account of color" on "every railroad in the District of Columbia."[2] But prejudice ran deep. The new law had to be claimed by people who were willing to risk insult and injury to bring change. That day Truth remained in her seat and rode farther than she needed to, for the pure joy of using her rights. "Bless God," she said as she left the car. "I have had a ride."[3]

Truth sometimes traveled the city with Laura Haviland, a white anti-slavery reformer and preacher. They used to go out and get supplies for the Freedmen's Hospital—bandages, bedding, and medicine. Haviland knew that long-held custom was against whites riding with Blacks. But she meant to defy Jim Crow.

Haviland got her chance on another day when she and Truth were waiting to ride. When a horse-drawn trolley drew near, Haviland signaled the conductor and waited for the car to stop. Sojourner kept walking, making it appear that only the white woman wanted a ride. But at the right moment, Truth doubled back and boarded the car. Immediately the conductor shoved Sojourner aside.

"Get out of the way and let this lady in," he ordered. Of course, "lady" to him meant "white."

"I am a lady too," Sojourner replied.

The conductor let her board, and Truth and Haviland rode on undisturbed. But soon they got off to transfer to another car, which would take them closer to the Freedmen's Hospital at Thirteenth and R Streets. Truth and Haviland were boarding again when a white man asked the conductor: "Have you got room for n*****s here?"

Seizing Sojourner's right arm, the conductor spun her around. "Get out," he ordered.

"I will not," Sojourner said.

"Don't put her out," said Haviland, placing one hand on Sojourner and the other on the conductor.

"Does she belong to you?" the conductor demanded.

"No. She belongs to humanity," said Haviland. "And she would have been out of the way a long time ago, if you had let her alone."

"Then take her and go," he said. The conductor shoved Sojourner and slammed her shoulder against the door.

"You will find out if you can shove me around like a dog," Truth said. Then she told Haviland, "Take the number of this car." Haviland did so.

When the two women got to the hospital, doctors examined Truth's shoulder and found it was dislocated. They treated her injury as best they could, but it pained her for a long time. Sojourner reported the incident to the president of the streetcar line. The police were informed, and they arrested the conductor on charges of assault and battery.

The Freedmen's Bureau hired a lawyer for Truth, and the case went to trial. This caused a "great sensation," Sojourner said later. The conductor was fired. After that, more Blacks were riding alongside whites, making the inside of the cars look to Sojourner "like pepper and salt."[4] She sent a letter to a friend about her experiences riding the streetcars. "It is hard for the old slaveholding spirit to die," she said, "but die it must."[5]

Truth's work to desegregate public transportation would be taken up almost a hundred years later by Rosa Parks, the Freedom Riders, and many others in the civil rights movement. Truth did not live to see the end of Jim Crow segregation, nor was she ever able to vote. Yet she believed equal rights must come for Blacks and women and never stopped working for change.

Sojourner Truth was born into slavery in upstate New York. As a young woman named Isabella, she left her place of bondage, and in her new freedom experienced a vision of Jesus. She felt called to be a preacher but could only support herself as a housekeeper. She went to New York City to work as a domestic and to conduct street evangelism on the side. Her quest for community led her to a cult whose leader claimed sole authority over right and wrong. Once more she had to free herself.

Isabella renamed herself Sojourner Truth because, as she explained it, God was calling her to travel and tell the truth about sin and slavery. She became a traveling preacher and then joined an abolitionist commune in Massachusetts. When the commune dissolved, she became an antislavery lecturer and an early advocate for women's rights. During the Civil War, Truth went to Washington to meet President Lincoln and to work among the freedpeople. After the war, she campaigned for lands in the West for freedpeople—a form of reparations.

Today, Sojourner Truth is remembered as a pioneer for equal rights. This was an expression of her faith in a God of justice and mercy. She was a preacher and a great singer of hymns, spirituals, and freedom songs. Sojourner loved Jesus and told many a crowd that since the Lord treated Blacks and women as fully human, men should do likewise. Truth had many charismatic gifts. She was an artist of spoken and sung word, and a talented improvisor who used her wit to subdue hecklers and change hearts.

Truth's life takes the reader through emancipation in the state of New York, the abolitionist movement, the women's rights movement, and the Civil War and Reconstruction. Many of the things she worked for, especially racial equality and women's rights, are still works in progress.

Since God created all people equal, Truth believed, it is a sin to treat any group of people as less than human. She practiced Christianity as a religion that changes individuals and society, through judgment and mercy. She held salvation and social reform together, believing that God's work of redemption takes place in *this* world. Her identity as a child of God gave her courage to claim her rights and fight for others' rights too. The many hardships she faced did not quell her joy. "Bless God," she said. "I have had a ride."

Isabella, a Northern Slave

Sojourner Truth was born into slavery in New York around the year 1797. She never knew her date of birth. Her parents named her Isabella, and many people simply called her "Bell." She grew up in the Hudson River valley, which was once part of the Dutch colony of New Netherland. Isabella's parents were born into slavery, and likely it was her grandparents who were captured in West Africa, forced onto slave ships, and brought to North America to be sold as slaves. The slave trade in New Netherland started in 1626, when the Dutch West India Company brought eleven African captives to be sold. Slave labor helped to build great estates along the Hudson River, roads throughout the colony, and of course, the city of New Amsterdam on Manhattan Island. New Netherland extended from New York to present-day New Jersey, western Connecticut, and parts of eastern Pennsylvania and Delaware. In 1664, the British took over the colony.

The British "replaced the Dutch as the world's leading slave traders" in the eighteenth century, writes historian Eric Foner. By 1790, seven years before Isabella was born, New York State had 21,000 slaves and 4,600 free Blacks, making it "the heaviest slaveholding region north of the Mason-Dixon line."[1] New York City had a large slave population, and in rural areas slaves "constituted a major part of farmers' wealth."[2] In Ulster County, New York, where Isabella was born, more than one in three households owned slaves. And, according to the 1790 census, a higher percentage of Dutch New Yorkers held slaves (nearly 30 percent) than did other groups.

The American Revolution inspired all the northern states to get rid of slavery; some did so quickly, and others gradually. New York's slowness to abolish slavery was attributed, at the time, to "the great body of Dutch [leg-islators], who hold Slaves in this government."[3]

Isabella was about two years old in 1799, the year the New York State legislature passed An Act for the Gradual Abolition of Slavery. It set the date of emancipation for July 4, 1827. New York's gradual approach allowed masters to keep younger Black people in bondage for their most produc-tive years. In addition, masters could extend servitude beyond emancipa-tion through "apprenticeships" until adulthood (women became free at age twenty-five, men at twenty-eight). The law freed all children born to slave women after July 4, 1799. This did not apply to Isabella, but in "1817 a new law passed that would free slaves born before 1799 but not until 1827."[4] This jumble of laws set in motion the slow and halting demise of slavery in New York, while at the same time shielding slaveholders from economic loss. There was, of course, no compensation for the enslaved. Isabella was born into what historian Deborah White called "the most vulnerable group" of Americans. She was "Black in a white society, slave in a free society, woman in a society ruled by men."[5] This she held in common with Black women of the antebellum South.

And yet, slavery in New York differed from southern slavery in some ways. The large cash crops of southern plantations—tobacco, rice, and cot-ton—required a great many laborers, who typically lived in slave quarters, set apart from the master's "big house." In contrast, New York's colder climate meant smaller and more diverse crops. Most New York slaveholders held two or three Black people in captivity, and a farmer who kept eight to ten was considered a large slaveholder. Instead of separate cabins or slave quar-ters, enslaved New Yorkers typically lived in the cellar of the master's house, where light was poor and the air was damp. The lack of slave quarters also spelled isolation. Isabella never had "a cohesive African-American neighbor-hood to return to," writes historian and Truth biographer Nell Irvin Painter. She often worked alone, and when she was "abused, violated or degraded, no Black neighbors could salve her wounds."[6] Isabella in her youth had only limited opportunity to form friendships with other Black people.

Isabella grew up when Dutch was still widely spoken in the Hudson Val-ley. Her parents spoke Dutch, and it was her first language. She may have carried a Dutch accent throughout life. Reporters often described her speech as "peculiar" and transcribed her words in what they supposed was a southern Black dialect. This gave a false impression. "Her dialect differs essentially from that of the Southern negroes," said the *New York Daily Herald* in 1878. "It is founded upon her early knowledge of the Low Dutch, which was her only language until she was twelve or thirteen years old."[7] The child who became Sojourner Truth grew up in an Afro-Dutch culture that combined European and African languages, food, and folkways. A Black abolitionist who knew Sojourner Truth said that she grew up among the "Low Dutch" people. In her youth, "she had been under no improving influences and scarcely knew her [right] hand from her left. With her half Low Dutch and half African accent, she [was] sent adrift to battle with the world as she could."[8]

Almost all of what is known of Truth's childhood comes from the *Narrative of Sojourner Truth*, first published in 1850. By that time, Truth was looking back on her childhood from the perspective of midlife, when she had been a free woman for more than twenty years and soon would join the antislavery lecture circuit. When telling about her early years, Truth wanted to show how far she had come in wisdom and understanding since her enslavement.[9]

The Revolutionary War was fresh in living memory when Isabella was born. In her old age, she told a crowd that she never saw George Washington, but, she added, "I lived when he did." She said this "with a great brightening of her face and an accent of reverential pride." She once saw the Marquis de Lafayette from a distance. When the famous French general made a triumphal tour of the United States in 1824, he traveled up the Hudson River in a steamboat. Truth was among the crowds standing on the banks to watch his boat go by. She heard that when Lafayette had dinner across the river in Duchess County, they roasted a whole ox for him.

Isabella's mother was named Elizabeth (or Betsey), but her family called her Mau-mau Bett. She taught her children to pray, work hard, and endure. According to historian Margaret Washington, slave-trade patterns imply that Mau-mau Bett came from West Central Africa, "the region of Kongo." Female leadership was well known there, and included religious leaders, queens, and "female warriors," as well as networks of female influence over clans, trade, and farming. Whether or not Isabella was told of this heritage, and despite a society dominated by white men, Isabella was born to lead.

Isabella's father, James, was several years older than Betsey. James had two wives before Betsey—"one of whom, if not both," were sold away from him.[10] He was "honest, dependable, and hardworking."[11] His family called him "Bomefree," a name that combined the Dutch word for tree (*bome*) with the English spelling of "free." In his prime, Bomefree was tall and strong and carried himself with dignity, like a true "Coromanti" of the Gold Coast.[12] To honor this family identity, some modern writers give Isabella the last name of Bomefree. In her own time, however, Isabella's last name followed that of her white owner. Each time she was sold, her name changed accordingly.

Betsey and James had perhaps a dozen children, who were sold away as soon as they were old enough to work. Isabella was the next to the youngest, followed by a little brother. She could recall six of her siblings,[13] but the older ones were sold before she was born. In her *Narrative*, Truth often noted her parents' enduring grief over being separated from their children.

Isabella's parents were enslaved by Colonel Johannes Hardenbergh, whose property she became at birth. Hardenbergh lived in the township of Hurley (present-day Esopus), near the Swartekill (Dutch for Black River). Descended from Dutch immigrants, Johannes still spoke Dutch. He had served in the New York colonial assembly and was a Revolutionary War colonel under George Washington; he was also a large landowner who ran a grist mill and several sawmills. He inherited this property from his father, and at his death it would be divided among his male heirs.[14] In 1790 Hardenbergh had seven slaves. He allowed James and Betsey to use a plot of land for growing their own crops, tobacco, corn, or flax, which they exchanged for food or clothing for themselves and their children.

One winter day when the countryside was deep in snow, Colonel Hardenbergh sold two children. Isabella's older brother Michael was just a small boy at the time, and he was excited to see a sleigh drive up the farm road and stop in the yard. He was happy when someone lifted him up onto it, but his glee turned to terror when he realized that he was being taken away. He wiggled free, jumped down, and ran indoors to hide, only to be dragged out and forced back onto the sleigh. This time he was held tightly. Then his little sister Dinah was stuffed into the sleigh box, and the lid closed to prevent her escape. The whip cracked over the horse's back, and the sleigh moved off down the road, swallowed up in white.[15] Mau-mau Bett wept as she told Isabella the story.

When Isabella was about two years old, the colonel died, and she and her family became the property of the colonel's son Charles Hardenbergh. He was building a new place, and when it was finished, Isabella's family moved there; by this time, Isabella had a baby brother named Peter.

Charles Hardenbergh's new home was also an inn, located on a turnpike convenient to travelers. Charles had a small farm to grow food for his own household and for paying guests. James probably worked the farm while Betsey did the cooking and cleaning. Isabella would have helped her mother with such tasks as a little girl could do. Isabella and her family lived in the cellar, where loose boards covered the dirt floor. There was no bed; everyone slept on the floor with "a little straw and a blanket" to cover them. In a heavy rain, water could be heard sloshing beneath the boards where the people slept. In addition to Isabella's family, two or three other slaves lived in this damp, dark cellar.

"My children, there is a God who hears and sees you," Mau-mau Bett used to say. "He lives up in the sky." She told Isabella and Peter, "when you are beaten or cruelly treated, or fall into any trouble, you must ask and God will always hear and help you." She taught her children to obey their masters and never lie or steal. This might make life a little easier; but if not, they could take pride in maintaining a good character.

Sometimes Mau-mau Bett gave way to lament. "How long, O Lord?" the old mother groaned, "how long?" Isabella asked what ailed her mother. "Oh, a great deal . . . a great deal ails me," came the reply. Slavery would come to an end, but not in time to free this family. At night Mau-mau would take Isabella and Peter outside and show them the stars. "Those are the same stars, and that is the same moon, that look down upon your brothers and sisters," she said, "though they are ever so far away from us, and each other."[16] When they could not see one another, they were still in the same natural world that God made.

Charles Hardenbergh died in 1808. Isabella saw her mother weeping for fear that the master's death meant her last two children would be sold when the estate was settled. "Bell's family remained together for a year or two" longer, waiting for the settlement.[17] Then the extended Hardenbergh family had to do something with the slaves that had belonged to Charles. They decided to free Isabella's father, not out of kindness, but because he was "growing weak and infirm," and nobody wanted the cost of his upkeep. They were planning to auction off Isabella's mother, but since the old woman was not worth much money, they decided to free her and let her take care of James. This relieved the Hardenberghs of any responsibility to care for the faithful couple who had toiled away their lives for nothing.

Along with the livestock from the estate, Bomefree and Mau-mau Bett's two remaining children were auctioned off. Isabella was sold for $100, along with a flock of sheep. Peter was sold to another farmer in the area, and the siblings were separated.

For a while Isabella's parents stayed on in the cellar, by permission of the new owners. Meanwhile Mau-mau Bett's health was failing. One day James was out doing chores for neighbors. He returned to the cellar to find his wife on the floor, in "a fit of palsy"[18] (some kind of shaking or tremor). She died a few hours later.

Isabella and Peter were allowed to visit their father and to attend their mother's burial. But they could not stay long to comfort their father, because they had to return to their owners. As Isabella and Peter were leaving, Bomefree "raised his voice and wept like a child," moaning, "What is to become of me?" For the rest of her life, Isabella would remember her father's cries.

Now that Bomefree was a widower, the extended Hardenbergh family said they would take turns letting him live on their respective farms; he would stay a few weeks at each place before moving on to the next.[19] If the journey was not too long, the old man walked, leaning on his staff; if the distance was more than Bomefree could manage, one of the Hardenberghs would give him a ride in a wagon.

Isabella's third owner was John Neely; she lived on his farm from about 1806 to 1808. Neely ran a store in the Kingston area, near the place where Roundout Creek meets the Hudson. Unlike Bell's previous owners, Neely and his wife spoke only English. Bell spoke only Dutch. They would ask her to fetch something, such as a frying pan, but if she brought the wrong object she was whipped. With the Neelys, Truth recalled, there was plenty to eat, but also plenty of whippings.

One Sunday morning she was ordered to go into the barn; she was not told why. There she found her master with a bundle of rods, prepared in the embers, and bound together with cords. When he had tied her hands together before her, he gave her the worst whipping she ever had. Neely "whipped her till the flesh was deeply lacerated, and the blood streamed from her wounds." She bore the scars from this whipping for the rest of her life. "Oh my God," Sojourner Truth recalled years later, "what a way is this of treating human beings?"

Isabella's mother had taught her to pray to God when she was in trouble. But Isabella thought that to pray, one must speak aloud. And to avoid being overheard, one must be alone. She never knew when the beatings would come, so she could not very well ward them off with prayer.[20]

She did pray that her father would visit her, and she watched and waited for him. One winter day he came to the Neelys' place. Bomefree could see that his daughter was being treated badly. She was thin and frightened, and, although the winter was cold, she had no coat or shoes. Isabella was overjoyed to see her father but afraid to tell him her troubles. As he was leaving, she followed him to the gate. He asked if he could do anything to help her, and she asked Bomefree to find her a better master. (Enslaved people could sometimes intercede for one who was cruelly treated, by asking a more humane white person to buy their loved one.) Bomefree promised to do all he could for Isabella, and they said good-bye.

Each day after that, Isabella would return to the place where her father had parted from her, "and walking in the tracks her father had made in the snow, repeated her prayer that 'God would help her father get her a new and better place.'" One day a Dutch man arrived at the Neelys' house and asked Isabella if she wanted to go with him. He bought her for $105 dollars "at the suggestion of her father"[21] and thus became her fourth owner.

The man who bought Isabella was Martinus Schryver of Ulster County. He lived in what is now Port Ewan, where he ran the Jug Tavern, a drinking establishment for Dutch folk of the lower and working class. Schryver was also a fisherman and a farmer. According to historian Margaret Washington, Schryver had not owned slaves before, but he bought Isabella "at Bomefree's bidding."[22] Isabella slept in the basement of the Schryver house but spent many of her days outside and had some freedom to come and go. Schryver would send Isabella to buy molasses or liquor at a nearby store, or into the woods to gather roots and herbs for beers. She hoed corn in the garden and carried fish caught in the nearby river. Bell was greatly relieved to be among Dutch speakers again. The Schryvers have been described as "a rude, uneducated family, exceedingly profane in their language, but, on the whole, an honest, kind and well-disposed people."[23]

Isabella stayed about a year and a half with Schryver. In 1810, when she was about thirteen years old, Schryver sold her for about $175[24] (worth nearly $4,000 today). Isabella's value went up as she grew older and could work harder.

The buyer was John Dumont, a farmer and trader. His house stood on the banks of the Hudson, and he kept a dock where boats could pick up or off-load goods. He had eight or nine slaves, a large holding by local standards.[25] Dumont descended from French Huguenots but spoke English—which Isabella was still trying to learn.[26] John was, by the standards of his time, a humane master. Isabella worked for Dumont for about sixteen years, during which time he was the most powerful person in her life. Many years later, when asked if Dumont ever whipped her, Sojourner Truth said, "Oh yes, he sometimes whipped me soundly, though never cruelly. And the most severe whipping he ever gave me was because *I* was cruel to a cat."[27]

John Dumont came to prize Isabella as an excellent farm worker and boasted that she could get more done than anyone else on the place. Dumont's wife, Sally, however, disliked Isabella and criticized everything she did. She made it a point to speak ill of Isabella in John's presence.

Sally may have been jealous of Isabella, suspecting a sexual relationship between her husband and the young enslaved woman, or fearing that such a relationship might develop. Whatever the reason, Sally lost no opportunity to make Isabella's life difficult. Olive Gilbert (who collaborated on the *Narrative of Sojourner Truth*) wrote that Sally Dumont's hatred was the source of "a long series of trials" in Isabella's life. "We must pass over in silence" some of these trials, Gilbert wrote, "from motives of delicacy." Gilbert explained that some of the worst things that happened to Isabella had to be "suppressed"[28] from the *Narrative of Sojourner Truth*.

It was Truth's decision to keep some parts of her enslaved life from becoming public. "There are some hard things that crossed Isabella's life while in slavery," wrote Gilbert, that Truth "has no desire to publish." Gilbert went on to give several reasons. First, some of the people who were cruel to Isabella had since died and gone to "a higher tribunal"; publishing their crimes would only hurt "innocent friends" still living. Second, the suppressed incidents were of a personal nature. Third, if Sojourner told "all that happened to her as a slave," she would not be believed. Olive Gilbert did say that Isabella suffered "what is usually called unnatural,"[29] a strong hint that a female owner sexually abused Bell. If so, Sally Dumont may have been that abuser. Historian Nell Irvin Painter notes that Sally Dumont died in 1846, four years before *Narrative of Sojourner Truth* was first published in 1850. Painter thinks that Isabella was sexually abused by Sally, not by John.[30] Truth stayed in touch with John Dumont for some time after slavery, and may have wanted to shield him from the shame of having his wife's behavior exposed.

There was, however, a story about Sally Dumont that Sojourner wanted to tell. Mrs. Dumont employed two white girls, and often claimed that their work was far superior to anything Isabella could do. One of these white servants, named Kate, enjoyed bossing Isabella and looked for ways to "grind her down."

Isabella used to cook potatoes for the family breakfast. One morning Kate complained that the potatoes looked dingy and dirty, and blamed Isabella. Mrs. Dumont gleefully told her husband to look at "a fine specimen of Bell's work." John saw the dirty potatoes and scolded Isabella, ordering her to be more careful. Isabella knew she had carefully prepared the food and sensed mischief afoot.

That night the Dumonts' daughter Gertrude approached Isabella, offering to cook the potatoes the next morning if Isabella would do the milking instead. Gertrude got up early and cooked the potatoes. Kate entered the kitchen and made up some reason why Gertrude should step out for a moment. But instead Gertrude went to the back of the kitchen and kept a sharp eye on Kate. She saw Kate scoop up some ashes from the hearth and dump them in the kettle with the potatoes. As the family came in for breakfast, Gertrude announced that she saw Kate put ashes in the potatoes. Mr. Dumont swore an oath, and Mrs. Dumont kept her face a perfect blank, while Kate blushed and looked "like a convicted criminal." By exposing the mean little plot, Gertrude vindicated Isabella. Looking back, Sojourner found a spiritual meaning in the story: "God shields the innocent, and causes them to triumph over their enemies."[31]

John Dumont now felt justified in praising Isabella. He would boast to his friends that Bell could work better than a man (a theme Truth later used in her speeches). Isabella worked hard to please Dumont. To prove her worth, she would go without sleep and do extra chores. When she received special favors from Dumont, the other slaves "taunted her with being the 'white folks' n*****."[32]

Many years later, Truth said that when she lived with the Dumonts, she "firmly believed that slavery was right and honorable." Young Isabella would do anything to please her master, whom she saw as almost a god. Sojourner Truth looked back with astonishment on her younger self, for having once believed all the lies and accepted the arrogance of her masters. Yet when everything and everyone around her reinforced slavery, what else was Isabella to think? However, she knew that slavery was set to end in New York in 1827, and as that time drew near, she began thinking more and more of freedom.

———

On a rare visit to Bomefree, Isabella saw that her father's strength was failing. She told him that in ten years all the slaves in New York would be free. She urged him to hang on until then, promising to take good care of him when they were free. But Bomefree said he could not live that long;[33] freedom was coming too late for him.

Around this time, Isabella fell in love with Robert, a young man who was enslaved on a nearby estate. Robert's owner was Charles Catton,[34] an English painter who had moved to Ulster County in 1804. Catton's artistic sensibilities did not soften his cruelty. Catton forbade Robert's visits to Isabella, lest Robert father a child that would become Dumont's property.

Robert was ordered to take a wife from among Catton's slaves, but he loved Isabella and used to visit her in secret. One day he was especially anxious to see her, having heard that she was "ill" (perhaps recovering from childbirth).[35] Determined to see her, Robert snuck over to the Dumont place. Isabella did not know Robert was coming until John Dumont came to warn her. "If you see [Robert] tell him to take care of himself," Dumont said, "for the Cattons are after him." Moments later Robert showed up on the Dumont place with Catton and his son in pursuit.

They caught him and began "beating him with the heavy ends of their canes" as Isabella watched from inside. They hit his head and face until Robert was covered with blood "like a slaughtered beast."

John Dumont intervened and ordered the Cattons to stop spilling human blood on his property. Then the Cattons tied Robert's hands behind him tightly, so as to cause much pain. Dumont made them loosen the rope, and then followed them to their home to protect Robert from further torment. Even so, Robert left a bloody trail in the snow. Later Dumont told Isabella that the Cattons' anger had cooled and the beatings would cease. Isabella "was greatly shocked at the murderous treatment of poor Robert, whom she truly loved, and whose only crime, in the eyes of his persecutors, was his affection for her."[36] Never again did Robert visit Isabella. His spirit was as broken as his body. He married one of Catton's slaves but did not live many years after the assault.

Robert may have been the only man Isabella ever loved, and she considered him her first husband. Isabella later married Thomas, an older man held in slavery by John Dumont (who likely arranged the marriage). Isabella did not love Thomas as she had loved Robert. Tom had been married twice before and may have been separated from his previous wives by sale. Slave marriages had no legal standing and could be broken up by white masters for any reason. Gertrude Dumont recalled in her old age that "Isabella and Tom argued about whether they were really married." Isabella said they were husband and wife, but Tom said "that they had merely been out on a frolic together and had agreed to live together as man and wife."

Isabella had five children. Robert may have been the father of her first child, and Thomas the father of three or four. This fits with a pattern described by historian Deborah White, in which "many [bonded women] established a more enduring relationship with someone other than their first child's father and went on to marry and have the rest of their children with him."[37] There is no strong evidence that Dumont fathered any of Isabella's children. "Nevertheless," writes historian Carleton Mabee, "the emotional ties between them seem unusually close for a master and slave, and a sexual relationship between them cannot be ruled out."[38] Truth's *Narrative* keeps things vague, saying only that "In the process of time, Isabella found herself the mother of five children."[39] Between the years 1815 and 1826, Isabella bore Diana, Peter, Elizabeth, and Sophia; another son, perhaps named James, died very young. Each child was named for one of Isabella's parents or siblings.

Sojourner Truth later said that during her enslavement she used to take pride in bearing children because they increased the property of her master, which, in turn, increased her own worth in the slave economy.[40] Later in life she realized that this was all part of the big lie of slavery. "I want to know what has become of the love I ought to have for my children," she said in a speech in 1851. "I did have love for them but what has become of it. I cannot tell you. I have had two husbands yet I never possessed one of my own. I have had five children and never could take any one of them up and say, 'my child' or 'my children' unless it was when no one could see me."[41] Truth recalled that as a young mother, she taught her children to work hard and not to steal, and that she punished them for doing wrong. She would even let her children go hungry rather than ask for more food and risk displeasing her master or mistress.

However, John Dumont seemed to have some feeling for Isabella's children. If he came in the house and heard one of the children crying because Bell "was doing something for Mrs. Dumont, Mr. Dumont would scold his wife . . . for not letting Isabella take care of her own child. 'I will not hear this crying,' he would say. 'I can't bear it, and I will not hear any child cry so. Here, Bell, take care of this child, if no more work is done for a week.'"[42]

When Isabella went to work in the fields, she would take a large basket with a rope tied to each handle. Then, putting her youngest child in the basket and tying the basket to a tree branch, she got another young child to swing it. In this way, Isabella could work while watching over two children at once.

The last time Isabella saw her father, Bomefree was still itinerating between the Hardenbergh farms. One day she found him seated on a rock by the roadside. His "hair was white like wool—he was almost blind," Truth recalled, "and his gait was more a creep than a walk." He sighed for his children, saying, "They are all taken away from me."[43] She tried to see him another time, in hopes of showing him one of his grandchildren. Carrying an infant in her arms, she walked twelve miles to see Bomefree. But when she got to the place where she thought her father was staying, he had already moved on.

When Bomefree was no longer able to travel between farms, the Hardenberghs sent him to live in a shack in the woods. He shared this mean dwelling with an old couple who had lived out their lives in slavery and were no longer able to work. These three elders were cast off with no provision for their care. Eventually the old couple passed away, leaving Bomefree alone. A Black woman who lived in the area sometimes went to see how Bomefree fared. She saw him hungry and cold, plagued by lice and unable even to wash himself. He could not gather wood or build a fire to keep himself warm. ("New York law required that owners provide medical care and support for slaves in old age,"[44] but the Hardenberghs did not obey it.) Bomefree died alone. When the Hardenberghs found out, they gave him what they called "a good funeral" with his coffin painted black and a jug of whisky and some tobacco for the slaves to pass around.[45]

———

Sojourner Truth's *Narrative* describes her religious faith during her enslavement. She did not mention attending any church, or having any religious instruction except that of her mother, who spoke of God as a great man in the sky. Mau-mau Bett told Isabella to call on God in times of trouble and trust God to help. This was Isabella's starting point.

She believed that God was a powerful man—like Washington or Napoleon. God kept a great book in which all of Isabella's actions were written, just "as her master kept a record of whatever he wished not to forget." She believed that God could see everything that happens on earth.

However, God did not know her thoughts until she spoke them aloud. That notion seems to have come from a story Isabella heard when she was very young. As the story goes, a wounded soldier was abandoned by a retreating army. Desperate and hungry, he knelt on the ground and prayed aloud to God until help came. Isabella thought that if she prayed out loud under the open sky, God would hear her.

Bell found "a small island in a small stream, covered with large willow shrubbery," where sheep grazed or lay in the shade.[46] The rush of waters allowed her to speak loudly "without being overheard by any who might pass that way." Isabella wove together some willow branches "to make a wall on the outside, forming a circular arched alcove, made entirely of the graceful willow. To this place she resorted daily, and in pressing times much more frequently." Isabella's leafy sanctuary calls to mind the so-called hush arbors made of woven branches, where enslaved people could worship without being seen or heard by the master.

Isabella would say the Lord's Prayer "in her Low Dutch, as taught by her mother." Then she told God all her troubles and sufferings, asking, "Do you think that's right, God?" She closed by "begging to be delivered from evil, whatever it might be."

As she got older, Isabella began to feel that God was "in some manner bound to do her bidding," as if God were her servant. It was a relationship she understood well, since Bell's masters kept her at their beck and call. She naturally wanted someone to serve her as she served her masters. But if God did not follow her orders, she assumed it was because she had done something wrong. Then she would bargain: if God would "help her out of all her difficulties, she would pay him by being very good."[47]

This was easier said than done. When Isabella could not fulfill her side of the bargain, she would make excuses. "She could not be good in her present circumstances," said Truth's *Narrative*. "But if [God] would give her a new place, and a good master and mistress, she could and would be good." She even promised to be good for just "*one* day to show God how good she would be *all* of the time," if only God would deliver her "from the temptations that then so sorely beset her." It never worked. The day would pass, and she knew that she had given in to temptations.

At least she had Pinkster to look forward to. The festival was the highlight of the year for the Afro-Dutch people. Pinkster was the Dutch name for Pentecost, a Christian festival that marks the Holy Spirit coming to Jesus's followers fifty days after Easter. As told in the biblical book of Acts, the Holy Spirit came to help the apostles spread the gospel to the world.

In colonial times, Dutch settlers observed Pinkster with worship services, followed by feasting and drinking. On the larger farms, enslaved Africans prepared the feast but then were given time off to celebrate with their friends and family. Pinkster evolved into a carnival blending Dutch and African food and music, and lasting several days. Pinkster "reminded Blacks that . . . they were a people sharing a common oppression, displacement, and heritage,"[48] writes historian Margaret Washington.

The carnival persisted long after the English took control. Around the year of Isabella's birth, a traveler wrote that "the settlements along the [Hudson] river are Dutch, it is the holiday they call pinkster & every public house is crowded with merry makers. . . . Blacks as well as their masters were frolicking."[49] This was a time when bondpeople could practice an African spirituality that found "joy in life in the face of every trial."[50]

The town of Albany held a big Pinkster festival atop the hill where the state capitol building stands today. People traveled for miles to attend, camping out on the festival grounds in the warm late spring. The festivities began with the appearance of "King Charles," an African-born slave dressed as a European monarch. The king paraded through the town with his court, collecting dues and giving orders in a comedy of reversal that was also, for those who could see it, a satire of slavery.

On the festival grounds, booths were built with green boughs. Here African-style food was sold along with tobacco and alcohol. Whisky and cider were easy to make and could be very potent. Gertrude Dumont recalled that Isabella "was fond of liquor and tobacco, and would use both when she could get them."[51]

The festival offered many entertainments. Athletes performed gymnastic feats and ran races. Storytellers held forth and jokesters played pranks. There was plenty of dancing, and as a young woman, Isabella was said to be a very good dancer. But the carnival's highlight was a dance called the Toto (or Guinea dance), performed to the music of drums, flutes, fiddles, and other instruments. Europeans considered the Toto to be indecent and were therefore eager to watch it. The more alcohol people drank, the wilder things got. At Pinkster Blacks and whites mingled more freely than usual—one reason the city of Albany banned Pinkster in 1811, just after John Dumont bought Isabella.

Pinkster continued farther down the Hudson Valley, though never with quite the abandon seen at Albany. Isabella loved Pinkster. It celebrated African culture and gave people a "break from the rigors of farm life."[52] Best of all, Black people who were scattered among relatively small, isolated farms could reconnect with friends and family.

Yet Pinkster also reinforced slavery, by releasing pent-up frustrations without bringing change. The great abolitionist Frederick Douglass wrote that slave holidays often involved drunkenness and other excesses, which kept "down the spirit of insurrection." Slave "holidays serve as conductors, or safety-valves, to carry off the rebellious spirit of enslaved humanity." Douglass thought that if slaves were denied some way to release their pent-up frustrations, there would be "an immediate insurrection."[53]

As the time for New York's emancipation drew near, Isabella looked forward to freedom. She began to make plans, little knowing that her resolve would be sorely tested by her need to celebrate Pinkster.

2

The Vision

Slavery was on borrowed time in New York State, with emancipation set for July 4, 1827.

As Freedom Day approached, the slave system was already breaking down. Many enslaved Blacks fled the state rather than spend more time in bondage. But a successful escape often meant leaving family. People caught trying to escape could be whipped, fined, or jailed—or even sold to the South. New York's abolition laws forbade selling anyone out of state, but some were willing to break the law in order to make money. Even legally free Black New Yorkers could be kidnapped and sold south. No wonder, then, that most enslaved people chose to wait in place with family and friends nearby, counting down the years, months, and days till emancipation.

Isabella was looking for a middle way between escaping and remaining enslaved. She wanted to be free without leaving her children. So she negotiated an early release, as did many others during this time of transition. Isabella had some bargaining power because she was the best worker on Dumont's farm. Knowing that Dumont could not well afford to lose her, Bell worked out a deal with him. If he would set her free one year early, she promised to work extra hard and not run away. In return, Dumont agreed to set her free on July 4, 1826. She could then work for wages on Dumont's farm or in the area, remaining near her children. When Isabella struck her bargain with Dumont, she had three living children: Diana was about ten, Peter was perhaps five, and Elizabeth a toddler.[1]

Around this time Isabella became pregnant for the last time. Like all enslaved women, Isabella worked straight through her pregnancies. She was in the field cutting grass or reaping wheat one day[2] when her scythe slipped and severed the index finger from her right hand. Pain seized her, and the wound bled freely. Someone—perhaps Isabella herself—had to apply pressure to stop the bleeding and then bind the wound.

As the shock of the injury wore off, Isabella feared that the deal she'd made with Dumont would fall through. She had promised to work hard, but how could she do heavy chores with her right hand so badly injured? Determined to be free, she tried to keep working as she had before. But using her injured hand caused pain and slowed down the healing. Try as she might, she could not work up to her full capacity.

Dumont was quick to take advantage. After all, he reasoned, why should he keep his part of the bargain if she was not keeping hers? He decided not to free her a year early. She must remain his slave until July 4, 1827. By Dumont's logic—the logic of slavery—Isabella had no right to be free. Her freedom was entirely up to him, and he could change his mind.

Looking back years later, Sojourner Truth saw that she had been caught in a game of bait and switch. "The slaveholders are TERRIBLE for promising to give you this or that, or such and such a privilege," she said in her *Narrative*. But when the promise comes due, the master forgets all about it. If you remind the master of the promise, Truth explained, you are called a liar or told that you did not keep your part of the bargain. The enslaved live in hope that the master will keep a promise, but, they said, when "it is almost in our hands [we] find ourselves flatly denied! Just think, how *could* we bear it?"

Isabella would not bear it. She decided to free herself before the official emancipation date. But when and how would she leave? She must plan well. Weeks passed, and she gave birth to a baby girl she named Sophia. Isabella would wait for her injured hand to heal a little more and for Sophia to get a little older. Isabella thought it was her duty to finish spinning the wool and to help harvest the crops, for she took pride in her work and desired to complete certain tasks before leaving. But around the end of 1826, John Dumont did something else that hurt Isabella deeply: he sold her son Peter to a local family. Dumont was within his legal rights, as long as the sale was in New York State. Legal or not, his actions caused pain and uncertainty for Isabella. The sale would make it harder for her to see Peter, and there was no telling how Peter's new owners would treat him or if they would keep him for very long.

As the days got shorter and colder, Isabella prayed over her departure. She told God she was afraid to leave at night. But if she left in daylight, she might be seen, caught, and forced back to Dumont's farm. According to her *Narrative*, a thought came to her: she could "leave just before the day dawned, and get out of the neighborhood where she was known" while it was still dark, then the sun would rise and help her find her way. "Yes," she said, "that's a good thought! Thank you, God, for *that* thought."

One chilly morning before the sun came up, Isabella tied up a few belongings in a kerchief and put little Sophia in a sling across her back. She had been taught that it was wicked to run away, so instead of running she walked. With the Hudson River at her back, she headed northwest toward the hill country. She had left three children behind, knowing that she would not get far if she took them. Now Isabella probably took the Poppletown road, a dirt track just wide enough for a small horse-drawn wagon. When the climb got steep, the road zigzagged its way up a ridge. Near the top Isabella stopped to look out across the countryside. As the sun rose, she could see the autumn fields stretched out like a quilt in the early light: black, brown, and tan patches bordered by gray stone walls. She knew the people on each farm. Soon they would hear that she was gone.

Isabella looked back down the road where she had come. Seeing no one, she sat down to nurse Sophia. She had been so intent on leaving Dumont's farm, but where should she go from here? As she prayed over this, a thought came to her: she would find Levi Rowe, a Quaker who opposed slavery. When she reached Rowe's house, he was sick in bed, being tended by his wife. Even so, these kindhearted people told Isabella where she might seek refuge.

She walked on through the short winter day. It was getting dark when she came to Roundot Creek. She saw a fieldstone house that she remembered from when she lived in this area as a child. "That's the place for me; I shall stop there," Bell said. It was cold, and she needed food and shelter for the night. An elderly woman came to the door and told Isabella to wait for the owners to come home. Before long, Isaac and Maria Van Wagenen returned and listened to Isabella's story. Devout folk who "never turned the needy away," they invited Isabella to stay and work for them.[3] Mr. Van Wagenen, it turned out, had "known [Isabella] since infancy"[4] because her first owners lived in that area.

If Isabella intended to get as far away from Dumont as possible, she would have sheltered only a night or two at the farm on Roundot Creek and then traveled on. She probably knew Dumont would come looking for her, and find her. Then she would give him a piece of her mind.

Sure enough, after some days of combing the area in search of Bell, Dumont showed up at the Van Wagenen farm. He probably drove a small wagon so he could take Isabella and Sophia back down the long, rough road to his farm on the Hudson River. He knocked on the door, and when Isabella appeared, he said, "Well, Bell, so you've run away from me."

"No, I did not *run* away," she replied. "I walked away by daylight, and all because you promised me a year of my time."

"You must come back with me."

"No, I *won't* go back with you."

"Well, I shall take the *child*."

Bell said Dumont would not take the child.

"I am taking you home," Dumont pressed. "You must come with me."

If Bell refused, Dumont could try to force her, or he could send someone to arrest her. But at that moment Mr. Van Wagenen spoke up. He said he did not believe in slavery and did not wish to *buy* Isabella and her child. However, he offered to pay Dumont for Bell's work for the time left until emancipation. Van Wagenen gave Dumont $20 for the work he claimed Bell owed him, plus $5 for baby Sophia. The transaction helped Dumont to save face, and he laid aside his claim on the mother and child.

"What should I call you?" Isabella asked the kind man who now stood before her.

Then Van Wagenen told Isabella something also meant for Dumont's ears: "Do not call me Master, for there is but *one* master, and he who is *your* master is *my* master." Dumont turned away his horse, pulling an empty wagon. "Call me Isaac Van Wagenen," said Bell's new friend, "and my wife is Maria Van Wagenen."

For the first time in her life, Isabella heard someone say that God alone is master. She could scarcely understand it in that moment, so deeply was her life formed by slavery. Remembering it years later, Sojourner Truth said that Van Wagenen's words brought a "*mighty change*"[5] in her life.

Isabella and Sophia were free. But money had changed hands between two white men, so in the eyes of the law, mother and daughter belonged to Isaac Van Wagenen until emancipation day, now less than a year away. Accordingly, Isabella took Van Wagenen as her last name.

On her journey to freedom, Isabella did not cross a frozen river in winter, nor evade bloodhounds by hiding in a swamp, as many Black people escaping southern slavery did. She did not crouch for years in an attic or stow away in the hold of a northbound ship, as other fugitives from the South did. She did not even follow the North Star, as so many others did. All the same, she took her own freedom, and she stood up to John Dumont.

Isabella believed that God helped her plan her escape and then guided her to the Van Wagenens. With this kind family, she could care for her baby and let her wounded hand continue to heal. She did chores for her keep but was never overworked. She began to receive some religious instruction from these Dutch Reformed Christians, who prayed and sang at home. Sometimes the Van Wagenens went to Methodist camp meetings and brought Isabella along.[6]

Everything at the Van Wagenens was "so pleasant, and kind, and good," she later recalled, "and all so comfortable, enough of everything; indeed it was beautiful." Isabella basked in the feeling that "her every prayer had been answered," and for a while she felt she had no more troubles.[7]

She noticed, however, that she prayed less as the weeks went by. Truth recalled in her *Narrative* that she felt guilty for treating the Almighty like a servant to be called on only in time of need. She missed her other children and perhaps even missed old Thomas. She was used to living by the great Hudson River with all its boat traffic, but now she lived on a farm carved out of the woods at the edge of the Catskill Mountains.

Isabella wintered with the Van Wagenens. Slowly the spring melt began, icy water burbling in every little stream. Yellow forsythia and pink dogwood came into bud. Warblers flocked homeward for nesting season, filling the forests and meadows with their songs. And the wild azalea (locally called the Pinkster flower) came into bloom—signaling that the Pinkster festival was at hand.

Pinkster was a time for Afro-Dutch people to gather and celebrate their culture and to rejoice in the spring. Pinkster was a Christian festival day, marking the outpouring of God's Holy Spirit in every language to all people on the earth. On the first Pentecost, as told in the biblical book of Acts, the Holy Spirit broke every boundary of race, class, or language to bring the gospel message to everyone. Pentecost is a great leveler. There is a wildness about Pentecost, for the Spirit blows where it will and gives God's power to the lowly. Which meant that enslaved people, who in Isabella's context seldom received baptism or religious instruction, could freely receive the grace of God. "Rural New York Blacks," writes historian Margaret Washington, were "a spiritual people." They saw nature and human community as one sacred whole, and this "informed their understanding of Christianity."[8]

In 1827 Pinkster fell on June 4, one month before slavery officially ended in New York. Isabella longed to join this celebration, but now, living at the Van Wagenens' place, she was far away from the festivities. Free but lonely and isolated, she found herself "looking back to Egypt" (a biblical reference to slavery) with intense longing. These turbulent emotions rushed her along, like a small boat in a swift current.

In her *Narrative* she says she had a premonition that John Dumont was coming back to get her. Somehow, she knew he would come. Whatever the nature of their relationship, she still felt strongly connected to Dumont. Isabella decided to go back with him so she could celebrate Pinkster with her people.

As Isabella told the story, it seemed that Dumont showed up, just as she knew he would (but his appearance may have been part of her vision). Oddly, Dumont said he would *not* take her back again. Isabella assumed he was joking; surely he would not come all this way for nothing! She went inside the house to get Sophia ready. She came back out carrying the baby, and was about to climb into the wagon—when a blaze of light overwhelmed her.[9]

A dazzling radiance surrounded Isabella, and she knew she was in the presence of God. Describing the experience later, she confessed a burning sense of shame: here she was—after God had guided her to freedom—about to go back to her old life! She felt it was a "great sin" to turn away from God's gift. Had she not promised to be faithful to God? But no sooner did life get easier than she forgot all about God. Looking into her own soul, Isabella said she saw "one mass of lies" writhing like snakes. She felt that God saw straight through her. If God did not look away, she felt she would be blown out like a lamp. How long this light searched her soul, she did not know.

When Bell became aware of her surroundings again, she looked around for Dumont, but he was gone. Where he went—or if he was ever really there in the first place—did not matter. What mattered was that she was about to return to slavery, but divine light intervened. "Oh God," Isabella cried. "I did not know you were so big."

Isabella retreated into the house and tried to resume her chores . . . but it was no use. She longed to speak to God like she used to, but the feeling of "her vileness" prevented her. "I have told nothing but lies, and shall I speak again, and tell another lie to God?" she asked herself. She needed someone to talk to God on her behalf. If someone truly worthy pleaded her case, God might listen.

Then, slowly, she felt a space was opening up between herself and God. "A friend" was there shielding her from that intense light, as if holding an umbrella between her and the burning sun. Her guilt and fear began to lift as she realized that this friend who shielded her from the burning light truly loved her.

"Who are you?" Bell asked. The presence seemed to take on a distinct form, "beaming with the beauty of holiness, and radiant with love."

Confused, Isabella repeated, "I know you, and I don't know you . . ."

When she said "I know you," the presence had a distinct form and remained quiet. But when she said "I don't know you," it blurred out of focus and seemed disturbed.

"Who are you?" Bell cried. Her *Narrative* says that she longed for this heavenly friend to stay with her. She struggled until she could hardly breathe.

When she felt she could bear it no longer, "an answer came to her, saying distinctly, 'It is Jesus.'"[10] Isabella had heard that name before. She assumed that Jesus was some great man "like Washington or Lafayette"—and such powerful men would not even notice, much less care about, a poor woman like Isabella. But waves of love swept over her until she knew deep down that Jesus loved her and "had always loved her." Isabella was filled with joy, and the world around her seemed "clad in a new beauty." She often said that on that day, Jesus took away the hatred she felt toward white people. As divine love bathed her, she asked herself, "What about the white folks, who have abused you, and beat you, and abused your people? What about them?" Another wave of love came over her, and she exclaimed, "Lord, I can love even white folks!"[11] This set a direction for her. Although at times she acknowledged the anger she still felt toward white people, she kept moving with God's Spirit in the direction of love.

Now she felt sweet union with Jesus, who was "altogether lovely," human yet exceedingly great. "I saw him as a friend, standing between me and God, through whom love flowed as from a fountain." Prayer was no longer just a plea for help; it was communion with the beloved. "Thank God, I shall always pray,"[12] she said. For the rest of her life she told the story of the vision that made her a follower of Jesus. And from that point on, she later said, "all she could say or think was Jesus."[13] Isabella missed the Pinkster carnival, but she was given her own Pentecost with salvation, sanctification, and ordination all rolled into one. Truth's vision inspired her to become a preacher.

She held this experience in common with other "Black female preachers [who] insisted that they had seen heavenly visions or heard angelic voices while they were fully awake and conscious," writes historian Catherine Brekus. "Black female preachers insisted that their authority to preach had come directly from the Holy Spirit," from "visions and voices that had come from outside of themselves."[14] And since her vision happened "outside the bounds of the church . . . she took little interest in conforming her experiences to the formal demands of theology or institutional affiliation."[15]

In her *Narrative*, Sojourner Truth recalled how, at the time of her vision, she did not know that Jesus was God's Son. When she learned that others knew him too, she was surprised and a bit jealous. Yet even before her vision, she may have absorbed some things at the revivals she attended with the Van Wagenens. And after her vision, in the twenty-plus years before her *Narrative* was published, she would have picked up a great deal from many worship services she attended. Some aspects of her visionary experience—such as the light of holiness, the sense of one's own sinfulness, followed by wave upon wave of love—call to mind the writings of Jonathan Edwards (divine light or glory) or the conversion of Charles Finney (waves of love filling one's being). Isabella's visionary experience became part of her, shaping her even as she shaped it. It could never be fully described or contained in one telling because it joined her to a love that transcended words.

Before this vision of Jesus, Isabella had little compassion for herself. She said she thought her longing for home was sinful, because it signified to her that she took too lightly the freedom into which God had led her. Her spiritual struggle may have been, in part, reckoning with the losses that she suffered in order to become free. The experience of divine love may have helped her to accept her longing for home and family as natural and normal. The fault was not with her, but with slavery.

In years to come, Isabella went to the Dumont place from time to time to see her children. A member of the Dumont family later said that Isabella became a "roaring Methodist" who went "around through the kitchen preaching as she went," and "kept on preaching all day."[16]

———

Isabella was now a free woman of faith. Little Sophia was free too, thanks to Mr. Van Wagenen. Isabella's older daughters, Elizabeth and Diana, remained apprenticed to Dumont. But her son Peter had been sold to the Gedneys (to whom Dumont was related by marriage). Under New York State law, Peter would remain apprenticed to the Gedneys until he reached the age of twenty-eight. Isabella could look forward to seeing him from time to time, since he was still in the area.

This hope shattered when Isabella learned that Peter had been sold to a plantation owner in Alabama. Her son was now one of "thousands of Black New Yorkers illegally sold into perpetual bondage in the South."[17] John Dumont sold Peter within the state of New York, but then Peter changed hands several times and ended up in Alabama, on a plantation owned by Eliza Gedney's husband.

Isabella knew that if she did not help Peter, no one else would. In her *Narrative*, Truth recalled her anguish over Peter. "Oh God," she prayed, "you know how much I am distressed, for I have told you again and again. Now God, help me get my son. If you were in trouble, as I am, and I could help you, as you can me, [do you] think I wouldn't do it?"

Leaving Sophia with the Van Wagenens, Isabella set out at a trot over the eleven miles of rugged road that led to the Dumonts' house. Although she had the tall, lean build of a runner and was known for her stamina, Isabella probably reached the Dumont farm dusty, sweaty, and thirsty. Mr. Dumont was not home. Isabella's old nemesis, Sally Dumont, came to the door. Isabella said, "Peter is too young to be so far away from his mother!"

"*Ugh!*" said Mrs. Dumont. She asked why Isabella was making all this fuss when she had more children than she could possibly take care of! And now here was Bell, "running like a fool uphill and down, making a hullaba-loo all for a paltry n*****!!!"

Isabella waited. Then slowly and with great dignity she said, "*I'll have my child again.*"

"Have *your child* again?" Mrs. Dumont jeered. Why the very idea struck Isabella's former mistress as absurd. "And just *how*, pray tell, can you get him?" And if Bell could get Peter, how would she support him? "Have you any money?" Mrs. Dumont scoffed.

"No," replied Bell. "I have no money, but God has enough, or what's better! I'll have my child again," she vowed. Inwardly Bell prayed, "Oh God you know I have no money, but you can make the people do for me, and you must make the people do for me. I will never give you peace 'till you do, God."[18] Isabella was sure God would help her. "Why, I felt so *tall within*—I felt as if the *power of a nation* was with me!"

Bell went next to the Gedneys—the family that bought Peter. There she found Sally Dumont's sister, Mary Gedney. (It was Mary's son Solomon who sold Peter into slavery in Alabama.)

Mary Gedney said Isabella had no cause to worry about Peter: he would "have enough of everything and be treated like a gentleman" (a sarcastic jibe, since "gentleman" was a term reserved only for white men of means). And besides, Mary said, Peter would be cared for by Eliza, Mrs. Gedney's daughter, whose husband owned the plantation where Peter was enslaved.

"Oh, I must have my child!" Isabella implored. But Mrs. Gedney laughed in a tone so cruel it sounded demonic.

Desperate, Isabella roamed the area and told her story to all who would listen. Finally, someone told her to seek the Quakers, antislavery people who "lived out the principles of the Gospel of Christ."[19] If anyone would help Isabella, the Quakers would. Bell walked several miles to Poppletown, where there was a Quaker settlement. There she met Edward Young, who listened to her story and "informed Isabella of Peter's rights."[20] Bell was invited to stay overnight with Mr. Young's family. To her surprise, they offered her a guest room, with a "nice, high, clean, white, *beautiful* bed," as she recalled years later. But Isabella always slept on a pallet on the floor. Could this bed really be meant for her? Unsure what to do, she lay down on the floor, but, not wanting to refuse the Quakers' hospitality, she climbed up and slept in a real bed for the first time in her life.

The next day, Mr. Young told Bell that she must go to the Ulster County Courthouse and bring her complaint to the grand jury. The courthouse was in Kingston, a town of about three thousand. Mr. Young took Isabella there in his wagon. They came to the courthouse, a large stone building in the federal style, its second story graced by a gable with a decorative fan window and its roof topped by a cupola—the most imposing building Isabella had seen in her life. Here was the place where her son's fate would be decided. Isabella got down from the wagon and went inside.

Isabella knew nothing of the legal system or how to navigate it. Twenty years later, she described her younger self as "poor and ignorant." Mr. Young had instructed her to bring her complaint to the "grand jury," which she assumed to be a large and powerful man. She scanned the crowded courthouse for someone who looked the part.

She found an important-looking man, but when she approached him, he said *he* was not the grand jury and that she must go upstairs, where the grand jury could be found. The wide staircase was crowded with people waiting in line to conduct their legal affairs. Bell had to make her way through them, and they let her pass, perhaps assuming that she was in the service of some lawyer upstairs. Reaching the top, Isabella once more found an important-looking person and began her story. At first the gentleman was amused—but then, seeing Bell's distress, he pointed out the room where the grand jury was meeting. "Oh God make the people hear me," Bell prayed. "Don't let them turn me off, without hearing and helping me."[21]

Bursting into the grand jury's chamber, she disrupted the meeting. "*My son has been sold South and I must get him back*," she cried. As the jurors muttered their annoyance, a justice of the peace (a Mr. John Chipp) took Bell into a side office.[22] He asked her to swear that the child stolen away was her son. "*Yes, I swear Peter is my son!*" she said, with all the passion she could muster. Laughter erupted from the law clerks in Chipp's office, so amused were they that Isabella did not know how to take a lawful oath.

Mr. Chipp helped Bell to take the oath. Then he gave her a writ and instructed her to give it to the constable in the nearby town of New Paltz (where Peter's illegal sale took place). Isabella then set off walking and trotting barefoot for several miles. Once in New Paltz, she found "the dull Dutch constable," a bumbler who served the writ on the wrong Gedney brother. Which gave the culprit (Solomon Gedney) a chance to row across the North River in a boat. Solomon consulted his lawyer, who told him to bring Peter back or pay a thousand dollar fine and spend fourteen years in jail.[23] Duly warned, Solomon went to Alabama to get Peter, but his errand would take several months.

Meanwhile Isabella, fearful that Peter's case would be forgotten, kept up a stir with her lawyers. She made several trips to the courthouse—a ten-mile trek from the Van Wagenens' farm to Kingston. She finally moved to Kingston, so as to be present when Solomon Gedney returned with Peter.

In Kingston, Bell supported herself by doing housework for the prominent Dutch lawyers, A. B. Hasbrouck and John Rutzer. She probably lived in the basement of one of their houses—the typical servants' quarters in that region. Of several lawyers who worked pro bono to help Isabella get Peter back, Hasbrouck seems to have been the most involved. His name appears on the court documents, discovered in 2022 in the New York State Archives in Albany.[24] These documents revealed that Isabella "sued both Peter's owner and the Albany Supreme Court for allowing the illegal sale of her son."[25]

Solomon Gedney, eager to avoid fines and charges, went to Alabama, where Peter's new owner decided to return the boy to avoid charges of kidnapping. With Peter in tow, Solomon then returned to New York State. However, Solomon had no intention of giving the boy to his mother. He seemed to think that bringing Peter back to New Paltz fulfilled his legal obligation and entitled him to keep Peter as his "apprentice." If the court agreed, Peter would have to work for Solomon Gedney until the age of twenty-eight.

This Bell would not accept. Her lawyer(s) advised her to have a writ served on Solomon Gedney once more, which she did. Solomon dallied but finally "gave bonds" of $600 to guarantee his appearance in court.[26] But he waited until the court was not in session so that he could continue to keep Peter in his custody. Bell's lawyer said nothing more could be done until the court was back in session—a wait of many weeks. "I *cannot* wait," she cried. "I *must* have him *now*, while he is to be had." She feared Solomon would take Peter away, Lord knew where. Bell prayed constantly: *Oh God, give Peter into my hands, and do so quickly.* And *Oh God, make the people hear me.* Like the widow in Jesus's parable (Luke 18:1–8), she kept on pleading.

Mr. Chipp advised her to take a settlement of $300—a large sum in those days—and let Peter go. But Isabella did not want money. She wanted Peter. She began to fear that her lawyers were getting tired of her and would drop her case. In distress, she paced the streets of Kingston. If only "you could have seen me," she later recalled in her *Narrative*, "trotting about the streets, meanly clad, bareheaded, and barefooted!" She clung to her faith that God could make the judge and jury hear her, and that God would answer her prayers.

Seeing Isabella's distress, a friend in Kingston urged her to find a lawyer by the name of Romeyn.[27] "*Stick to him*," the friend urged. She must give Romeyn no peace until he helped her.

So Isabella found Romeyn and told her story. He promised that if she would give him five dollars he would get her son back. Isabella had no money, so she walked to Poppletown, where her Quaker friends gave her much more than $5. Trotting back to Kingston, she gave all the money to Romeyn. Isabella's friends later said she should have paid only the required $5 and used the rest to buy shoes for herself. But she did not want shoes. Besides, she reasoned, if $5 could get Peter back, then more than $5 would *surely* get him!

Romeyn took the money (not for himself, but to pay someone to apprehend Peter and Gedney). He told Isabella he would get Peter back within twenty-four hours. But what did that mean? Bell did not know. She kept returning to Romeyn's house—knocking on the door. Finally a servant told Bell to come back in the morning. At first light before Romeyn was out of bed, Isabella was back. After a while, Romeyn came to the door. He told Isabella that he had sent Matthew Styles (a Kingston constable)[28] to apprehend Gedney and Peter. Styles would bring them back, dead or alive, Romeyn said. With that unsettling promise, Bell was told not to return until sent for.

That evening Romeyn summoned Bell. They now had Peter and Gedney, but Peter claimed that he had no mother nearby. So Romeyn said Isabella must go to the courthouse and declare whether this boy was her son. (The court was not yet in session, but Romeyn apparently did a work-around by finding a judge to come in and hear the case.)

Isabella and Romeyn went to the courthouse. Peter and Solomon Gedney were brought in. When Peter saw Isabella he burst into tears—but not tears of joy. He begged to stay with "his dear master, who had brought him from the dreadful South, and been so kind to him," according to Truth's *Narrative*. Peter had been brainwashed to see Solomon Gedney as his hero and savior, and to fear Isabella as a bad person who was not really his mother. Peter was also told to lie about his injuries and was threatened with punishment if he told the truth.

The lawyer now questioned Peter about his wounds. The boy said the bruise on his forehead was from being kicked by his master's horse, and the scar on his cheek was from "running against the carriage."

Isabella was asked, "Is this your son?" She said yes. But Peter denied that she was his mother. Even so, lawyer Romeyn pleaded that the boy be returned to Bell, "on the ground that he had been sold out of the State, contrary to the laws."[29]

Romeyn now consulted with Isabella and told her that if she chose to prosecute, Gedney would have to pay her a pretty sum. (Solomon Gedney, once he saw how things were running against him in court, renounced all claims to Peter and denied having any interest in his services.)[30] Isabella declined to press further charges, saying she did not want money, but only her son. As she later explained in her *Narrative*, she feared she had made many enemies of local whites, which would make it hard for her to find work. She wanted Peter and dared not ask for anything more.

Now it was time for the judge to decide the case. He declared that Peter was to "be delivered into the hands of the mother—having no other master, no other controller, no other conductor, but his mother." Isabella had won! The judge told Peter to go with Isabella. "She is not my mother!" the boy wailed. "My mother does not live here." Peter begged to stay with Gedney, as Isabella sat in a corner of the courtroom feeling "helpless and despised." Patiently the lawyer, the court clerks, and then Isabella herself convinced Peter that she was his real mother and she would take good care of him.

Isabella led Peter away from the courthouse. Then she examined her son and found that his whole body was covered with scars and welts, some as thick as her finger. "Heavens! What is all *this*?" she asked Peter. He told her this was where Mr. Fowler, the plantation master, whipped, kicked, and beat him. "Oh Lord Jesus, look! See my poor child!" Isabella prayed. "Oh Lord, 'render unto them double' for all this!"[31]

Turning to Peter, she said, "Oh my God! Pete, how *did* you bear it?"

"Oh, this is nothing, mammy," said Peter. He told her about Phillis, another slave on Fowler's plantation. "She had a little baby, and Fowler cut her till the milk as well as blood ran down *her* body. You would *scare* to see Phillis, mammy."[32]

Isabella asked what Miss Eliza (Fowler's wife) said when Peter was beaten. He answered that Miss Eliza said she "wished I was with Bell." He told his mother that Eliza was the only one on Fowler's plantation who was kind to him. After Peter got a whipping, Eliza would wait till everyone else was asleep, and then she could come to put salve on Peter's wounds.

Isabella's court victory in March 1828 is today hailed as "the first time in history a Black woman successfully sued a White man for a family member's freedom."[33] It emboldened her to stand up for her rights, and the rights of others, later in her life. But her most immediate need was to support her family, with both Sophia and Peter in her care. She continued to do housework in Kingston, but since her daughters Elizabeth and Diana were still appren-

ticed to John Dumont, Isabella went there for an extended visit. To pay her
expenses while there, she hired herself out to do chores for nearby families.
John Dumont was surprised when Isabella agreed to go and help a neighbor
who was part of the Gedney clan. But Isabella said she wanted to mend fences,
so that everyone would "forget their anger toward her" over Peter's court case.
Isabella needed a good reputation in order to keep on getting work.

One day when Bell was working for the Gedneys, one of their daughters
burst in, all out of breath. "Heavens and earth, Isabella! Fowler has murdered
Cousin Eliza!" A letter had just arrived with the grim news. Bell was horrified,
but she was not surprised that the man who whipped a little boy so cruelly
could kill his own wife. The family was called together. As the letter was read
aloud, Isabella stood in the doorway and listened. The letter said that Fowler
knocked down Eliza, "broke her collarbone and tore out her windpipe." Now
he was in jail, and his motherless children were being cared for by friends.

Isabella slipped away from the somber family gathering. That she had
been present when the dreadful news came seemed to her "a special providence of God." But she took no delight in retribution, since poor murdered
Eliza had been the only person to treat Peter with kindness. Later Bell heard
that Eliza's mother, old Mrs. Gedney (who mocked Isabella for wanting to
get Peter back), was now "deranged" by grief. Isabella's conscience smote as
she recalled her prayer after seeing Peter's scars: "*Oh, Lord, render unto them
double.*" Now she wished she could take back that prayer. "O, my God! That's
too much," she said. "I did not mean quite so much, God!"[34]

So far, emancipation was not turning out as Isabella had hoped. For years,
she and her husband, Thomas, longed for a small house where they could
raise their children together. John Dumont had promised them "a log cabin
for a home of their own."[35] That promise was not kept. And anyway, freedom came too late for Thomas. He was much older than Isabella and in fee-
ble health. He was free, but his strength was spent, and he could earn only a
pittance by doing odd jobs and farm chores.[36] Around the time Isabella was
in Kingston trying to free Peter, Thomas died in a "poorhouse." The older
daughters (Diana and Elizabeth) were apprenticed to John Dumont. That left
Isabella in charge of Peter (about seven years old) and Sophia (a toddler).

To support herself and these two children, Isabella kept house for wealthy
families in Kingston. But she could not get ahead no matter how hard she

tried. And what was she to do with the children while she worked? She might bring Sophia with her and leave Peter to fend for himself; or she could put Peter in charge of Sophia. But Peter often got into trouble when Isabella was not watching him, so she found him a job as a lock-tender on the nearby Delaware-Hudson canal.[37] She did the best she could for Peter and Sophia. She took them to religious meetings, talked with them, and prayed for them. She disciplined them according to the standards of her time: "when they did wrong, I scolded at and whipped them,"[38] Truth said years later.

While in Kingston, Isabella found fellowship with the Methodists. On her way to attend worship in a private home one evening, she wondered if she would be allowed inside. If so, would she, a Black person, have to sit apart from the whites? As she approached the house, she heard singing: "There is a holy city, a world of light above, beyond the starry regions, built by a God of love." Unsure whether to enter, she stood outside and listened through the open windows. Someone inside the house beckoned her to come inside and join the singing. The hymn proclaimed that the lowliest "child of God outshines the sun." Isabella believed in the leveling power of divine love and held this moment sacred for the rest of her life.

Revival Christianity prized conversion over social status, and spiritual power over hierarchy and credentials. Some Methodist camp meetings even allowed women and Blacks to preach or lead the prayers. This suited Isabella Van Wagenen well. "To foster holiness, Methodists scorned ostentatious living and public displays of wealth and status," attracting "many poor people into their churches."[39] This Methodist simplicity and egalitarianism appealed to Isabella, who held these values throughout her life.

The Dutch Reformed church had long been established in the area, but not until 1823 did the Methodists build their first church in Kingston, New York. The building was made of rough timber and looked like a country schoolhouse. Preaching at the church's dedication was Freeborn Garretson, a Methodist minister who freed slaves he inherited in Maryland and wrote a biblical argument against slavery—*Dialogue between Do-Justice and Professing Christians* (1805). Isabella began attending this church in 1827.[40] Here she sang and prayed and perhaps testified about her vision of Jesus.

At this church, Isabella met a white woman named Mrs. Grear who knew Methodists in New York City—wealthy businessmen who supported evangelism and reform. Mrs. Grear told Isabella that if she worked for one of these families, she could expect better pay than she was getting in Kingston. Better still, Isabella might find ways to use her spiritual gifts in some of the outreach ministries run by Methodists in the big city. Mrs. Grear asked Isabella to go with her to New York City and promised to introduce her to potential employers. [41]

At that time, New York City was a hub for benevolent reformers, evangelists, and wealthy patrons who sought to convert sinners and reform society. In this way, they hoped to prepare the world for the second coming of Christ. Many Protestants shared such ambitions, and the network of organizations and reform movements they created became known as the Benevolent Empire.

Isabella may not have known about the Benevolent Empire, but she knew she wanted to use her freedom to follow her calling. She could not make a living as a preacher, but in New York City she might find more opportunities to preach the love of Jesus. She would still have to do housework, but if her employers were like-minded believers, so much the better.

If she left Kingston, what would she do with Peter and Sophia? She had to keep Peter with her. His body and mind scarred by slavery, the boy needed his mother. Perhaps in New York Peter could find work, or even go to school. And what of Sophia, the child Isabella carried to freedom? Isabella would have to decide whether to take Sophia with her or leave her with the Dumonts, where she could be with her sisters. Isabella could scarcely earn a living in Kingston, but if she moved she could not keep her family together. Wanting more from freedom, she decided to go to New York City.

3

Lost Sheep in Gotham

Isabella set out for New York City on a passenger boat heading down the Hudson River. She took Peter with her, but little Sophia probably stayed on the Dumont place along with her sisters Diana and Elizabeth.[1] If Isabella's friend Mrs. Grear traveled on the same boat, segregated seating would have kept them apart on the journey.

The trip from Kingston to New York was about one hundred miles. The boat traffic traveling southward increased steadily, until the river teemed with barges, sailing ships, and steamboats. When Isabella arrived in 1829, New York City had a population of about 200,000 people, making it the largest city in the United States. Because lower Manhattan *was* New York City in those days, Gotham (a nickname for the city based on Dutch for "goat home") did not come into view until the end of the boat trip.

Church steeples defined the skyline, their bells pealing the hours, calling to worship, and tolling for funerals. Church bells sounded the alarm when fires broke out. Accidental blazes spread quickly among the wooden buildings, all the more combustible because they were heated with coal or wood and lighted with oil lamps. When the Great Fire of 1835 consumed seventeen blocks, it could be seen as far away as Philadelphia.

Horses defined the streets. Horse-drawn vehicles clattered over cobblestone, but since many streets were as yet unpaved, traffic sent up clouds of dust or spattered mud on passersby. The stench of horse manure and urine was ever present, becoming most intense in the warmer months. Cleaning up after the horses was a job typically done by Black men. Animals ran loose in the streets: pigs wallowed in the mud or rooted through garbage, and chickens pecked in the refuse as rats and mice darted everywhere in search of food.

Some parts of the city boasted wealth: fine homes of the merchants, stately churches, and swanky shops that sold luxury goods from all over the world. The pounding of hammers and rasping of saws together with the shouts of workers hailed a city always building and growing.

When Isabella arrived, Black New Yorkers spoke the languages of Africa and Europe, often blending them together. Some were freeborn, and others, like Isabella, were recently freed. Slavery had officially ended in New York, but equality was a distant hope. Black men could not vote. "Blacks were not allowed on [horse drawn] street stages, and when a Black man hailed one of the new omnibuses going up Broadway, the driver warded him off with a whip, convulsing white bystanders with laughter."[2] Restaurants, barbershops, and tearooms did not admit Blacks, and larger venues like theaters and churches either denied entrance to Blacks or restricted them to balconies or back rows. Even the cemeteries were segregated.

"New York was the most potent proslavery and pro-South city" in the North, writes historian Jonathan Wells, "due in large part to the lucrative trade between Manhattan banks and insurance companies and the slaveholders of the cotton South."[3] Although the transatlantic slave trade was outlawed in 1808, New York was one of several port cities in the North that outfitted slave ships and profited from the illegal slave trade.

Despite these dangers, many fugitive slaves lived in town or passed through. Some stowed away on ships that came to New York Harbor from southern ports. Fugitives would slip into town by night and blend into the city's Black population. Slave catchers prowled the streets and the harbors in search of runaways, and each person captured was worth a cash bounty when returned to the owner. Many legally free Black people were kidnapped and sold south, especially children. Kidnapping was rampant in New York City, and, thanks to a complicit court system, politicians, and police department, perpetrators could make a great deal of money with little fear of punishment.[4]

Black New Yorkers fought back. Taking the lead in the struggle was David Ruggles, a freeborn Black man who would later become a mentor to Sojourner Truth. Ruggles ran the first Black bookstore and reading room in the city and edited *Mirror of Liberty*, the first magazine written by and for Black people. He was a prominent member of Mother Zion Church,[5] where Sojourner Truth attended during part of her time in the city. A sketch of

Ruggles shows him sporting a fashionably tailored coat, with white top hat and black silk bow tie, spectacles perched on the end of his nose.

Ruggles knew that New York City was a dangerous place for fugitives from slavery.[6] So he organized vigilance committees to keep a sharp lookout for slave catchers and to warn those who were at risk of capture; hiding places were prepared and kept ready. Activists (called "conductors") were trained to move fugitives on to safety. Today, David Ruggles "is thought to have helped convey as many as 600 people to freedom."[7] Ruggles and his associates also organized "a legal defense for all cases of Black residents who were accused of being fugitives."[8] This made him an enemy of the kidnappers and their cronies.

Ruggles was jailed several times, threatened by mobs, and stalked by kidnappers. After years of dangerous work, Ruggles's debts were mounting and his health was failing to the point where he suffered "seasons of mental anxiety."[9] Author and activist Lydia Marie Child arranged for Ruggles to move to an antislavery commune in Massachusetts, where he later met Sojourner Truth; but during the years she lived in New York City, their paths are not known to have crossed.

Isabella arrived in Manhattan as an Afro-Dutch domestic worker from upstate. Unused to urban life, she had to pluck up her courage. As she told the story later, she resolved "that even if she was despised she would go among the white people and learn all she could."[10] But why despised? Because of the color of her skin, her Dutch accent, her country ways and low status as a housekeeper. Fortunately, she had Mrs. Grear to help her find work.

Mrs. Grear introduced Isabella to potential employers—Methodist merchants who could afford to pay a housekeeper and were active in revival and reform work. Employment was Isabella's most practical need, but she longed to follow her calling to preach. To pay her expenses and save a little money, she would need more than one job. Like many other domestic workers, she stayed overnight with employers and got her meals wherever she was working. Wealthy people typically had rooms where hired help could stay.

Isabella's son Peter stayed with her to begin with. Although Peter was traumatized by slavery and kidnapping, Isabella had high hopes for her son. According to Truth's *Narrative*, Peter was growing up to be "a tall, well-formed, active lad." He was quick-witted and cheerful, with "much that was open, generous and winning about him."[11]

Unfortunately, racial prejudice closed most doors to Peter. Schools were for whites only (except for the African Free School, funded by charity). All trades requiring a license were for whites only. Factories typically employed whites only. A younger Black boy might get work cleaning stables, sweeping chimneys, or running errands, and when he got older, he could be a waiter, drive a wagon or a coach, or become a day laborer.[12]

Many Black males went to sea, where they could get better pay. But life at sea required submission to a strict chain of command enforced by the lash, as well as exposure to harsh weather and the risk of shipwreck. Once the voyage was over, the sailors got their liberty and their pay. Even young boys could join a ship's crew to learn life at sea, doing menial chores to earn their keep. Isabella urged Peter to consider it, but in vain.

When Isabella worked or attended religious meetings, Peter made friends with boys much like himself. They taught him how to pick pockets and steal from shops and market stalls. Peter might have found a better path at the free African school, but he was not interested in doing so. His new friends "did not improve either his habits or his morals," and, according to Truth's *Narrative*, Peter had "little power to withstand temptation." Peter was clever and learned to "conceal from his mother and her friends"[13] anything that might worry them.

Before long Peter was caught stealing. When her son got into trouble, Isabella would plead with the authorities for leniency, on account of Peter's age or circumstances. Then, getting Peter alone, she would confront, warn, and punish him. He always said he was sorry and promised to do better next time. But when Isabella turned her back, Peter rejoined his friends on the streets.

Isabella enlisted the help of others to turn Peter around. A white woman (unnamed in Truth's *Narrative*, but perhaps one of Isabella's employers) took Peter aside and tried to reason with him. He admitted his faults and impressed her as being very intelligent. She offered to pay for Peter to attend a navigation school for Black boys. If Peter learned basic seamanship, he could find work on a ship's crew. There might even be a future in it, for "many Black men still took to the sea, as sailors, stewards, or cooks, so many that in the late 1820s the African Free School added navigation to its curriculum."[14]

Peter feigned interest long enough to please his mother and her patron. Then he skipped classes to roam the city with his friends, making excuses at school to cover his absences. Soon the ruse was discovered.

So Isabella and her patron found "an excellent place" for Peter as a wagon driver for a wealthy merchant. The job required Peter to wear livery (uniforms worn by coachmen to display their employers' wealth). Peter quickly sold the livery along with a few other things purloined from his new employer. Peter was fired, but the boss declined to prosecute because Peter was so young.

When Peter got into trouble, Isabella confronted him. Peter said he was sorry and promised to be good. But the more this happened, the harder it was for Isabella to believe Peter's excuses. Before his tears of repentance dried, he was out on the street selling "stolen loot on street corners and at tavern hangouts."[15]

Peter was jailed several times. Isabella feared that his crimes would escalate to something worse than theft. She pleaded with him to take a job with a ship's crew, but he was having too much fun with his friends.

While Peter became an artful dodger on the streets, Isabella became a respected housekeeper in the homes of wealthy merchants. One of her employers was James LaTourette, a successful dealer in furs who lived in the Bowery (a street named for the "Boers," or Dutch farmers). LaTourette believed that women should be able to preach in public and to conduct reform activities without male supervision.[16] When Isabella first came to the city, the LaTourette family attended the John Street Church,[17] the oldest Methodist church in town.

Isabella decided to go there too. She had a letter of reference from the Methodist church in Kingston, and, after presenting it to the John Street Church, she was received as a "colored" member. In those days Methodists had small fellowship groups called classes; at the John Street Church, these classes were segregated by race, and so was seating during worship. On Communion Sundays, whites were served first and then Blacks. Only white men could be ministers, and other forms of leadership were for whites only. Even though the church was antislavery, it practiced a racial caste system. And unlike the more down-to-earth Methodists Isabella had known in Kingston, the John Street Church had become more wealthy and status-conscious over the years.[18] Isabella did not stay there long.

She found an African Methodist church where she was welcome. The congregation was started in 1796 by Black artisans from the John Street Church who rejected its discriminatory practices. They built Zion Church at the corner of Leonard and Church Streets, near the Five Points area, a "working class slum." Entering the church, "Zion's members . . . would see a brothel next door."[19] In 1821, Zion Church became known as Mother Zion, because it was the founding church of a new Black denomination: the African Methodist Episcopal Church Zion.

At Mother Zion, African Americans could worship freely under their own leadership. At this "church of the Black working class," Isabella may have heard "debates and speeches" on slavery, abolition, and other issues of the day,[20] writes historian Margaret Washington. At Mother Zion, women "engaged in self-help, provided for sick and shut-in members, supported the adult night school and the children's African Free School, aided the poor, and worked for the Underground Railroad."[21]

One day at Mother Zion, a well-dressed woman approached Isabella. She introduced herself as Sophia, Isabella's older sister who had been sold away before Bell was born. Their mother, Mau-mau Bett, had told Isabella about Sophia, and later on Isabella named her youngest daughter Sophia. Now the sisters met and embraced with joy. Perhaps they swapped stories of how they each became free and what brought them to the big city. Sophia said that their brother Michael also lived in the city and arranged for Isabella to meet him. At this meeting, Michael told Isabella that another of their siblings—a sister named Dinah—used to worship at Mother Zion. Michael told Isabella what class (prayer group) Dinah used to attend and described her. But Dinah had recently died.

Then Isabella remembered a woman she had recently prayed with at Mother Zion. "The peculiar feeling of her hand, the bony hardness," so like Isabella's own, impressed her strongly at the time, but she did not know why. Now she understood that this woman was not only a sister in Christ—she was Bell's own flesh and blood. Isabella knew that she had an older sister named Dinah, and, although she was sold away before Isabella was born, the name would have registered. Unfortunately, Dinah had changed her name to Nancy, so Isabella had no idea of her identity.

"Damn," Isabella swore through tears. "Here she was; we met . . . and yet I could not know she was my sister; and now I see she looked so like my mother!" Then the reunited siblings, Sophia, Isabella, and Michael, wept. "Oh Lord," Isabella cried, "what is this slavery, that it can do such dreadful things? What evil can it not do?"[22]

Mother Zion's arms held them through the joyful reunion and the pain of loss. The church reached out to offer hope and help to people in New York City's toughest neighborhood, called Five Points.

Five Points was once a swamp and then a water collection pond. After it was poorly drained and filled with rubble, it became a place for folk who could not afford to live anywhere else. Located between Broadway and the Bowery, the area was home to many African Americans and Irish. Overcrowded buildings with little or no sanitation invited cholera and tuberculosis, yellow fever and smallpox. But New Yorkers from other neighborhoods came to frequent the dance halls, sex houses, and theaters of Five Points. Drunks and prostitutes shadowed the doorways and alleys. Pigs and feral dogs roamed the streets along with gangs and homeless children. The neighborhood had a large municipal jail, rebuilt in 1838 and called "the Tombs" because its façade looked like an ancient Egyptian burial place.

Five Points attracted missionaries and reformers, and Isabella joined their ranks. After putting in a day of work, she went to Five Points to evangelize. She sometimes felt the sting of rejection. Years later she told how, as a newcomer to New York City, she wanted "to get among her own colored people and teach them" about Jesus. Bell "used to go and hold prayer meetings at the houses of the people in the Five Points." But sometimes they rebuffed her, preferring instead "to hear great people," not an unknown preaching woman. The *Narrative of Sojourner Truth* says that Isabella invited a Black woman to pray with her, but the woman said she already had all the ministers she needed. Rejected, Isabella "went off weeping."[23] It seems that many Blacks as well as whites "preferred educated male ministers to unlettered female exhorters."[24]

Female preachers were rare in those days, and they were often met with scorn—even from other women. One of the few to gain lasting renown would be Sojourner Truth—the person Isabella was becoming. Isabella also attended a house church in the elegant home of her employer, James La-Tourette, who left the John Street Methodist Church in order to develop an independent, lay-led ministry. LaTourette "opposed both the consumption of alcoholic beverages and the institution of slavery," writes historian Nell Irvin Painter. His followers "became itinerant preachers who were not connected with any formal church."[25]

Isabella preached in LaTourette's house church and at camp meetings in what was then rural Manhattan. A contemporary of Isabella's said that she was "known among the Methodists, and . . . much respected by them." On one occasion when she was "preaching on the same ground at the same time" as the famed Irish preacher John Newland Maffitt, she drew a bigger audience.[26]

The prostitutes were her toughest audience. New York had legions of them working in back-alley shacks and saloons and also in stylish "parlor houses" and hotels. Their customers were sailors and laborers, merchants, bankers, and businessmen. The Five Points area was "the summit of public sexuality," with prostitutes walking "the streets day and night" soliciting.

Women had few ways to make money in those days. Middle-class women who were single or widowed might be teachers or governesses; poor women could sew and wash clothing, cook or clean—for very low pay. Desperately poor women took "to the streets to hawk fruits or vegetables, or themselves."[27] Madams and pimps kept a sharp lookout for new "girls" to staff their brothels. In the New York slang of the time, prostitutes were called "dolly mops" or "fallen women" or "dirty puzzles." But to evangelists like Isabella, they were "lost sheep" straying from the Good Shepherd's fold. If someone preached the gospel to them, they might repent and be saved.

The mission to the prostitutes was one of several reform movements embraced by the perfectionists, who strove to banish all sin from self and society and thereby prepare the world for the return of Christ. Isabella became involved through LaTourette, who promoted spiritual perfection and social reform.

Perhaps Isabella felt compassion for the prostitutes. Like them, she had been cast adrift from her family. She knew poverty, abuse, and slavery. But unlike them, Isabella took pride in honest labor. She had a good reputation and carried herself with dignity, knowing that she was a preacher called to seek and save the lost. According to her *Narrative*, Isabella ventured into the slums in the company of two white women, Mrs. Grear (who brought Bell to New York City) and Mrs. LaTourette (Bell's employer's wife). But these proper white ladies "dared not follow"[28] into some of the places Isabella went in search of lost sheep.

One can imagine Isabella, her wool cloak about her shoulders and a white kerchief on her head, searching Five Points for lost women. Holding her plain long skirt carefully to one side as she stepped around horse manure and garbage, or ascended flights of grimy stairs, Isabella ignored taunts from those in "the trade" who held do-gooders in contempt.[29]

Some of the prostitutes she invited to prayer meetings accepted. At these gatherings a few women became "delirious with excitement." Truth's *Narrative* recalls one person who "in a fit of ecstasy . . . jumped upon [Isabella's] cloak" and dragged her to the floor. Believing that Isabella "had fallen in a spiritual trance," the worshipers got to "jumping, shouting, stamping, and clapping" their hands, trampling over Isabella while "rejoicing over her spirit." Isabella struggled to her feet, bruised and shaken. From that point on she "refused to attend any more such meetings," doubting whether "God had anything to do with such worship."[30] It was hardly a sweet hour of prayer.

Isabella was invited to preach at the Magdalene Asylum on Bowery Hill, a halfway house for ex-prostitutes. It was named after the biblical character Mary Magdalene, who, according to tradition, turned from a life of sin to follow Jesus. Now Isabella no longer needed to search out the lost sheep; she could simply go to the Magdalene Asylum, where a little flock was already gathered.

It was Katy, a friend of Isabella's from Mother Zion Church, who brought Isabella to the asylum for the first time. Katy had been enslaved in Virginia, and, like Isabella, she left children behind in order to work in the city. Now Katy was keeping house for Elijah Pierson, a merchant who ran the Magdalene Asylum. Pierson was part of the perfectionist network that sought to bring in the kingdom of God through social reforms and holy living. At the Magdalene Asylum, Katy introduced Isabella to Pierson.[31]

"Are you baptized?" Pierson asked Isabella.

"By the Holy Ghost,"[32] she replied, to Pierson's delight.

Pierson saw Isabella as a person with divine gifts, someone he wanted to join his inner circle of followers. Isabella probably saw Pierson as a man of faith whose beliefs dovetailed with her own. He cared about the poor. He rejected the Christian denominations in favor of free house churches. He followed personal inspiration rather than doctrine. Since the friendship of Isabella and Elijah led down a strange path, some background on Pierson may be helpful.

Long before Isabella met him, Elijah Pierson was seeking "a simpler and more spiritual approach to life."[33] Although he was rich, no curtains graced the windows of his spacious home on Bowery Hill. The floors had no rugs, and the walls were bare. Instead of luxuries, the place was fitted out with a schoolroom, a chapel, and guest rooms for Elijah's followers.[34] He and his wife, Sarah, were part of the "retrenchment movement," which shunned luxury in favor of self-denial and reform. They had formed a network of like-minded friends to meet for worship and to support reform projects like the Magdalene Asylum.

One day Pierson was riding through the city on an omnibus (a large horse-drawn coach that carried passengers inside and on top). As the vehicle trundled along, Elijah thought he heard God say to him: "*You are now 'Elijah the Tishbite*'" (a biblical prophet from Tishbe). Pierson took this to mean that the spirit of the ancient biblical prophet now dwelt within him. Then he seemed to hear this command: "*Gather all the members of Israel at the foot of Mt. Carmel.*" Elijah obeyed. He tried to gather his friends to live with him at his Bowery Hill home.[35] Some moved in with him, but others, doubting his sanity, declined the invitation.

Meanwhile, Elijah's wife, Sarah, was dying of consumption (tuberculosis). Elijah thought he could heal her if he had enough faith. He summoned his followers, and together they anointed Sarah with oil, laid their hands on her, and prayed for healing. Six days later she died. Elijah shocked his friends by promising to raise Sarah from the dead at the funeral.[36] On July 1, 1830, a large crowd gathered for the funeral. Pierson "extended his hands over [Sarah's] coffin, and asked all those present to pray that the Lord would raise her up."[37] The women fanned themselves, and the men shuffled their feet, unsure how to respond. Elijah prayed. Nothing happened. After the coffin was closed and taken away for burial, friends took Elijah home.

Elijah would not accept Sarah's death. He insisted that God would raise Sarah very soon, or else send her spirit back clothed in another body. Elijah believed Sarah would return one way or another. Pierson's Christian friends, distressed by his denial of death, parted company with him. However, Pierson found new friends who believed in him and began to gather them into his house.[38]

Around this time, a slave revolt in Virginia shocked the nation. On August 21, 1831, Nat Turner and his followers killed more than fifty white people. In a fury of retribution, whites rounded up and slaughtered two hundred Blacks and beat hundreds more—the vast majority of whom were not involved in the Turner rebellion. Harsh new laws were put in place to make Southern slavery even more restrictive. In response, William Lloyd Garrison started the Boston-based abolitionist paper the *Liberator* and founded the

American Anti-Slavery Society. The antislavery movement became more militant and better organized. One day Sojourner Truth would join it and become renowned for her public speaking and singing.

However, in the fall of 1831, Isabella became Elijah Pierson's temporary housekeeper and a member of his commune. Bell's friend Katy normally kept house for Elijah, but since she was in Virginia visiting her children, Elijah needed help managing his household of two motherless daughters and several lodgers.

Isabella accepted Pierson's offer and moved into his house. (Where Peter was at this time is not clear; he could have been living with his friends, or visiting back at the Dumont place, or possibly in jail.) Isabella left her other employers and no longer worshiped at LaTourette's church or even at Mother Zion. Instead she became "one of the 'spirits' in Pierson's Kingdom."[39] She prepared the meals, did cleaning and laundry, and supervised Elijah's daughters; she continued her ministry at the Magdalene Asylum because it was part of Elijah's work.

Isabella was more than a housekeeper. Elijah called her a "master spirit" and sometimes took her on preaching missions to New Jersey.[40] The opportunity to preach was not open to women at Mother Zion, which may be one reason she moved toward Elijah's ministry. Isabella was "at once both the domestic and the equal, and the depository of very curious, if not valuable, information," says the *Narrative of Sojourner Truth*.[41] Elijah may have linked Isabella's race with powers of healing, prophecy, and awareness of the spirit world so often associated with Africa, according to Margaret Washington. Perhaps Elijah saw Isabella's lack of formal training in Christianity as a strength, insofar as it made her more receptive to unorthodox teachings.[42]

Elijah treated everyone under his roof as an equal. All meals were taken together at a common table. This mattered to Isabella. She was used to a social order in which Black people (whether enslaved or employed) prepared the food for whites to eat first. Blacks ate later, usually at a different table. Elijah's open table signaled a new kingdom.

When she joined Elijah's household, Isabella had a small savings account. He now told her to withdraw her money from the bank and turn it over to him, so that he could invest it in a common fund for the community. This fund was supposed to supply all of Isabella's needs for the rest of her life. Trusting Elijah, Isabella took her money out of the bank and handed it over. After years of scrimping and saving, she may have been relieved to stop worrying about money.

Isabella's friend Katy returned in the late winter of 1832; at that point, Isabella could have sought work with her former employers. Instead, she chose to stay where she was treated as an equal and respected for her higher talents. She wanted to pursue her quest for perfection, and Elijah seemed like a good mentor.

He fasted for part of every week, sometimes going three whole days without eating. When Isabella asked why Elijah fasted, he explained that it "gave him great light in the things of God." If fasting gives "light inwardly and spiritually," she said, "I need it as much as anybody—and I'll fast too." For three days she took no food or water. For the first day or two, "she did get light, so light . . . that she could 'skim around like a gull,'"[43] she recalled. By the end of the third day, she was weak. On the fourth morning when she tried to rise, she fell down. She struggled to her feet and went to the pantry, where she ate an entire loaf of bread and guzzled water. Fearing that her extreme hunger would offend God, Isabella was relieved when nothing happened.

Pierson held beliefs that set him apart from the religious circles Isabella had moved in up to that point. In particular, his "belief in transmigration of souls, direct teachings of the Holy Spirit, the presence of devil-spirits, and [spirit] possession were too bizarre even for Isabella's Perfectionist associates."[44] Isabella may not have been aware that by casting her lot with Elijah, she was moving away from the fellowship she had known at Mother Zion; not even perfectionists like James LaTourette would follow Elijah's teachings.

At least Elijah was kind and tried to treat everyone as an equal. The same could not be said of a stranger who was coming to Elijah's house. Once this man appeared, Isabella's life would take a very strange turn.

4

The Kingdom of Matthias

On the fifth of May 1832 Isabella went to answer the door of Elijah Pierson's home. A tall middle-aged man stood before her, dressed in outdated clothing. His hair was pulled back and tied behind his head, and a long, grizzled beard sprawled down his chest. His gaze was so intense that Isabella wondered for a moment if Jesus stood before her.

The visitor said he was looking for Elijah Pierson, but Isabella said, "Mr. Pierson is not home." Even so, she showed the man into the parlor, where he introduced himself as Matthias the Prophet. As Isabella told the story later, Matthias said he was "a Jew" (by which she thought he meant "a converted Jew"), perhaps sent by God to bring in the kingdom that Elijah Pierson expected.[1] The visitor questioned Isabella about Elijah's beliefs and was pleased to learn that Elijah did not align with any of the churches. Matthias promised to return when Elijah was home.

Matthias the Prophet was one of many religious innovators in nineteenth-century America who gathered followers from Christianity's margins. Isabella's journey from the Methodists to the perfectionists had led her to those margins. Her ties to perfectionists taught her to distrust the churches, which often failed to live out their creed. Her quest for a community of pure and perfect religion made her willing to listen to someone like Matthias.

Matthias's real name was Robert Matthews. He was born in 1788 in upstate New York and orphaned at an early age. Relatives raised him in a strict Scottish Presbyterian sect, whose minister gave the young child a blessing. From that time on, Matthews thought God gave him a special destiny. As a young man, he taught himself carpentry and then sought work in New York City.

A carpenter could always get work in Manhattan, but *keeping* work was much harder for Matthews. When other workmen swore prodigiously and drank on the job, Matthews told them: "Repent or be damned." The workers mocked Matthews, and the boss fired him. The same thing happened at his next job, and the next.

Matthews returned to his hometown of Coila, New York, where relatives helped to set him up as a storekeeper. He made trips to New York City to obtain flour and seed, tools and cloth for his store. In 1813 Robert Matthews married Margaret Wright. They started a family and seemed to be living a normal life, but at the store people began to notice that Matthews had "strange seizures of intense peevishness."[2] He borrowed money to expand the store, but a failure of credit put him out of business.

Robert Matthews took his family to Manhattan, where he tried again to support himself as a carpenter. But two of their children fell ill and died. Then Matthews got sick and could not work for months. As his family sank into poverty, he suffered from "headaches, violent fits and sudden rages." Matthews took to beating the children and shouting at Margaret. He started building a model of Solomon's Temple as he imagined it to have looked in Bible times. He claimed that "wandering Hebrews" were abroad in the land and vowed to join them. Margaret was beginning to doubt her husband's sanity.[3]

The family drifted north to Albany, where Matthews again found construction work. He heard the preaching of Charles Finney, a revival minister who demanded conversion and sanctification (which to Finney meant perfection or the complete absence of sin) in the Christian life. Deeply shaken, Matthews decided that all of his own religion was worthless. Then smallpox swept through the town, and the Matthewses' youngest child died—the third they had lost. Robert blamed Margaret, beating her with a rawhide whip to drive the bad spirit out of her.[4] He started preaching at his construction job and was fired.

Now Matthews took to ranting at people on the street. He would barge into public meetings and church services, where he shouted until someone dragged him away. Beards were not in fashion then, but Matthews stopped shaving because he thought the practice was against the Bible. With his long beard and piercing eyes, he must have looked, to others, like a madman.

By this time Margaret and the children were living on charity. When churchwomen brought them food or clothing, Matthews was enraged. As the patriarch, he claimed the right to let his family starve if it suited him. Matthews was in and out of jail for beating his wife and disturbing the peace. Poor Margaret could not seek a divorce because the laws of that time did not give her sufficient grounds.

In 1831 Robert Matthews began to call himself "Matthias, Prophet of the God of the Jews." In the Bible, Matthias was chosen to replace Judas and thus became the last of Jesus's disciples. And now Matthews claimed that the ancient spirit of Matthias dwelt within him. In other words, Matthews believed in the transmigration of souls, meaning that a spirit or soul from the past can inhabit the body of a person now living.

Matthias took his message on the road, traveling as far south as Washington, DC. When in New York City, he lived in "a rooming house near the Battery." A fellow lodger heard Matthias claim to be a prophet in succession to Moses and Jesus, yet thought Matthias had only a poor knowledge of the Bible. The lodger saw Matthias as "more of a knave than a fool . . . a dupe to his own fraud." He was vain "and quite charmed with his beard." Another eyewitness saw Matthias wandering "the streets of lower Manhattan, predicting the end of the world or the coming of Christ, or some other humbug."[5]

Some other humbug included Matthias's claim to have been on earth for more than eighteen hundred years; and that all who "eat swine's flesh are of the devil," and that whoever eats pork will tell a lie less than a half hour later; and that the world will soon burst into flame. Matthias taught that prayer is a mockery and Holy Communion a hoax and that all religions except his own were wrong. Matthias held women in contempt. "Everything that has the smell of woman will be destroyed," he proclaimed. He believed it was wicked for men to teach women, and that women who dare to teach men were condemned to hell. Women can only be saved by serving men.

On the day Matthias was to meet Elijah for the first time, Isabella hurried to finish the housework. Matthias was brought into the parlor, and Elijah, not yet knowing Matthias's views on women, invited Isabella to stay and listen as the two men talked. Each man claimed to have a spirit from ancient times inhabiting his body. Finding that they had received these spirits on the very same day, they concluded that God wanted them to bring in the kingdom together.

However, as Matthias claimed he was "the spirit of God" come to earth, he outranked Elijah.[6] Elijah then agreed to make way for Matthias, and they sealed their agreement by washing each other's feet. Witnessing this display of brotherly love, Isabella saw Matthias's coming to Pierson's house as an answer to prayer. Matthias was invited to dinner. He stayed overnight and made himself at home.

The next day Elijah preached for the last time. Matthias stopped all prayer and social reform work. No longer could women testify or pray aloud when men were present. They must remain silent. Isabella no longer preached or led others in prayer. This seems very strange to anyone who knows of Sojourner Truth's career as a public speaker, but then Isabella was not yet Sojourner Truth. Isabella was not that far out from slavery. She was used to an authoritarian system in which obedience to a master's whims, no matter how cruel or bizarre, was a matter of survival. Yet Matthias also attracted white people who were educated, some of whom were wealthy.

Not everyone in Elijah Pierson's house believed in Matthias. A schoolteacher named Mr. Sherwood lived in Elijah's house and rented space to teach his students there. Calling Matthias an imposter, Sherwood reached out and pulled Matthias's beard.[7] Meanwhile Isabella was harassed by Mrs. Bolton, an ex-prostitute who did all the sewing for the Pierson household. She taunted Isabella with tales of her former exploits. Elijah told the two women to wash one another's feet in an act of humility. It didn't work. The tension in Elijah's house built up to the point where someone had to leave.

So Matthias moved into an elegant home in lower Manhattan, and Isabella went along to keep house for him. The home belonged to Sylvester Mills, a wealthy merchant, widower, and former Presbyterian. Mills became a follower of Elijah, through whom he met Matthias and believed in him.[8] Mills was delighted to lodge Matthias and opened his home so others could come listen to the prophet's teachings. As word got around that all guests would be fed, attendance grew. All were warned that anyone who challenged Matthias's teachings would be driven away.

Sylvester loaned a fine carriage to Matthias, who liked to drive through the city, alighting here and there to preach to passersby. Sometimes he would enter shops "and shout warnings at the merchants and their astonished customers."[9]

These warnings seemed to come true in the summer of 1832, when cholera swept New York City and killed more than three thousand people. Nobody knew that cholera spreads through contaminated water—so places with poor sanitation were hardest hit. Matthias explained it all as the wrath of God, touting the good health of his friends and followers as proof of God's favor. But they were spared only because Sylvester Mills, like other wealthy people, got his drinking water from upstate.[10]

Matthias continued to spend Sylvester's money freely. He bought clothes of silk, fur, and velvet and ordered a silver table service engraved with Bible verses and symbols. These expenditures alarmed Sylvester's relatives; they also worried that his house would be mobbed. To prevent this, the Mills family decided to have both Matthias and Sylvester "arrested on the charge of lunacy."[11] They got the police to assist them; they also rounded up some of Sylvester Mills's business friends, recruited some clergymen, and enlisted several neighbors.

When this delegation came to the front door, Isabella refused to let them in. Not so easily put off, they went to a side door, where another servant let them in. Isabella rushed to block their entry, only to be shoved aside. She sprang up and kept putting herself between the intruders and Matthias. Then one of Sylvester's brothers struck Isabella a hard blow to the neck, and she fell to the floor. Fighting through her pain, she got up and continued to resist the intruders until several men held her down.

Some of the invaders grabbed Matthias, "shaved [him] clean, cut his hair, took his money and his watch, stripped off most of his clothing and generally humiliated him."[12] He did not fight back. Outside the house a mob was calling for Matthias's arrest; they cheered when he was brought out. By this time Isabella had been let go. She went out into the street, where she saw clergymen in the crowd and concluded that Christians were persecuting Matthias. This tightened Isabella's loyalty to Matthias and loosened her ties to Christianity.[13]

Matthias and Sylvester were taken to the lunatic asylum at Bloomingdale Hospital, north of town. Isabella went to Elijah Pierson's house and begged him to help Matthias. She must have been persuasive, for Pierson got a lawyer, put up some bail money, and got Matthias released. Matthias stood accused of blasphemy, but it was a difficult charge to prove, and he was not convicted.

Matthias needed somewhere to go, but Elijah, not wanting his own house to be mobbed, gave Matthias a monthly allowance and told him to rent other lodgings. Isabella went along with the chastened prophet to keep house for him. In April 1833, Elijah Pierson, in a flash of common sense, stopped paying Matthias's rent. Matthias then took rooms in a hotel. Isabella found work as a housekeeper with another family but continued to do Matthias's laundry.

Matthias's luck turned when a wealthy businessman offered him a house in the country where he could gather some followers. The benefactor was Benjamin Folger, a businessman who belonged to the same network of perfectionists as Elijah Pierson. Folger lived in the city but also held property some thirty miles north of Manhattan, on the Hudson River, near the little village of Sing Sing. It was secluded and yet within easy reach of the city, the perfect setting for a commune.

It was Elijah Pierson who introduced Benjamin Folger and his wife, Ann, to Matthias. The Folgers must have seen a change in their old friend Elijah. He used to be a Christian (albeit an eccentric one), but now he told the Folgers that "Christianity was the work of devils. . . . God the Father, in the person of Matthias, had returned to set things right." Elijah said the Folgers must leave their church, avoid prayer meetings, and stop teaching Sunday school. Females must be subordinate to males. "Ann must not preach or teach," Elijah said, declaring that "Benjamin must get control of his house."[14] The Folgers could see that Elijah no longer looked like a businessman: he had stopped shaving and no longer cut his hair or his fingernails. Despite these oddities, the Folgers "believed themselves under the teaching of the Spirit"[15] and joined the cult of Matthias.

The Folger estate on the Hudson became the new center for the kingdom. Matthias called it Zion Hill (or Mount Zion). The Folgers gave up ownership of the property, which was held in trust first by Elijah and then by Matthias.

Meanwhile, Isabella was still working in the city. One day Matthias came to tell her that Elijah Pierson was living at Zion Hill on the Hudson. However, Elijah was "sick and throwing fits," and Ann Folger needed help taking care of him. When Matthias asked Isabella to come and see the place for herself, she agreed to pay a visit.

Isabella liked what she saw: an elegant home and a small farm close to the river. After several years of Manhattan's grit and noise, the quiet, rural setting appealed to Isabella. "Even well-off blacks rarely took summer retreats up the Hudson or lounged in the confines of uptown parks."[16]

After her son Peter drifted out from under her care, Isabella longed to be part of a family and seemed willing to accept Matthias's role as "Father."

Isabella returned to the city to give notice to her employers. In October 1833, she joined Zion Hill, which came to be called the Kingdom of Matthias.

There was a semblance of equality in the Kingdom, for all members ate at the same table. They "fasted often and followed a diet that emphasized fresh fruit and vegetables and prohibited alcohol."[17] But such practices did not change the fact that some members were wealthy and some were not. The little savings Isabella had turned over to Elijah were now absorbed into Zion Hill, along with a few simple furnishings she owned. Isabella and the others received no pay for their work but were given food and a pleasant house to live in, and perhaps some new clothing as needed. Meanwhile, the wealthy members of Zion Hill who kept their own property in the city could travel back and forth with ease.

As the patriarch, Matthias insisted that everyone call him "Father." Just below him were Elijah Pierson and the Folgers, whose wealth underwrote the commune. Most of the drama swirled around these four people. Supporting characters included Isabella and Catherine Galloway, a white kitchen maid who had worked for Sylvester Mills. A few other members came and went, including some children of the principals. The only Black person in the house was Isabella, and from her vantage point as a housekeeper, she kept watch on the main characters and their foibles.

Matthias ruled in all things. He assigned the chores in the house and on the farm. He also ordered Kingdom members to bathe one another and decreed who should bathe whom. "The household revolved around Matthias's power, his anger, and obedience to him in all things."[18] To do anything without asking Matthias was to provoke his outrage. "We regarded [Matthias] as God the Father," Ann Folger later said. He was in charge of "the Holy Ghost" and could "bestow it on whom he would."[19]

It was dangerous to cross Matthias. Those who offended him received a beating. Matthias whipped those who became ill for letting an evil spirit into their bodies and then shouted commands to cast out these evil spirits. He did not allow the sick to see a doctor or take medication. One day Matthias was beating one of his young sons, presumably for discipline. Isabella intervened to spare the boy. Turning from his son, Matthias struck Isabella with his cowhide lash and roared, "Shall a sick devil undertake to dictate to me?"[20]

Fortunately for the others, Matthias liked going to New York City. He would ride around town in a fancy carriage or stroll along the Battery. He wore "a green frock coat heavily embroidered with gold . . . a crimson silk sash around his waist, well-polished Wellington boots, and a gold watch." Thus adorned, he moved with slow deliberation to attract attention to himself.

Ann Folger preened herself to attract the peacock who ruled Zion's roost. Isabella noticed that Ann dressed up for Matthias and that she perfumed herself heavily. For hours at a time Ann sat with Father, flattering him and claiming that his thoughts were just like hers. One day when Benjamin was away on business, Ann took Matthias to the bathing room. Isabella remarked later that the bath took a very long time.

That Ann was married to Benjamin Folger did not deter Matthias. He said that since Christian ministers were devils, all marriages performed by them were false. Matthias taught that only "match spirits" could be truly married, and he alone knew if two people were match spirits.

Benjamin returned from his business trip, and Matthias told him that he must give Ann up. Benjamin wept and argued. "Benjamin, behave yourself," Ann chided. Then she broke the news that she belonged with Matthias as his match spirit. Benjamin gave in, but Isabella said Benjamin "looked like a dog with his tail singed, or one who had been dragged through a gutter."[21] Matthias said that Ann must now be called "Mother" by everyone. She was striving to conceive a "holy child" with Matthias and no longer did any other work. Isabella had to pick up the chores that Ann used to do. The community was supposed to take all its meals together, but now Father and Mother were often busy at mealtimes.

Matthias and Ann decided that Benjamin needed a match spirit of his own. Father had someone in mind for Benjamin: Matthias's own eighteen-year-old daughter, who was married to a Mr. Laisdell. (Her first name was Isabella, so to avoid confusion, she is here referred to as Mrs. Laisdell.) Her marriage to Charles Laisdell was easily dismissed as just another false union.

It seems that Benjamin Folger already knew Mrs. Laisdell rather well. Earlier that year Benjamin had gone down to Albany to fetch Matthias's children, and on the return trip he shared a room with Mrs. Laisdell. Back at Zion Hill, Benjamin told Father that he and Mrs. Laisdell had committed "an act upon the road." The wily prophet, needing to placate the man whose wife he had stolen, proclaimed that Mrs. Laisdell and Benjamin were match spirits.

The wedding took place in January 1834 with all members of the Kingdom in attendance. Matthias officiated, and all were asked to give their consent. Matthias gave his daughter, Mrs. Laisdell, to Benjamin Folger. Then Matthias gave a lengthy lecture on morals and wifely obedience, which Isabella later said was quite amusing.[22] Finally the newlyweds were released to enjoy some privacy upstairs. But Isabella saw that Catherine (a white woman who worked in the kitchen) was in distress. Catherine had some time ago slept with Benjamin, only to be passed over for a younger woman.

Meanwhile back in Albany, Charles Laisdell wondered why his wife had not yet returned from visiting her father. She had been gone for several weeks. Laisdell decided to go up to the Kingdom and find out for himself. But when he arrived, he was not allowed into the house. So he stayed overnight in the nearby town, returning the next morning to seek his wife. Someone, perhaps Isabella, told him that Mrs. Laisdell married another man and went with him to New York City.

Enraged, Mr. Laisdell spread the word in Sing Sing that Matthias gave his own daughter—who was already married—to a married man! The townsfolk already sensed something amiss at Zion Hill, and now they were on high alert.

Laisdell went to Manhattan in search of his wife. He beat on the door of Folger's house and was refused entry. Next he went to Albany (the state capital) and showed his marriage license to a judge. The judge gave Laisdell a writ empowering him to reclaim his wife. This he took back to the village of Sing Sing, where a tribunal met in a tavern and agreed that Mrs. Laisdell must go with her lawful husband immediately.

Rather than face arrest and jail, Matthias and Benjamin complied. Mrs. Laisdell returned to her husband. The townsfolk gathered in the tavern and the streets, threatening to mob the commune, but local authorities dispersed the crowd.

Benjamin, having lost both his wife and his match spirit, pined away. His former wife, "Mother" Ann, told him that the kitchen maid Catherine could be his new match spirit. Isabella, observing all this, knew it wouldn't work. Catherine was neither beautiful like Ann nor young like Mrs. Laisdell. Sure enough, Benjamin soon tired of Catherine.

By now Ann was pregnant by Matthias, but Benjamin still wanted her back. Benjamin saw that he was "a ruined man" if Matthias was a fraud.

Benjamin took to going into the village tavern to tell his troubles there. His friends offered to storm the commune and cast Matthias out, but Benjamin hesitated. Back at the commune, Benjamin called Matthias an imposter and demanded to have Ann back. Matthias cursed Benjamin.

Words turned to blows. Once, in the presence of Isabella and others, Benjamin threatened Matthias with a fireplace poker, shouting, "I'll split your brains out." Someone (Isabella?) grabbed the poker away. Benjamin lunged at Matthias, threw him down on a sofa and tried to throttle him. Matthias sprang up and ran for the door. Benjamin tried to follow, but Isabella seized his arms and pinned him against a door.

Matthias returned with a sword. Swinging it in circles, he intoned: "Let that spirit be destroyed,"[23] as if performing an exorcism.

Isabella continued to hold Benjamin's arms, while Elijah Pierson tried to calm him down. When Benjamin's rage cooled, Matthias put down the sword and Isabella released her hold. Benjamin then turned to Ann and begged her to come with him. She refused. But she took him to her room for a while, and when Benjamin came out again, Isabella said he looked "like a tamed elephant."

Ann must have been persuasive, for Benjamin's faith in Matthias was temporarily restored. He went into the village to quell the anger he had stirred up against Matthias, but in vain. Several men followed Benjamin back to the commune and then left, only to return the next day.

Rumors swept through the neighborhood: Matthias was to be deposed from his lunatic Kingdom. People filled the road leading to the commune, hungry for drama. Some even went onto the property and climbed trees to get a better view, while others kept watch from the hilltop overlooking the house.

A prankster from the town boasted that he would go inside the Kingdom and get the beard of Matthias. Posing as a constable, the intruder rapped on the door and was let inside. He announced that Matthias was in grave danger and must leave the house, but first Matthias must shave off his beard lest the villagers recognize and attack him. Matthias "wisely determined to sacrifice his beard" to save his own life. The faux constable offered to do the honors, but Matthias insisted on cutting off his own beard. Catherine stood close by and "received the locks in her apron," while Elijah Pierson diverted the "constable" with talk. Isabella took Catherine's apron, now full of beard clippings, rolled it up and stuffed it under the kitchen carpet. The prankster left empty-handed.

Meanwhile out in the barn, other Kingdom members harnessed the horses to the carriage. Matthias climbed in and made his getaway sans beard. Ann stayed behind, mourning for Matthias. That night, Isabella heard Benjamin say to Ann, "Come, let's go to bed. I've had a great deal of trouble to get you."[24]

With Matthias absent, Elijah Pierson declared himself "Father of the Kingdom." He sat at the head of the table and waited for the others to treat him with deference. No one did. Instead, Isabella, Benjamin, and Ann decamped to New York City, leaving Catherine to care for "the deranged Elijah and the children of the Kingdom."[25]

Before long, Ann and Isabella returned to Zion Hill. Soon Matthias slunk back to resume control. The hapless Benjamin Folger shuttled back and forth between Manhattan and Zion Hill, unable to make up his mind about Matthias.

———

Meanwhile Elijah Pierson's health was failing. For years he had seizures, which he called "fitty devils." He asked Isabella to put him on the floor when a fit came on, so he would not fall and injure himself. As his fits got worse, he would cry out for his deceased wife, whom he fully expected to return in another body as his match spirit.

When Elijah was feeling up to it, he did some light chores around the farm. On one fateful day, he was picking blackberries with Matthias. That night at supper, Elijah ate two plates of berries, and the next day became violently ill. No doctor was called because Matthias believed sickness was caused by evil spirits. On August 6, 1834, Elijah died.

A coroner's team examined the body and concluded that Elijah died of natural causes. But local animosity ran so high that county officials took control of the farmhouse and evicted all the Kingdom members. Local authorities pressured Matthias to renounce any legal claim to the property, which now fell to Elijah Pierson's heirs. They took Elijah's body and buried it in the family plot in Morristown, New Jersey.[26]

Back in their Manhattan home once more, Ann Folger decided that Benjamin was her husband after all. However, a second honeymoon was

awkward because of their houseguests. Matthias and his sons, plus Isabella and Catherine, had all fled to the Folgers' town house when they were
evicted from Zion Hill. Matthias still desired Ann, and Catherine still pined
for Benjamin.

Desperate to shed these unwanted guests, the Folgers did a buyout. They
gave Matthias $500 (a large sum in those days) to buy a farm somewhere in
the West. To Isabella they gave $25 as wages (she gave it to Matthias, but he
told her to keep it). In September 1834, Matthias and his sons went by boat to
Albany, where his legal wife, Margaret, still lived. Catherine stayed on with
the Folgers as a domestic servant, but was soon dismissed.

Isabella went to visit her children on the Dumont place upstate. Word
reached her that Matthias, charged with theft by Benjamin Folger, was arrested and sent to Bellevue Prison. Folger was now claiming that Matthias
had murdered Elijah Pierson by serving him blackberries, which were poisoned by Isabella.

Now Isabella was in trouble. No formal charge had yet been brought against
her, but that could change at any moment. Soon the Folgers claimed that Isabella tried to murder them by serving them poisoned coffee. The Folgers were
trying to "fix the blame for their own folly and humiliation on Matthias and
Isabella, both persons it would be easy for the public to distrust."[27]

This was a very bad time to be a Black person accused of a crime in New
York. As Elijah Pierson lay dying in the summer of 1834, the city was beset
by rioting, looting, and burning. The New York City Abolition Society was
falsely accused of promoting mixed marriages (then called "amalgamation").
White rage ignited several riots that engulfed the city in flames. A reporter
for the *Times* wrote on August 8, 1834, that the real cause of the riots lay
"in the hatred of the whites to[ward] the Blacks." When abolitionists called
for an end to slavery, "ignorant whites" formed mobs that "attacked the
churches, the dwelling-houses, and the stores of the prominent abolitionists." They also attacked the homes and stores of "the leading colored people,
destroying their furniture and stealing their goods."[28]

Black churches were damaged, especially St. Philip's Episcopal Church,
whose rector, Peter Williams, would one day help Isabella's son Peter. An article in the *New York Post* described a mob of thousands attacking St. Philip's,
tearing out the doors and windows and ransacking the interior before moving
on to destroy the homes of Black people. "Their rage appeared to be declared

against the Blacks,"²⁹ said the *Evening Post*. Mobs lashed out at Rev. Williams because he supported the antislavery movement, but also because many of his members had prospered—and "Black displays of affluence greatly irritated common white men who cherished their racial supremacy." St. Philip's was also "high church," and its formal style of worship did not fit the stereotype whites held of Black worship. On top of all this, "a false story circulated" that Rev. Williams had conducted a wedding for "an interracial couple, leading rioters to target the church."³⁰ It took military intervention to restore order.

In the fall of that tumultuous year, charges were brought against Matthias for the murder of Elijah Pierson. Isabella found for Matthias a lawyer named Mr. Western. This lawyer did not believe Matthias to be guilty of murder. Aware that Isabella might be charged with aiding and abetting Matthias, Western urged her to obtain character references.

Isabella procured letters of reference from employers in New York City. She went back to Ulster County and got letters from John Dumont, Isaac Van Wagenen, and others, as well as references from Kingston. These employers described Isabella as faithful, honest, industrious, hardworking, trustworthy; one called her "a woman of extraordinary moral purity."³¹

Meanwhile, the "holy child" of Ann Folger and Matthias was born. It was a girl, and that seemed to convince Ann that her faith in Matthias was misplaced. Now the Folgers tried to salvage their reputation. In addition to the lawsuits, they commissioned a book called *Matthias and His Impostures*. The writer, William Leete Stone, portrayed Ann and Benjamin as innocent dupes. As for Isabella, she was "the most wicked of the wicked," an accomplice to the murder of Elijah Pierson.³² Nothing could be easier than to blame a Black cook for the crime of murder by poisoning.

Isabella was not going to let them win. "I have got the *truth*, and I know it," she vowed, "and I will *crush* them with the *truth*."³³ With the help of her lawyer, she pressed charges of slander against Benjamin Folger. Now there were two court cases dealing with the Kingdom of Matthias.

First, Matthias was tried in April 1835 for the murder of Elijah Pierson. The trial lasted three days and was conducted before a packed courtroom in White Plains, New York. Several newspapers published accounts of the trial. Matthias entered the courtroom "dressed in an open green frock coat, with frog buttons, buff cassimere vest, and a red sash round his waist."³⁴ His beard had regrown to an impressive length.

Having been told that a grand jury had met before the trial to discuss the proceedings, Matthias shouted that the grand jury and its findings were "dissolved . . . dissolved . . . DISSOLVED!" Then he pronounced "the curse of Almighty God" against the grand jury.[35] Which then examined Matthias for insanity. Finding him sane, they gave him thirty days in jail for contempt of court.

The mortal remains of Elijah Pierson were much discussed in court, but a new autopsy yielded no conclusive evidence of poisoning. In Matthias's defense, Mr. Western argued that Pierson had died of epilepsy, and that he would have died with or without medical treatment. Matthias was acquitted of the charge of murder. Isabella was relieved but also disappointed that she could not testify on his behalf.

Public opinion now demanded that Matthias be punished for *something.* So he was charged with "assaulting his daughter," Mrs. Laisdell. When she visited the commune, Matthias beat her with a cowhide strap—which was illegal, since, in the eyes of the law, a married daughter belonged to her husband and not her father. Mrs. Laisdell wanted to drop the charge, but her husband, Charles, insisted on pressing it. Matthias was found guilty and sentenced to three months in prison, plus another month for contempt of court. The judge did not believe Matthias to be guilty of murder, but he called him a "barefaced impostor."

In the second trial, Isabella charged Benjamin Folger with slander on two counts. (First, Folger had accused Isabella of theft, claiming that she stole the $25 he paid her for housekeeping services; second, Folger had accused Isabella of feeding poisoned blackberries to Elijah Pierson, thereby aiding Matthias in the supposed murder.) When confronted in court, Folger admitted that these accusations were false. Isabella "was awarded the [then] large sum of $125.00 plus costs." Isabella won, but she wanted more from the trial than she got. She had character witnesses at the ready, but they were not asked to speak on her behalf. Nor was she, a Black woman, allowed to speak for herself. This was the second time Isabella brought charges against a white man and won, and it would not be the last.

Shortly after the two court cases, a small book appeared under the big title: *Fanaticism: Its Source and Influence, Illustrated by the Simple Narrative of Isabella, in the Case of Matthias, Mr. and Mrs. B. Folger, Mr. Pierson, Mr. Mills, Catherine, Isabella, &c. &c. A Reply to W. L. Stone, with the Descriptive*

Portraits of All the Parties, While at Sing-Sing and at Third Street.—Containing the Whole Truth—and Nothing but the Truth. This book is the main source for our account of Isabella in the Kingdom of Matthias.

The author was Gilbert Vale, a British journalist and antislavery freethinker. Vale sought to discredit fanaticism, which he said occurs when people "mistake *feelings* for divine impressions."[36] Isabella was not the only one to succumb to fanaticism. Elijah Pierson and Ann and Benjamin Folger had more education and money, yet they fell for Matthias. The more they invested, the more they had to lose if the whole thing turned out to be a humbug. But unlike Isabella (and Catherine the kitchen maid), wealthy folk had a safety net.

Gilbert Vale spent many hours interviewing Isabella and cast her as the central witness. Knowing that white readers would discount a Black person's testimony, Vale cross-checked Isabella's story with so-called white evidence. The more he investigated, the greater grew his respect for Isabella. Although Vale thought Isabella was duped by Matthias, he respected her personal integrity and her powers of observation, and admired her wit. "Hers is a peculiar and marked character,"[37] he wrote. He was deeply impressed with Isabella and made a point of vindicating her character.

Matthias served his four months in jail. Then he traveled to Kirtland, Ohio, to meet the Mormon prophet Joseph Smith. Matthias introduced himself as a Jewish teacher named Joshua. Smith discovered Matthias's real identity, said his doctrines were of the devil, and banished him from Kirtland.[38] Matthias is said to have died in the Iowa Territory, date unknown.

To those who are reading about the life of Sojourner Truth for the first time, the story of Isabella in the Kingdom of Matthias may come as a surprise. But Isabella was not yet Sojourner Truth. When she met Matthias, she was a housekeeper trying to make a living in Manhattan. She longed for a community where she could be a valued member. Isabella was also a religious perfectionist who wanted to be closer to God. When she met Elijah Pierson, she appreciated his efforts to treat her as an equal and his compassion for the poor. Yet Pierson was subject to delusions, and his lack of theological moorings left him vulnerable to the claims of Matthias. Isabella was loyal to Pierson, and if Pierson believed Matthias, Isabella would follow.

If this was the biggest mistake in Isabella's life, she learned a great deal from it. Later on, as Sojourner Truth, she excelled at deflating pompous

men, exposing hypocrites, and facing down bullies. But her sharpest wit
she saved for white men who used religion to justify their power over others.
Truth could take them down so deftly, they scarcely knew what had hit them,
except that the people they once intimidated were now laughing openly at
them. Isabella learned that humor, especially satire, is a great leveler. But if
she learned anything good from Matthias, perhaps it was this: how to make
astonishing claims with such boldness that people believe something new.
For in nineteenth-century America, what could be more bold than the claim
that all people are children of God and deserve to be free?

5

"Why Sit Ye Here and Die?"

Isabella remained in New York City for about eight years after the Kingdom of Matthias fell. It was a period of turmoil for the antislavery movement. In 1837, a white minister, Elijah Lovejoy, was murdered for publishing an abolitionist newspaper in Alton, Illinois. In 1839, a mutiny aboard the slave ship *La Amistad* stoked transatlantic furor over the slave trade. During that time Isabella was "getting an honest living by work," and was "respected for her services and integrity."[1] But she was worried about her son Peter, and how to save him from a life of crime.

Peter was not alone. "Look at our young men, smart, active and energetic, with souls filled with ambitious fire," said the Black reformer and author Maria Stewart in 1832. Racial prejudice limits these youth to the worst jobs, Stewart told the New England Anti-Slavery Society, so that "many of them lose their ambition, and become worthless."[2]

This was Peter's story. Isabella knew that Peter must face the consequences of his own deeds, but he was a master of evasion. If caught with stolen goods, he gave a false name to the police. His favorite alias—Peter Williams—appeared frequently in police records alongside the theft of silver spoons, shoes, and lumber.[3]

The *real* Peter Williams was a clergyman[4] at St. Philip's African Episcopal Church in the Five Points neighborhood and cofounder of *Freedom's Journal*, "the first Black newspaper in the United States."[5] As noted above, Rev. Peter Williams had suffered persecution along with his flock during the race riots in New York City.

In January 1839, Peter Van Wagenen was arrested and locked in the Tombs (formally known as the Halls of Justice and the House of Detention), where the ceilings leaked and sewage seeped through the floors.[6] Peter sent word to his mother asking her to visit him, but weeks passed and she did not come. Finally, he asked the police to contact the *real* Peter Williams, "whose name he had been wearing."[7] So Rev. Williams went to the Tombs to visit Peter. Williams often visited the jail, and sometimes helped young men like Peter find employment on a ship's crew.

Going to sea was "a school of hard knocks and tight discipline that would quickly shape up a young miscreant,"[8] writes historian Nell Irvin Painter. After a voyage of a few years, with berth and board provided, the sailors were paid and free to go. This could be the fresh start that Peter needed. Rev. Williams knew of a whaling ship called the *Zone*, which was in the harbor and sailing in a week's time. The minister said he would post Peter's bail on condition that the young man join the crew of the *Zone*. Peter agreed. He went to tell his mother the news, but she did not believe him because he had deceived her so many times.

To prove he was telling the truth, Peter took his mother to meet Rev. Williams. Isabella was relieved when the minister confirmed Peter's story. Even so, she worried: What if Peter was lying to Rev. Williams? What if the *Zone* sailed and Peter was not on board? One day Rev. Williams came in person to tell Isabella that the *Zone* had left port with Peter aboard. Yet for several more weeks, Isabella expected Peter to turn up. Only after time passed with no sign of him could she believe that he was really gone. It was the summer of 1839, and Peter was about eighteen years old.

More than a year went by before Isabella received a letter from Peter. In due time she received three letters from her son (although he said he had sent five). Peter wrote that the *Zone* had hard luck at first; perhaps there was illness on board, bad weather, or, most likely, no success in hunting whales. One letter said he was "severely punished" but did not explain why. Peter asked about his sisters and wanted to know how things were "at home" (meaning the Dumont place).

Peter begged his mother to send him a letter. "I am your only son, that is so far from your home, on the wide, briny ocean," Peter wrote. "I have seen more of the world than I ever expected, and if I ever should return home safe, I will tell you all my troubles and hardships. Mother, I hope you do not forget me, your dear and only son."[9] In a letter dated September 19, 1841, Peter reported success (probably in catching whales). This was the last Isabella heard from him. Shipping records indicate that, after a voyage of almost four years, the *Zone* returned to New York Harbor on May 8, 1843, with 2,063 barrels of whale oil. Peter was not onboard.[10] Whether or not Bell knew that the *Zone* had returned, she never found out what happened to Peter. He could have died at sea, or deserted the ship at some faraway port. Isabella held on to the hope that he was safe and living a good life somewhere. She always remembered him saying that he would do better.[11]

Isabella wanted to do better too, and her call to preach stirred within. Women were denied ministerial training and locked out of ordination. Yet women did preach in settings like camp meetings and revivals, where the ability to make converts mattered more than formal credentials. Ever since the Great Awakening, there were women preachers. Jerena Lee (1783–1864), a freeborn African American, obtained a preaching license (but not ordination) from Richard Allen, the first bishop of the African Methodist Episcopal Church. A religious visionary and foe of slavery, Lee was one of several Black female preachers of that era whose names are still known.[12]

In addition to preaching, Isabella was drawn to lecturing. The lecture was a popular medium that could be used for entertainment, education, and even social reform. But like the pulpit, the lectern was for men only.

Among the first women to break that barrier was Fanny Wright. The Scottish-born reformer traveled in the United States in the 1830s giving anti-slavery lectures. Large crowds assembled to witness the strange spectacle of a woman speaking in public to a large audience. Women were warned against "Fanny Wright-ism" and told that a woman who spoke in public was a freak of nature and would never catch a husband.

Isabella may not have heard Fanny Wright speak, but she did hear an even more famous lecturer. William Miller, a self-taught Bible student and Baptist minister, proclaimed the end of the world and the literal second advent (coming) of Christ. Many forms of Adventism percolated through the country in those days, but Miller traveled and gave lectures that made his predictions a national sensation.

Miller made it all sound reasonable. During his lectures he used charts to align historical events with biblical prophecies on a timeline, seeming to prove that the end was near. Drawings of a seven-headed dragon and other strange beasts brought a thrill of fear to Miller's followers.

In New York City, Isabella attended one of Miller's lectures. She saw many strange pictures hanging on the wall but said she did not understand them and they "failed to interest her"[13] (in part because she could not read). Yet Miller made a lasting impression. When Truth was about eighty years old, she recalled that she had "listened to the preaching of William Miller, who prophesied the end of the world."[14]

Isabella believed Jesus would return. Not to fulfill a chart or to rescue the righteous from doom; no, Jesus was coming to turn things right-side up. He would right wrongs and set people free. The Millerites "included some Blacks" who saw the world as a "conflict between the forces of good and evil, the forces of liberation and enslavement."[15] Isabella would soon combine Adventism with the abolition of slavery.

Isabella may have done some public speaking in the weeks before she left New York. The *National Anti-Slavery Standard*, dated May 11, 1843, carried this report, which has been connected with Isabella by scholar Margaret Washington: "Last Sabbath afternoon, we had the pleasure of listening to a very touching discourse from a colored woman, in the Sixth-street Methodist (colored) church. She was once a slave, and is a fine specimen of natural oratory. In propriety, energy, and grace of action, she beats any teacher of elocution we ever heard."[16]

Isabella was a talented speaker. Yet many obstacles and setbacks tempted her to despair that she could ever fulfill her calling. "Where [Isabella's] hopes had been raised the highest," says her *Narrative*, "there she felt [her] failure had been the greatest, and the disappointment most severe." She saw others "hoard up treasures for themselves and children" with far less effort. She began to see life as a play in which the rich rob the poor, and the poor rob each other, in "one great system of robbery and wrong."[17]

One winter after a heavy snowfall, Isabella's employer gave her a half dollar to "hire a poor man" to clear the steps and walkways. This man had cleared the snow before on this property, and expected to do it again. But Isabella rose early, removed the snow, and kept the money. Then along came the very man she was supposed to hire. Seeing the work was already done, he said, "you should have hired me." But Isabella "hardened her heart," saying, "I am poor too." Years later Truth described her own behavior as "selfish grasping."[18] She wanted to be kind to others, yet she needed to survive.

Her struggle was part of a larger one: the financial panic in 1837 that ushered in years of economic hardship. "Competition among the destitute grew more stark," writes historian Nell Irvin Painter. And Isabella, though poor, "was appalled by her own lack of charity toward those more in need."[19]

In a bad economy, Black workers had even fewer options than usual. Isabella did the essential work of housekeeping and was paid poorly for it. Around this time, the Black reformer Maria Stewart said that few white people "are willing to spend their lives and bury their talents in performing menial, servile labor." Black people should not have to spend their lives this way either. "Why sit ye here and die?"[20] Stewart asked.

That question (or something like it) welled up inside Isabella until she could ignore it no longer. Isabella "felt called in spirit to leave [the city] and to travel east and lecture," says Truth's *Narrative*.[21] It was the first of June 1843: Pentecost Sunday. The day when the Holy Spirit empowered the disciples to preach the gospel to all nations. Isabella remembered the vision of Jesus that came to her at Pinkster, after she had walked away from slavery. Now was the time for her to walk away from drudgery that was not her true calling. She told her employer, Mrs. Whiting: "The Spirit calls me and I must go."

"But Isabella, why are you leaving?"

"My name is no longer Isabella . . . but SOJOURNER."

Mrs. Whiting went to tell her husband, who came and kindly suggested that Isabella should eat breakfast first.

"No, I must go right now. I can't wait."

Then Sojourner took most of the coins she had saved and handed them back to Mrs. Whiting—who was now certain that the housekeeper had lost her mind. What Sojourner lost was a mind-*set*, imposed by slavery and prejudice, that kept her treading narrow, dead-end paths.

From that time on she was free to go wherever God's Spirit called her. The new name, Sojourner, marked a great change in her life, the sequel to her vision of Jesus when she first got her freedom.

Sojourner's new name echoed the Scriptures. The "strangers and sojourners" of Bible times (1 Pet. 2:11) were wanderers and exiles seeking a better country (Heb. 11:16). "The Lord gave me Sojourner," she explained later on, "because I was to travel up an' down the land, showing the people their sins, and being a sign unto them." When someone asked Sojourner if she always had that name, she said: "When I left the house of bondage, I left everything behind. I wanted nothing of Egypt on me" (Egypt was a biblical metaphor for slavery). Black people often took new names after escaping from slavery. Not only did this make it harder for slave catchers to trace them; it was also a way to shape their new identity as free people.

Soon after Sojourner began her journey, she introduced herself by her new name and was asked, "Sojourner what?" Then she started to pray for a last name. "O God, give me a name with a handle to it!" And it came to her "in that moment, like a voice . . . just as true as God is true: 'Sojourner *Truth*' and I leaped for joy—Sojourner *Truth*."[22] Elsewhere she said, "Everybody else had two names and the Lord gave me Truth, because I was to declare the truth to the people."[23] When she was enslaved, her last name declared which white person legally owned her. By taking Truth as her last name, she declared herself to be a child of God. "God, that is a good name," she prayed. "Thou art my last Master, and Thy name is Truth, and Truth shall be my abiding name until I die."[24]

Sojourner chose a name that was antislavery. "No slave holder can lay any claim to Sojourner Truth," she later said, "for the truth does not stay where there is any kind of slavery."[25] For the rest of her life, Sojourner lived into her name.

6

The Lever of Truth

Before dawn on the day of Pentecost, Sojourner Truth left the Whitings' house in lower Manhattan and walked to the South Street Seaport, carrying a small basket of food, a change of clothes, and a few small coins she had kept to pay her fare. Then she boarded the boat that took her across the East River to Brooklyn, a city of thirty-seven thousand on Long Island.

Stepping ashore, Sojourner *almost* looked back across the river at New York City. Then she remembered the Bible story about Lot's wife, who fled the wicked city of Sodom but looked back—and was turned into a pillar of salt. Truth waited until she had walked a fair distance before she looked back toward Manhattan—now a mere haze of smoke in the distance. Satisfied, she walked toward her future and "her true work," which she said was to preach "the hope that was in her—exhorting people to embrace Jesus, and refrain from sin."[1]

Truth set out as an Adventist preacher preparing people for the return of Christ, and "quite possibly a Millerite,"[2] according to Nell Irvin Painter. The Millerites were one sect that not only allowed but encouraged female preaching. Truth left New York City in 1843, the year the Millerites expected the return of Christ. (When Jesus did not return, the date was recalculated to October 22, 1844.) So great was their expectation that many Millerites ceased farming; others signed away their businesses and gave up their belongings; Isabella, too, left her housekeeping job and gave up her savings. Believers suffered a "Great Disappointment" when Christ did not return at the expected time. The *Narrative of Sojourner Truth*, published six years later, gently distanced Truth from Millerite Adventism.

Truth began her ministry on Long Island, which was at that time mostly rural and still carried a strong Dutch and Afro-Dutch imprint. After slavery ended in the state, many Black people worked on farms or made their living from fishing or gathering oysters to sell in the market. Others, like Peter Van Wagenen, went to sea on whaling ships or worked in the harbors outfitting those ships. Sojourner Truth "remained in the predominately Dutch western area of Long Island . . . for about one month."[3] Here she could speak her first language and enjoy the company of people with similar background.

Sojourner walked through town and country. She "followed a Millerite network on Long Island" and sometimes received invitations "at Second Advent meetings at which she preached."[4] At other times she announced her own meetings and gathered her own audience. She believed that God showed her the people she should talk to.

One day, as Sojourner walked down the road, a man approached her. "Are you looking for work?" he asked.

"No," she said, "that is not my purpose," adding that she could work a few days if someone needed her. The stranger said some of his family were sick, and he needed help to keep his household running. Sojourner went with him and did cleaning, cooking, and organizing for several days. The family pleaded with her to stay and offered good pay.

"No," she said. "I must go." The grateful family gave her "what seemed in her eyes a great deal of money." She accepted only enough "to pay tribute to Caesar" and nothing more, for Jesus said: "Render unto Caesar that which is Caesar's and unto God that which is God's" (Matt. 22:21). To Truth, this meant using money only for bare essentials like food, lodging, or passage on a ferryboat.

She was used to having a decent place to sleep each night, and now she did not know where she would lay her head. She might pay a coin or two to sleep overnight in a tavern, but she preferred staying in a private home. If she had just spoken to a crowd, or held a conversation, it was easy enough to ask for lodging. Failing that, she could ask people she met in the road, or even knock on doors to find a place to stay.

The poor opened their homes to Truth more readily than did the rich. She had many "religious conversations with people who were strangers to her,"[5] and usually these were poor people. Religion was easy to find among the poor and hard to find among the rich, Sojourner observed.

As an itinerant preacher, Truth had to suffer the uncertainties and hardships of the road—hunger, exposure to the elements, and a lifestyle akin to homelessness. She later recalled a time when she did not know where she would spend the night. As afternoon faded into evening, she still did not have a place, although she had asked many people. Night came, and she walked along guided by starlight and the glimmer of a new moon. Two Native American men approached and spoke to Sojourner as if they knew her. (There were still Native American communities on Long Island.)

"How far is the nearest tavern?" Sojourner asked.

"Two miles that way," they said, pointing down the road.

She walked on alone until she reached the tavern. It was in the same building as the courthouse and jail. She was told she could stay the night but only if she agreed to be locked up in the jail. She refused, declaring that she would rather walk all night than "to have a key turned on her."

She walked on until she heard someone call out to her, then she stopped and met a woman and man who greeted her in a friendly way.

"Can I stay the night with you?" Sojourner asked.

"Yes," they said, "but first we are going to a ball. You can come with us if you don't mind waiting for us at the dance."

Sojourner agreed and followed the couple. The dance was held in "a dirty hovel" that reeked of whisky; Truth's *Narrative* says that the people came from "the dregs of society." Wary and weary, Sojourner found a corner to sit down and wait. By the time the couple were ready to leave, they were drunk. Sojourner followed them to "a miserable cabin," where she was offered a bed so dirty she could not lie down in it. After a sleepless night, Sojourner arose early and walked toward Huntington, a harbor on Long Island Sound. From there she went to the whaling village of Cold Spring to celebrate the Fourth of July.

The national holiday was, for many, a time to get drunk and to fire guns and cannons. In response, temperance societies promoted the Fourth of July as a sober, pious holiday. The Cold Spring festivities were to be conducted "on the principles of temperance," an ad in the *Long Islander* promised. Instead of drinking to excess, the people would praise God for the blessings of liberty and prosperity.

The day began with a gunfire salute at sunrise. At 10 a.m. the people gathered at the Methodist church, where a grand marshal led a parade to the Grove, a campground where the event took place. The "exercises" began with prayer, followed by a local dignitary reading the Declaration of Independence. Then came a few speeches and the singing of hymns and patriotic anthems.[6] A highlight was "dinner on the grounds," for which Sojourner made "dishes *a la New York*," enjoyed by all. After the meal, "several speakers of celebrity" held forth, and there was more singing.

Sojourner Truth stayed in Cold Spring for three weeks. The village had a large Black population, many of whom worked in the whaling industry. Truth probably preached to groups and held "religious conversations" with individuals. She may have done housework and cooking in exchange for lodging, but no record of where she stayed has been found.

When she felt it was time to go, Sojourner took a ferryboat across Long Island Sound to Bridgeport, Connecticut. From there she walked northeast, "lecturing some, and working some, to get wherewith to pay tribute to Caesar." At New Haven she attended "many meetings" (probably Adventist revivals and temperance meetings). Truth's *Narrative* reports that she "found in [New Haven] many true friends of Jesus with whom she held communion of spirit." Sojourner did not favor one religious group over another but was "satisfied with all who gave her evidence of having known or loved the Savior."[7]

As word spread about this Black preaching woman and Truth began to get more invitations to speak, she impressed people as "a preacher who gloried in divine inspiration." Her use of biblical language gave her authority in a time when people knew the Scriptures by heart. She had been free for about sixteen years, but she "presented herself as a woman who had been a slave." For the rest of her life, her experience in slavery was part of her testimony.[8]

People started recommending Truth by word of mouth and in writing. In one introduction that Truth carried with her to Hartford, the writer described her as a "living messenger" whom "God loves." The writer advised his "sister," to whom the letter was directed, to receive Truth and "give close attention, and you will see she has got the lever of truth, that God helps her to pry where but few can."[9]

Meanwhile, back in upstate New York, Sojourner's daughters worried about her. Diana, Elizabeth, and Sophia had heard disturbing rumors about their mother. If they tried to contact her through her employer, Mrs. Whiting, that lady would have given them an earful. The daughters had somehow heard that their mother had become "a wandering maniac." They wept for her, fearing that she might commit suicide.[10]

Sojourner had not told her family of her name change or of her travels, lest they try to stop her from following her call. Now that she was well launched, she reached out to her daughters. In Berlin, Connecticut, she found someone to take dictation, and then sent a letter to her daughters at the Dumont farm. She said she was in good health, sent her love, and gave a temporary address. The letter relieved the daughters' fears for their mother, whom they now looked forward to seeing again.

Although Truth could not read or write, she dictated and sent letters to stay in touch with her family and friends. Later she would send letters to newspapers to share her experiences with—and sometimes to ask for financial support from—the antislavery network. Although she did not form the words with her own hand, she used her considerable agency to send messages and accomplish her aims.

———

Truth continued preaching in Connecticut and had some tense exchanges with Millerites in the Hartford area. At one large camp meeting, she was grilled on her orthodoxy. When someone asked if she believed that Christ was returning soon, she replied, "It has not been revealed to me." Then, perhaps referring to Miller's technical charts, she allowed that, if she could read, she might see things differently.

"Don't you believe the Lord is coming?" someone demanded.

"I believe the Lord is as near as he can be, and not be it," was Truth's enigmatic answer.

Then she asked the people what *they* really believed. Did they have good reasons to expect the Lord's return, knowing that it would shake the foundations of the world? After some discussion, the people asked Truth to join in their devotions. More people drew near as Sojourner prayed, spoke, and sang. The people accepted her as "a lover of God and his cause." But Truth thought these folk were "laboring under a delusion." (She had so labored when she followed Matthias, and resolved never to do so again.) So she tried to "calm the fears of the people, and pour oil upon the troubled waters."

As she walked around the meeting grounds, Sojourner saw that many people had worked themselves into a high pitch of excitement. She stepped up onto a stump and shouted, "Hear! Hear!" Once she had their attention, she said, "Children, why do you make such a to-do? Didn't Jesus tell you to 'watch and pray'? But you are neither watching nor praying." Like a mother, she told them to go back to their tents and "watch and pray quietly." Remember, she counseled, "the Lord came still and quiet. Why would he visit a scene of such confusion?" Many were soothed by Truth's words and "suppressed their noisy terror." Some went to tell others to "listen to the advice of the good sister," and many went back to their tents.

Moving on to another part of the campground, Truth heard some preachers working the people into a state of alarm. After listening a while, she stood up and spoke her mind to the preachers.

> You are talking about being "changed in the twinkling of an eye." But if the Lord came now, he'd change you to *nothing* for there is nothing in you. You think you are going to some parlor *away up* somewhere, and when the wicked have been burnt, you are coming back to walk in triumph over their ashes—this is to be your New Jerusalem! Now *I* can't see anything so very *nice* in that, coming back to such a *mess* as that will be, a world covered with the ashes of the wicked! Besides, if the Lord comes— and burns [the world] as you say he will—*I* am not going away; *I* am going to stay here and *stand the fire*, like [the Bible story of] Shadrach, Meshach, and Abednego! And Jesus will walk with me through the fire, and keep me from harm. Nothing belonging to God can burn, any more than God himself. True believers have no need to go away to escape the fire! No, *I* shall remain. Do you tell me that God's *children can't stand fire*?

The ministers were shocked by Truth's speech. How could this woman not fear the judgment? Then "one of them, in the kindest possible manner," tried to persuade her, and failed. He admitted that Truth knew "much that man had never taught her." One thing she knew was that true religion was not based on fear but on love.

Truth's confrontation with the Adventists may reflect her beliefs in 1843 (before the Great Disappointment) or her views in 1850 (when the *Narrative* was published). The way people tell stories can change over time, Sojourner Truth included. The exact chronology of this story may never be known, but it says that Truth's faith was based not on fear but on hope for justice and redemption. Sojourner was not looking to escape the judgment. She would rather "stand the fire" and trust in God.

Truth now made her way north, moving up the Connecticut River valley to Springfield, Massachusetts. "When she arose to speak . . . her commanding figure and dignified manner hushed every trifler into silence," wrote someone who heard Truth preach in Springfield. Even those who did not agree with her "listened eagerly to Sojourner and drank in all she said." She preached to many "who believed in the second advent doctrine" and quickly became "a favorite among them." Sojourner said that "the world is topsy-turvy" with everything in confusion, but someday when all is right-side up, how beautiful the world will be![11] An abolitionist wrote a letter reporting to a friend that "there is also a colored woman astonishing the Springfielders"; she could not read or write, "but the Spirit has taught her."[12]

Truth was warmly received in Springfield, but she longed for a place to put down some roots, a community where she could be a spiritual leader. Experimental communities sprouted up like dandelions: almost fifty of them started between 1841 and 1850. Different as these groups were from each other, they all rejected greed and competition in favor of simplicity and cooperation. They sought to "perfect themselves" and to change "the world by the moral force of their example."[13] Some of these communes, like Fruitlands in Massachusetts, lasted less than one year, while others lasted longer.

The Shakers (so-called because they danced and shook with fervor in worship) had more staying power than other groups. Their movement began in England and migrated to North America around the time of the Revolution. Their formal name was the United Society of Believers in Christ's Second Appearing. Unlike the Millerites, the Shakers believed that this "second appearing" *had already happened* in the person of their founder, "Mother" Ann Lee. The Shakers believed that God was a duality of male and female, and therefore both sexes were equal. Since Shakers were celibate, their communities could grow only through conversion or adoption of orphans. Shakers opposed slavery, welcomed Black people into their fellowship, and were known to harbor fugitive slaves. Shakers were perfectionists who sought to live simply, much like Sojourner Truth.

Sojourner Truth traveled ten miles south to visit the Shaker community at Enfield, Connecticut. According to her *Narrative*, she went to see "whether there was any opening for her." Why she did not join is unknown.

Perhaps the Shakers were too withdrawn from the world for Truth, or perhaps she was too much involved with the world for them.

Returning to Springfield, Sojourner resumed preaching. She did some housework for people who needed her, but she took no money for it. She felt a longing for "a quiet place," says her *Narrative*, "where a way-worn traveler might rest."[14] Truth may well have felt ill or depleted from her traveling; when she did settle down, she took steps to improve her health.

Friends in Springfield had heard of an abolitionist commune just outside of Northampton, Massachusetts, that might be the right place for Sojourner. Founded in 1842 in the little hamlet of Florence, the commune was a hub for antislavery activity and other reforms. This commune did not have a poetic name like New Harmony, Brook Farm, or Pleasant Hill. It sounded more like a business: the Northampton Association of Education and Industry (NAEI). For short, it was called the Northampton Association or, simply, "the community."

Each word in the NAEI name was carefully chosen, starting with "Northampton." The Calvinist preacher Jonathan Edwards once sparked the Great Awakening there, and a century later a new movement sought to ignite a moral awakening against slavery. The word "association" meant that leadership was shared. Members could speak freely and could stay or leave according to conscience. "Education" included old and young, men and women, Black and white. The Northampton Association had a school for young children and a "boarding school directed by a former professor of literature at Harvard."[15] Community members could learn practical skills, enjoy spirited conversation, and attend lectures. Most important, the NAEI hoped to educate the American public to promote free labor and abolish slavery. "Industry" meant that the community would support itself by free labor and the sale of products made in the commune. Free labor should generate fair wages for all and time off for rest and recreation.

This grand scheme hung by a silken thread, because the main industry of the community was the manufacture of silk. Unlike Southern cotton, silk was "a 'free' product untainted by the evils of slavery." By using only free labor to make textiles, the community hoped to "speed up social change,"[16] writes historian Christopher Clark. The NAEI founders bought a failed silk farm that they meant to transform into a successful business.

Silk farming in New England began in colonial times. This delicate process started with feeding silkworms on mulberry leaves. The silkworms spun cocoons, which were then unwound to harvest the silk. The fiber was spun into thread (which could be dyed) and wound onto spools. The silk could be sold as thread or woven into fabric.[17]

The community silk farm had 470 acres of land, including fields for growing crops and a grove of mulberry trees to feed the silkworms. A small river powered the silk factory and a few lesser mills. The factory was equipped and ready for use, along with various outbuildings and a few cottages. Stockholders advanced money to buy the property; those who had no money but wanted to live in the community could contribute their labor in exchange for food, lodging, and wages.

Those who joined the Northampton Association were fervent abolitionists. It was here that Sojourner Truth rubbed shoulders with some of the most famous—or soon to be famous—abolitionists. William Lloyd Garrison, editor of the *Liberator*, lived in Boston and made frequent visits to the community, where his sister and brother-in-law were members. Frederick Douglass spoke there several times. Parker Pillsbury and William Stetson, "two of the abolitionists who would later become Sojourner's partners on the speaking circuit,"[18] were friends of the community. David Ruggles, pioneer of New York City's underground railroad, was a member.

Sojourner Truth may not have thought of it this way, but she was about to enroll in a school of social reform. Abolition was the main course of study, but related subjects included women's rights, temperance, and health reform. Other communities sought to reform marriage and family structure: the Mormons had polygamy, the Shakers chose celibacy, and Matthias called for "spirit matches." The Oneida Community (founded after the NAEI closed) had open or "complex" marriage. But Sojourner was joining an antislavery commune, whose constitution stated that the marriages and families of its members were to be respected. They did not want anything to rival or distract from the antislavery cause. Truth must have known that, by joining the NAEI, she was by no means risking a repeat of Matthias's Kingdom.

The NAEI was the closest Truth came to a formal education. She would become its most distinguished graduate, bringing honor to the community long after its doors had closed.

7

The Moral Reform Depot

Sojourner Truth came to the place where the rest of her life began, late in the fall of 1843. She traveled by horse-drawn wagon from Springfield, Massachusetts, to the commune on the outskirts of Northampton. Sojourner was not feeling well after the journey, perhaps having caught a chill.

Arriving at the Northampton Association of Education and Industry, Truth saw a brick factory building four stories high with a stout bell tower. Inside the factory were large industrial rooms with machinery for spinning, dyeing, and weaving silk thread. The building was also home to many community members, who slept in an unheated dormitory, ate in the common dining hall, and bathed in the nearby river. (Some members of the NAEI lived in cottages on the property, but most lived in the factory dormitory.) As she later recalled in her *Narrative*, Truth at first decided that the Northampton Association was not for her. "I'll stay one night and go back to Springfield," she told herself.

Then the people she met changed her mind. They had left behind their old lives as farmers, artisans, and merchants. There were also "a few clerks, teachers, ministers, and intellectuals, two physicians, one lawyer, and a professional portrait painter."[1] The members were mostly white, but a few Black people joined; other Blacks were long-term visitors, and many more passed through briefly because the NAEI was a stop on the Underground Railroad. These people were drawn together by their commitment to free labor and abolition. The community constitution proclaimed equal rights "without distinction of sex, color, or condition, sect or religion."[2] The general goal—to raise labor "to its true dignity"[3]—appealed strongly to Truth.

However, the community did not reduce human beings to mere workers. It nurtured "whole-souled" people and promoted the health of body, mind, and spirit.

Each adult did some work to help the community function. In addition to the silk factory, there were small workshops, a kitchen, a laundry, and a school; gardens, fields, and livestock also needed tending.[4] Almost everyone was involved in antislavery work and other reforms. Truth's *Narrative* says "the choicest spirits of the age" lived in this community. Here was "an equality of feeling, a liberty of thought and speech, and a largeness of soul" that appealed to Truth. Many members had left security and comfort behind for the sake of a greater cause. "Well," Truth told herself, "if these can live here, *I* can."[5]

Here Truth met visiting lecturers that linked the NAEI to a broader community of reformers throughout the North.[6] So dynamic was the exchange of reform ideas and strategies, and so steady the comings and goings of reformers, that the community was dubbed "the moral reform depot." A depot was where steam locomotives came and went with their great chuffing smokestacks and shrieking whistles. They took on fuel and water and passengers, and dropped off people and goods, all the while connecting people in ever wider networks. In those days nothing could match the power of a steam train barreling down the tracks. No wonder the antislavery movement ran an Underground Railroad that had conductors and passengers.

Sojourner Truth had much to contribute to the moral reform depot. Surviving letters and journals from the NAEI show respect for Truth's "wisdom and advice."[7] A person who grew up in the community saw Truth as "tall, weird and impressive." She was "very religious and had a firm reliance on God's providence," this eyewitness recalled. She spoke "with great force and power of the wrongs and sufferings endured by members of her race." She would often break into "singing the Negro songs" that moved people to tears.[8]

These talents marked her as a spiritual leader, but like others in the community, she did her share of common labor. She was tasked with running the laundry, which was set up in the basement of the factory building in order to draw water from the nearby river. Dirty laundry was boiled in a large kettle and stirred with a wooden paddle; heavily soiled clothes got scrubbed on a washboard. Then came the rinsing, wringing out, and hanging up to dry. Once dry, many items had to be pressed with heavy flat irons heated on a fire.

Mercifully, clothing was not washed as often in those days. The laundry only operated one or two days a week. Sojourner was her own boss and had at least one assistant. If she fell ill, she could rest and recover for as long as needed. If she wanted to preach at camp meetings or visit friends or family, she was free to go, knowing that others would take over. Truth probably did other work as needed, such as caring for the sick.

The community paid more money for "necessary but unpleasant" work, and less for easier jobs.[9] However, Sojourner declined her wages for the laundry. She expected "Providence" to supply her needs for the rest of her life and saw money as a temptation to greed.[10]

With or without money, Sojourner got a new pair of shoes from the community store. She borrowed a horse and rode throughout the area, holding meetings. If denied permission to speak inside any church, she "preached from a stump, a wagon, or a hastily constructed platform." Outdoor preachers were sometimes harassed, and the risk of violence—especially against a Black preacher—was real. Thus, if Truth was absent longer than expected, Samuel Hill (a community founder) would send out a driver and wagon drawn by a pair of white horses to search for Sojourner.[11]

She could have used that kind of backup when, in the spring of 1844, she was almost mobbed at a revival meeting near Northampton. But this particular revival was the kind where people stayed overnight at a campground, and Truth's friends at the NAEI expected her to be absent for a while.

According to Truth's *Narrative*, "wild young men" harassed the revival, "hooting and yelling" during the worship services. The camp meeting leaders could not persuade their persecutors to leave.

Sojourner slipped into a tent and hid behind a trunk. "I am the only colored person here," she said to herself, "and on me, probably, their wicked mischief will fall first." Then, as Truth recalled later, she confronted her fears. "Shall I run away and hide from the Devil? Me, a servant of the living God?" She challenged herself: "I know I am a servant of the living God. I'll go to the rescue, and the Lord shall go with and protect me." She prayed and felt, she said, "as if I had *three hearts!* And that they were so large, my body could hardly hold them!"[12]

Leaving the tent, Sojourner told some friends she was going out to calm the storm. She asked if anyone wanted to go with her; they declined and said Truth was "wild" for daring to confront the ruffians.

By now night had fallen, and a full moon shone over the meeting ground. A woman was supposed to preach that night; perhaps that is what attracted the disturbers of the peace. They carried clubs and smoked cigars to foul the air of the meeting ground. The preacher went up into the preaching stand and trembled with fear as the invaders jeered. Sojourner, seeking to draw the intruders away from the preaching ground, walked in the other direction to the top of a small hill nearby. Standing alone in the moonlight, she began to sing a hymn that she composed herself:[13]

> It was early in the morning
> Just at the break of day
> When he rose—when he rose—when he rose,
> And went to heaven on a cloud.

Her deep, powerful voice reached the meeting ground. The hecklers turned like a pack of feral dogs and started moving toward Sojourner. They surrounded her, menacing. Sojourner stopped singing and waited. "Why do you come about me with clubs and sticks?" she asked. "I am doing no harm to anyone."

"We aren't a going to hurt you, old woman," they called. "We came to hear you sing. Sing to us, talk to us, pray, old woman! Tell us your experience," they mocked. Though she had much to fear, Sojourner did not seem fearful.

"How can I talk to you," she demanded, "when you crowd up so close?"

"Stand back," called one of the leaders. He raised his club in the air, and the others stepped back, making a large circle around Sojourner. "Sing," they demanded. "Preach and pray." The ring leaders promised to "knock down" anyone who gave her trouble.

Sojourner sang and preached and tried to answer their questions.

"We cannot hear you," came shouts from the back. "Climb up on that wagon and speak."

"No," Sojourner said. "You'll just tip over the wagon."

"I'll knock down anyone who tries to harm you," someone said. Arms reached out to help Truth climb up onto the wagon. From this rough preaching stand, she held forth.

"There are two congregations on the ground," she said. "The sheep shall be separated from the goats. The other preachers have the sheep, *I* have the goats. And I have a few sheep among my goats, but they are *very* ragged." That brought laughter.

As she spoke the men listened, but whenever she paused they clamored. She was getting tired and wondered how she could dismiss them. So she motioned for them to be quiet and said, "Children, I have talked and sung to you as you asked me; and now I have a request to make of you: will you grant it?" Some said yes.

"If I will sing one more hymn for you, will you then go away, and leave us this night in peace?" A few muttered agreement. Not satisfied, Sojourner repeated her question, adding, "and *I* want you all to answer." She kept asking until everyone shouted yes. "AMEN! It is SEALED," she proclaimed, repeating this in low tones as if to draw everyone into a sacred and binding vow. Then she sang: "I bless the Lord I've got my seal . . . I mean to take the kingdom in the good old way."

As she sang, the invaders turned away. They walked and then they ran, and kept running until "every rioter was gone, and not one was left on the grounds, or seen there again during the meeting."[14] It was not the last time Sojourner Truth would face down a mob. After this confrontation, she must have been glad to return to the community and be among friends.

One of these friends was David Ruggles, the Black abolitionist leader from New York City. For health reasons he came to the Northampton Association in November 1842, about a year before Truth. Ruggles welcomed Truth to the community and mentored her in "abolitionist views and methods."[15] He helped launch her career as an antislavery lecturer, giving her an opportunity to speak in the nearby town of Northampton.[16] This may have been the first time Truth spoke against slavery to a group outside the community.

Before Ruggles reached out to Truth, he had also helped Frederick Douglass. Back in 1838 Douglass (whose last name was then Bailey) was newly escaped from slavery in Maryland. Finding temporary refuge in New York City, Frederick married his fiancé, Anna Murray, in Ruggles's home. The newlyweds were going to Canada, but Ruggles convinced Bailey to change his last name and remain in the United States to work for abolition.

Douglass was still a fugitive in the eyes of the law when he first visited Ruggles at the Northampton Association. Douglass was saddened to see his old friend "blind" and "measurably helpless," but pleased that Ruggles, who had helped so many others, "received support and comfort in the Community." Douglass praised the egalitarian spirit of this community where "there was no high, no low, no masters, no servants, no white, no Black."

Frederick Douglass became a traveling lecturer for the American Anti-Slavery Society—a dangerous business, since these meetings were often mobbed. In one melee Douglass's hand was permanently injured. He returned to visit the Northampton Association in 1844, to give several lectures. Joining him were the Hutchinson Family Singers, a white group that performed music at antislavery rallies. Fresh from their first tour of Philadelphia, Baltimore, and Washington, they spent two days in the community and performed alongside lectures given by Frederick Douglass.[17] Truth was almost certainly present at these events. She must have enjoyed hearing the Hutchinsons—three brothers and a sister who sang in harmony and played the violin and cello. One of their most popular songs, "Get Off the Track!" warned politicians, priests, and lawyers to clear out of the way: they could not stop the abolition train.[18]

Truth and Douglass met in 1844 at the Northampton Association. Decades later, Douglass recalled meeting Truth "for the first time." He described her as a "strange compound of wit and wisdom, of wild enthusiasm and flint-like common sense." Over the years, their paths crossed at antislavery events. She "seemed to feel it her duty to trip me up in my speeches and to ridicule my efforts to speak and act like a person of cultivation and refinement," Douglass recalled.

In his reminiscences about the Northampton Association, Douglass described Truth as "a genuine specimen of the uncultured negro [who] cared very little for elegance of speech or refinement of manners." Still, he admitted that Truth "was much respected at Florence" for her honesty, industry, and friendly manner. "Her quaint speeches easily gave her an audience, and she was one of the most useful members of the Community in its day of small things."[19] The "day of small things" remark may sound condescending, but Douglass penned these comments after the Civil War, to which everything was small in comparison.

Douglass and Truth both looked up to Ruggles, whose health was failing when he joined the community. Seeking to rebuild his strength, he embraced the water cure, a regimen of bathing, exercise, and hydration popular among reformers. The water-cure diet called for grains, fruits, and vegetables, instead of the greasy, salted meat that was so common in those days. Water-cure patients also had to quit taking opiates, mercury, and other poisons commonly used as medicines. No wonder so many who "took the cure" got better. Ruggles, though nearly blind, taught himself to be a water-cure therapist and physician. It was said that he could diagnose illness and prescribe treatment through touch and the art of listening.

Ruggles opened his own water-cure practice and gradually built it up until it had a wash house, a gymnasium, and a boarding house. His patients included William Lloyd Garrison, Frederick Douglass, and Sojourner Truth. During the first year of Truth's time in the community, "Ruggles treated her for stomach and bowel problems, swollen and abscessed legs, and joint and muscle ailments," writes Ruggles's biographer. These illnesses suggest that Truth bore within her body the effects of many hardships and privations. Some of her wounds, physical or emotional, probably began in her enslavement, then continued in her life of hard domestic labor and then her homeless life as an itinerant preacher. She was about forty-six years old when she arrived at the Northampton Association; by the standards of her day, she had already lived a long life. (The average life span of Black women in the mid-nineteenth century is estimated to be as low as twenty-one or as high as thirty-six.) Thanks to Ruggles, a better diet seems to have helped Truth's digestion, while "constant wet-sheet packing and cold baths slowly provided relief from her leg problems." After about ten weeks of treatment, Truth could resume working in the laundry.[20]

Besides Ruggles and Truth, the NAEI had at least two other Black members: Stephen Rush and George Sullivan. Little is known about them except that both had been enslaved. Other Black people passed through the community as visitors. Black membership may have been unintentionally limited by the requirement that "a candidate had to be known and recommended by a member or friend of the group."[21] Another obstacle may have been that Ruggles and Truth "were vigilant in confronting slackers, especially Black ones."[22] Truth was a perfectionist and quick to chide those who failed to live up to her standards. Truth once "turned . . . [an] old colored man out of doors" because he was not working hard enough, wrote a community member to her husband. That same week, another Black man left "because he [was] not a good workman"[23] (Truth was not mentioned in connection with this departure).

The Northampton Association had safe places to shelter fugitive slaves. It offered food and clothing, and a guide to bring people safely to their next destination. Truth's *Narrative* does not say that she worked in the Underground Railroad. However, the *Narrative* came out in 1850 when this work was illegal. Truth would not have wanted to expose herself or her friends to arrest. One can only imagine Truth washing and mending clothing for escapees from slavery, or bringing food to those in hiding. She may have prayed and sung with the sojourners and listened to them talk about their experiences of slavery in the South.

Slavery was no longer legal in the North, but many white Northerners rejected abolition and saw abolitionists as fanatics. To avoid the stigma of radicalism, many people identified themselves as antislavery but not abolitionist. If an antislavery meeting was mobbed, the abolitionists were blamed for stirring up trouble.

Many Northern churches were conflicted about slavery. Some openly condemned slavery and encouraged their members to become activists. But most churches chose to avoid controversy. Some abolitionists left their churches rather than commune with folk who tolerated slavery or profited from it. Other abolitionists were disfellowshipped from (kicked out of) their churches for subversive activities—like handing out antislavery literature, criticizing the minister, or trying to hold antislavery meetings on church property. Exiles of conscience were called "come-outers." They came out not only from churches but also from political groups, businesses, and even families. Many tried to come out from the slave economy by boycotting slave-grown products like cotton, sugar, and tobacco.

The term "come-outer" derives from Scripture. "And I heard another voice from heaven, saying, Come out of her [the wicked city of Babylon], my people, that ye be not partakers of her sins, and that ye receive not of her plagues" (Rev. 18:4). America's plague was slavery.

The Northampton Association was a magnet for come-outers. Alongside abolition, a commitment to women's rights likewise led some people to leave their churches. The Northampton Association was a place where women could speak and vote at meetings and even become "spiritual leaders."[24]

Sojourner Truth belonged with the come-outers, having herself come out so many times. She came out from slavery and from churches that practiced discrimination. She came out from the authoritarian Kingdom of Matthias, and from her old life as Isabella the housekeeper. By speaking in public, she came out from the silence imposed on women. And although she never quite succeeded, she tried to come out from the need for money.

Like many come-outers, Truth wanted to decide for herself what to believe. The Bible presented a special challenge to her, since she could not read it for herself. She tried getting adults to read the Bible to her, but they spoiled it by telling her what each passage meant. She preferred having children read to her, because a child would read a passage over as many times as Truth wanted to hear it, without trying to explain it to her. In this way she could study Scripture and decide for herself what it meant.[25]

Unlike some in the community who identified as "freethinkers," Truth believed in core Christian teachings—such as salvation by faith in Jesus, the gift of the Holy Spirit, and the return of Christ, not in some far-off future, but soon.

Truth sometimes attended and preached at Adventist meetings in the Northampton area. After one meeting in West Springfield, she became convinced that the world was ending, and she did not want to be among strangers when it happened. She was very relieved when Samuel Hill sent his wagon drawn by white horses to bring her home. "She said she felt like running out into the road to kiss the horses," according to the account of Hill's son, Arthur. That night she woke up thinking about the end of the world. She got out of bed and went to the window, opened it, and leaned out. She gazed up and around looking for signs of the world's ending—and just then a few shooting stars or meteors shot across the sky. She went outside to the house of Mr. Hill and shouted, "Samuel Hill, Samuel Hill, come out here!" Samuel came to the window and asked what was the matter.

"The world's coming to an end! Come out quick!" Sojourner said.

"Well," said Samuel, "wait until I dress and I'll come out."

"Never mind your breeches, Samuel! Come right out!"

Telling the story later, Truth said: "Lord, I was sure the world would end before he could get out and I wanted to go up with somebody that I knew."[26]

Sojourner Truth was an Adventist Christian when she came to the community, but she got along well with the "freethinkers" there who did not share her beliefs. She later defended them from charges of "infidelity" (unfaithfulness to the Christian faith). "If any were infidels" at the NAEI, Sojourner said, "I wish the world were full of such infidels. Religion without humanity is a poor human stuff."[27]

The members of Truth's new community were "stigmatized" as irreligious—yet many were "deeply religious people."[28] The community defined true religion as "perfect spiritual liberty and universal benevolence" and therefore did not require "a particular creed." Instead, "each person must answer to their own conscience before God."[29]

The community held Sunday meetings at which anyone could speak, pray, or sing. In the winter these meetings took place in the dining hall inside the factory building. In warm weather the meetings were held in a grove of pines overlooking the river. One towering pine in that grove was almost sacred. Sojourner used to stand beneath that pine when she preached or sang with the community.

When visitors attended these Sunday meetings, they were likely to hear about abolition, women's rights, or health reform. They might also hear critiques of clergy who failed to take a stand against slavery. The *Newburyport Watchtower* called the NAEI an asylum for "extreme Abolitionists, Come-outers, broken down politicians, negroes, ladies and children." Indeed, the community was "a persistent thorn in the side" of some of the local ministers.[30]

That was intentional. The community was "a base for lecturing and campaigning" against slavery, and, as such, it intended to "aggravate and annoy" anyone who supported slavery. Historian Christopher Clark writes that "the very existence of a community of radical, nonsectarian" reformers made "a moral witness to the cause for which they were working."[31]

And of course, reformers could also needle one another. People of strong convictions and high moral standards were bound to have conflicts. To relieve tensions between members, the community held "mutual criticism meetings." At these meetings, anyone with a concern or a grievance could speak up. The goals were to give and take criticism with a humble spirit, and to seek reconciliation. The criticism meetings were an opportunity for personal growth and for building up the community. Yet there was always the risk of hurt feelings and damaged relationships.[32]

Truth was not shy to speak at criticism meetings. On one occasion she scolded a teacher for using playing cards in the classroom. Truth perhaps saw cards as a temptation to gambling, and therefore the first step on a slippery slope to ruin. Some agreed with Sojourner, but others defended the teacher, insisting that the cards were used only to teach arithmetic. The argument resulted in one person leaving the community.[33]

Another conflict was about dancing. Many in the community saw no harm in dancing, reasoning that it was good recreation and exercise. Dances were held in the dining hall in the old factory building. When there was a break in the dancing, young people saw a chance for courtship. The youth could be seen "lolling on each other squeezing each other's hands or sitting in each other's laps."[34] When two young couples behaved amorously, some members took offense. "Last week we had a regular blow up from Sojourn[er] . . . about the young people," one woman wrote to her absent husband. Truth was not the only objector. A man at that meeting "used most unjust language and produced a great deal of disgust."[35] In response to this, one member threatened to leave the community.

Sojourner Truth (in her youth as Isabella) was known as a good dancer. But now she may have worried about her two daughters. They arrived in the community in July 1844. Elizabeth (about eighteen years old) and Sophia (about seventeen) were still indentured to John Dumont, but he may have given them leave to visit their mother, or hired them out to someone else who gave leave.[36]

The reunion of Sojourner with Elizabeth and Sophia was "very affecting," wrote community member Dolly Stetson. She described Elizabeth and Sophia as good-looking and "energetic like their mother."[37] Yet something was amiss, reported Stetson. It seems that, back in upstate New York, Sophia had "disobeyed her mother and [gone] to live with a man." This man was a widower who "kept [Sophia] to take care of his family . . . [but] she became afraid of him and he abused her shamefully." Sophia got pregnant. The widower promised to marry her but never followed through. Sophia's pregnancy was the catalyst for the girls' coming to visit their mother, for, according to historian Margaret Washington, "some of Sojourner's friends had wrested Sophia from the man's grasp and sent the two daughters to Northampton."[38]

At the community dances, Sophia and Elizabeth taught the others a new dance called the waltz. Unlike reels and other folk dances, the waltz involved partners holding on to one another and was therefore called the "touching dance." One girl in the community wrote that Sojourner's "daughters waltz and it was quite a wonder to the people here."[39]

By the fall of 1844, Sophia was obviously pregnant. If Sojourner rejoiced to see her family grow, she may also have wondered how Sophia would support herself and the baby. Near the end of the pregnancy, Sophia had to quit her community job in the kitchen. That winter, the baby was born and named Wesley—probably after John Wesley, the founder of Methodism, who took a strong stand against slavery.[40]

In March 1845 the community held a dedication for its newly renovated dining hall. The large room was decked with evergreens, and hanging lamps were brought in from the silk factory. After dinner came the speeches. Sojourney (as some folks called her) spoke in praise of the new room and its decorations. Then some of the founders spoke. They warned against ingratitude and complaining, extolled orderly living and moderation in eating, and praised "rational enjoyments." The last speaker dedicated the new dining hall to free speech.

Meanwhile, the younger folks bided their time, hoping there could be a dance when their elders went home. There was a piano in the dining hall, and someone ready to play it once the coast was clear. Finally the older folks left. But no sooner had the music and dancing started than one of the elders returned to tell the young folks that it was nine o'clock, high time for reasonable people to go home to bed. "And thus ended the matter," Dolly Stetson wrote. "And yet it didn't end, because there was a great deal of grumbling" from those "not permitted to dance."[41] Sojourney gets no mention in this letter, perhaps because she, a reasonable person, had already gone to bed.

Long after these little skirmishes were forgotten, Truth would give thanks that the community connected her with William Lloyd Garrison. He put wheels on the abolition train by founding both the New England Anti-Slavery Society and the American Anti-Slavery Society. He was known nation-wide as the editor of the Boston-based *Liberator*, one of the best-known abolitionist papers. Truth became friends with Garrison, who encouraged her to become a public speaker in the national antislavery movement.

Garrison was a familiar figure at the Northampton Association. With his genial smile, balding head, and round spectacles, Garrison looked more like a schoolteacher than a radical reformer. His moral crusade against slavery made him one of the most hated people in America, but at the community he could relax among friends. The community members were "practical and questing people who formed the backbone of the *Liberator*'s subscription list."[42]

Garrison wrote countless editorials and articles, and even a few song lyrics to be used at abolitionist meetings. This verse, sung to the tune of Auld Lang Syne, expressed Garrison's militance and was likely sung by Truth herself:

> I am an Abolitionist!
> No threats shall awe my soul,
> No perils cause me to desist,
> no bribes my acts control;
> A free-man I will live and die,
> In sunshine and in shade,
> and raise my voice for LIBERTY,
> of naught on earth afraid.[43]

The editor of the *Liberator* was controversial within the antislavery movement. Today it is easy to assume that the antislavery effort was all of a piece. In truth, it was a loose coalition with many organizations, leaders, and strategies. Often there were rivalries and arguments, with people changing their allegiance from one group to another.

There was much to disagree about. How and when should slavery end? Should full citizenship and social equality for Blacks be the goal, or was it enough to end the institution of slavery and leave Blacks as a lower caste? Should abolitionists stay out of politics because it was corrupted by slavery, or use politics as a lever to end slavery? Was the Constitution of the United States inherently proslavery, or was it, at least potentially, antislavery? Should women be public speakers and leaders within the movement, or should they remain silent on the sidelines? Were the churches allies or enemies, or merely irrelevant to the antislavery cause?

Garrison taught clear doctrines to settle these and other questions. He believed that slavery must end immediately with no compensation to slaveholders. Slavery must end nonviolently, through moral suasion. Black people deserved full legal and social equality. Women were equal to men in every respect and should be leaders and speakers. (Controversy over women's role contributed to a split in the antislavery movement in 1840.)

Like Sojourner Truth, Garrison had a strong perfectionist streak. If ever there was a come-outer, it was Garrison. He shunned politics as hopelessly corrupted by slavery; he would not endorse any political party, nor would he vote. Because there should be "no union with slaveholders," he thought the North should secede from the Union. Garrison denied the authority of Scripture because it was quoted to support slavery; yet he often used verses that called for justice. He lambasted churches whose members supported slavery, profited from it, or acquiesced to it. Yet many of his allies were Christians, including several radical ministers.

Truth learned abolition from Garrison and his followers in the community. She believed his teachings and respected his leadership. Likewise, he saw her abilities, trusted her integrity, and gave her opportunities within the antislavery movement. Their connection outlasted the Northampton Association of Education and Industry, which closed in 1846.

Sojourner had hoped to spend the rest of her life in the community, but it was not to be. The silk products from the factory did not make enough money to pay off the debt on the property; there was also some dissent among members. As debts mounted, members began to leave.[44]

At a deeper level, the community closed because "the world was not ready for the experiment," wrote historian Charles Sheffeld. The Northampton Association set "a lofty ideal of social and industrial life" and human equality. For four years the members strove to overcome obstacles and hardships. Although they were forced to abandon their experiment, "they did not wholly fail"[45] because the principles of the community lived on in labor reforms, the women's movement, and, above all, the antislavery movement.

Sojourner Truth remained in Florence for some years after the community closed, as did some other former members of the NAEI. They continued their work for reforms, but did so as private citizens. The village of Florence grew up around the old factory site and "remained a center of the reform tradition, in a region still often hostile to it."[46] Today Florence is a neighborhood within greater Northampton.

The moral reform depot, though short-lived, broadened Truth's calling. She was still a preacher, but now she fused the message of salvation with a passion for justice.[47] For her, the end of the world was not an excuse to ignore suffering and injustice. Instead, her Adventism made her want everybody to get their rights and use them while there was still time. And the friends she made in the community she treasured for the rest of her life. "I was with them heart and soul for anything concerning human right, and my belief is in me yet and can't get out," she recalled. "What good times we had."[48]

8

"Make Me a Double Woman"

When the Northampton Association closed, Sojourner went to live in the nearby home of George and Helen Benson, who, like herself, had been members of the community. Truth kept house for the family, but the arrangement was temporary, for George Benson was slowly "going bankrupt" and would soon have to sell the house. When that day came, Truth would need another place to live.

Meanwhile, Samuel Hill, a wealthy founder of the NAEI, took steps to pay off the community's debts and to help members who were displaced by the closing. Using his own money, he bought land once owned by the NAEI and divided it into housing plots. Then he arranged for several houses to be built and offered loans on easy terms to former community members, including Sojourner Truth.

Samuel Hill entrusted Truth with a $300 mortgage (worth around $10,000 today) with no down payment. Her house was a basic two-story frame structure, built near the old silk factory on Park Street. The name on the deed was "Isabella Vanwagner . . . sometimes called 'Sojourner Truth.'" On April 15, 1850, Sojourner signed her "X" and became a homeowner.[1]

At long last Truth could offer her daughters a home. They were now adults with their own lives, but their mother's house gave them a safety net and a gathering place. Sophia came to live with Truth in 1850 with her little boy, Wesley. Diana arrived later that year and took in washing to earn her living. Elizabeth came to live with her mother in about 1852, bringing her child, Samuel Banks. Though each of the daughters would move on to other things, their mother's house offered stability.

Around the time Truth became a homeowner, she got her life story published. The idea probably came from William Lloyd Garrison during the time Truth lived with Garrison's sister Helen Benson. When in town to visit the Bensons, Garrison would have had opportunity to talk with Truth. Well aware of the success of Douglass's autobiography, Garrison wanted Truth's story to reach a wider public too.

The great obstacle was that Truth did not read or write. When she tried to learn the alphabet, she said "the letters all got mixed up" and she "couldn't straighten them out." When friends offered to teach her, she said her brain was "too stiff now."[2]

Yet she was gifted in oral language and had more experience in public speaking than most white women of that time. "You know, children," she used to say. "I don't read such small stuff as letters. I read men and nations. I can see through a millstone, though I can't see through a spelling book."[3] The biblical prophets could read the hearts of people and discern the meaning of events. These prophetic gifts—together with her talent for speaking and singing—were her strengths. One historian observed that Truth "might actually have preferred orality to literacy, as an African woman 'who professed a spiritual calling.'"[4]

Truth knew the Bible well, from close listening, prayer, and meditation. She could quote it with ease, but hers was more than rote knowledge. She understood God as the source of grace, of glory, and of judgment, and expected divine power to make all things new. The Scripture to her was not a compendium of theology but a living word to be proclaimed, prayed, and lived. Like other Black preachers, Truth was inspired by "the low earthly station of the Son of God."[5]

Sojourner Truth did not apologize for her nonliteracy but made it part of her persona. In her old age she told a reporter that her message came "fresh from the fountain of all truth." It was not borrowed from books, for she could not read them. "I dictate my letters, but a friend's hand moves the pen. People oft times express sorrow that I cannot read and say: 'Sojourner, you ought to learn to read the Bible.' I tell them I have a Bible in me."[6] If she needed help to get her story on paper, so be it. That help was near at hand.

Olive Gilbert was a staunch abolitionist, having seen slavery up close when she worked as a tutor in the South. She came to the Northampton Association to visit family, and, after the community closed, she remained in the area. Olive had met Sojourner before, little knowing that they would collaborate on a book.

White, single, and childless, Miss Gilbert lived modestly on a small inheritance. She was raised to be an enlightened Protestant who followed the teachings of Jesus, preferred simple worship, and practiced "moral responsibility."[7] Sojourner Truth believed in moral responsibility too, but she also believed in miracles and prized the baptism of the Holy Spirit, quite a contrast to the worldview of Olive Gilbert. Gilbert's "choice of language [in Truth's *Narrative*] suggests that she held Truth's religious ideas at a great distance," wrote Jean Humez, a scholar of women's history and literature whose work informs these remarks. Gilbert was sympathetic to Truth but may have wanted to distance Sojourner from religious views that were too far beyond Gilbert's view of respectability.

Above all, Gilbert wanted Truth's *Narrative* to strike a blow against slavery. Truth, on the other hand, saw her experience in slavery as part of a bigger story, an ongoing spiritual journey. She wanted her story to be about something more than how terrible slavery was. She wanted to testify to divine guidance that brought her out of slavery into a new life. In other words, Truth was antislavery *and* she wanted "a story of spiritual awakening and guidance by divine inner voice."

Olive Gilbert never claimed to be a professional writer or historian. She didn't check basic facts, and she included stories and opinions of her own. And Truth didn't always tell her story with strict accuracy—indeed, no human really can, since we reinterpret our experience as we go along. It is not surprising, then, that the *Narrative of Sojourner Truth* contains mistakes, leaves out parts of the story, and sometimes tells things out of order. Olive Gilbert's voice comes through, but Truth "as storyteller exercised significant control" over the end result.[8]

Olive Gilbert was a true friend. She asked for no share of the profits from book sales. Nor did she want her name to appear as editor or coauthor. Most important, she offered the reading public a "dignified portrait" of Truth. Unlike others who wrote about Truth, Gilbert did not impose a crude plantation dialect on Truth's words. Instead, she used standard English to set Truth's words before the reader. Humez thinks that Gilbert's choice "may reflect a genuine respect for Truth's eloquence in speaking." After the book came out in the spring of 1850, Gilbert followed Truth's career with great interest. "I get to glimpse you often through the papers," Gilbert wrote to Truth years later, "which falls on my spirit like bright rays from the sun."[9]

William Lloyd Garrison wrote a foreword for the book and endorsed it in the *Liberator*. He got a Boston publisher to print Truth's book on credit and then "lined up a number of speaking arrangements" where Truth could sell her *Narrative* at twenty-five cents per copy. With the proceeds she would eventually repay both the printer's loan and her mortgage.[10]

The *Narrative of Sojourner Truth* was published in 1850, a slender volume of 128 pages. It included a sketch of Sojourner Truth, wearing a plain dark dress trimmed with a white collar, her hair covered with a simple white wrap. Her face showed her dignity, strength, and intelligence. On the back cover were several endorsements from abolitionists, and inside was an unattributed quotation meant to describe Truth's story: "To meanest matters will I stoop, for mean is the lot of mortal; I will rise to noblest themes, for the soul hath a heritage of glory."[11]

The first part of Truth's *Narrative* is about Isabella's enslavement and how she freed herself. Most slave narratives end shortly after the protagonist becomes free. Truth's story, however, keeps going long into her free life, so that the reader sees a "vast gulf" between Isabella's young life and the mature Sojourner Truth. Her book is a spiritual memoir with an antislavery core.[12]

Truth chose to end the story with her last encounter with John Dumont, her former master, in the fall of 1849. Truth had gone to Dumont's farm to visit her daughter Diana, who was working there. Truth probably asked Dumont his opinion of slavery. He said that he once thought that owning slaves "was as right as holding any other property," but now he saw slavery as "the wickedest thing in the world, the greatest curse earth had ever felt."

"Well," countered Truth, "those who are now slaveholders still think it is right, or they wouldn't do it."

"How can they keep on thinking slavery is right," Dumont asked, "with so many people speaking and writing against it?" He claimed that if he had only known better, he would not have *dared* to hold slaves! Indeed, he would have "emancipated every one of them." Easy words to say, now that more than twenty years had passed since New York's emancipation and Dumont had nothing to lose. Then Truth recalled Dumont telling "his slaves not to lie and steal, when *he* was stealing all the time himself and did not know it!" Stealing her labor, her youth, her children. None of it could be paid back.

Truth had every reason to doubt Dumont's sincerity. Yet, like a preacher, she rejoiced over his testimony. "Oh! How sweet to my mind was this confession," she said. "A slaveholding master turned to a brother!" She wished that all slaveholders would "partake of his spirit."[13] Did Truth's antislavery readers find it strange that her *Narrative* ended with a story of forgiveness? Perhaps, but her choice shows that she was an abolitionist whose "religious worldview" was the core of her identity.[14]

Truth returned home rejoicing in John Dumont's change of heart. Some weeks later, Diana sent word to her mother that Dumont had moved away, taking with him some furniture that belonged to Truth, which she had left with Dumont for safekeeping. "Never mind," said Sojourner, "what we give to the poor, we lend to the Lord." John Dumont used to be the most powerful person in her life. Now she saw him as a "poor old man." So shall the first be last, and the last first.

———

In the late spring of 1850, Sojourner Truth went to Boston for a large antislavery convention. Abolitionists there were alarmed by the new Fugitive Slave Bill under discussion in Congress. Dubbed by critics "the bloodhound bill," this was the lightning rod in the Compromise of 1850, a bundle of legislation meant to keep the Union from falling apart.

If passed into law, the new Fugitive Slave Bill would require Northerners to help capture fugitive slaves, and anyone caught helping runaways would face steeper fines and longer jail terms than before. Black people accused of being runaways would be forced back south into slavery without the opportunity to defend themselves in a court of law. Legally free Blacks had never been safe from kidnappers, who sold them south into slavery, but the new law raised their risk of falling prey to traffickers. To avoid this fate, many chose to move to Canada.

Tensions over the Compromise were rising in the Senate. On April 17, 1850, amidst a heated argument, Senator Benton of Missouri suddenly rose from his seat and rushed toward his opponent, Senator Foote of Mississippi. Foote drew a pistol on Benton. "Let the assassin fire!" shouted Benton. "I have no pistols. I disdain to carry arms." Just in time, someone wrested the pistol away from Foote and locked it in a desk.[15]

News of this confrontation between two senators was still fresh in May, when the antislavery meeting convened in Boston. With the Fugitive Slave Bill likely to pass, the abolitionists vowed to keep the Underground Railroad going at all costs. As Senator William Seward had said in a speech earlier that spring, if Congress passed a law that told people to go against God and conscience, then they must obey the higher law. Truth listened to earnest speeches and joined in the singing. During breaks she sold copies of her newly published *Narrative*.

On the third day, Garrison introduced Truth to the convention. Having preached at many revivals and at smaller abolitionist meetings, Truth was ready. But the chairman worried that Truth, being a woman, might speak too softly to be heard. Before she even began, he encouraged her to speak up. "I have got a voice like a trumpet," she assured him.

Truth spoke for thirty minutes. The *Anti-Slavery Bugle* described her as a "tall, middle aged colored woman, with her head wrapped in a white handkerchief." (Many accounts of Truth mention her white headwrap, sometimes also called a turban. This was commonly worn by Black women, whether enslaved or free, who performed menial labor.) The *Bugle* went on to say that Truth spoke "with great earnestness" and with "natural shrewdness and wit."[16] No record of what she said survives, but the *New York Daily Tribune* said Truth "brought down the house and the galleries."[17]

Not amused, the *Richmond Enquirer* called the convention "rant and madness . . . a disgusting burlesque." The reporter singled Truth out for contempt. In the same terms used on handbills for slave auctions or rewards offered for the capture of runaway slaves, the *Enquirer* described Truth as "an immense negro wench of the blackest ebony with towering white turban on her head." He found Truth's attack on slavery "disgusting" and marveled that no one rose to "constrain Truth's disruptive presence."[18] And this was just the beginning of the madness, opined the *Enquirer*, for now the abolitionists were plotting a convention on the most absurd thing: "The Rights of Women."[19]

Sure enough, when the antislavery convention ended, nine women and two men met at Boston's Melodeon Theater to plan the first national convention on woman's rights.[20] (Two years earlier, in 1848, the Seneca Falls convention had laid the cornerstone for the woman's rights movement.) Now it was time to create a national organization. Among the planners of the first national gathering were Abby Kelley Foster, Paulina Wright Davis, William Lloyd Garrison, and Lucy Stone.

The first American woman to hold a college degree, Stone was also a veteran public speaker—a rare combination in 1850. "We *need all the women* who are accustomed to speak in public," Stone told a friend, "every stick of timber *that is sound.*"[21] Those who had heard Truth speak recognized her as one of those rare "sound timbers" who could support women's rights through public speaking. They invited her to speak at the first National Women's Rights Convention, to be held in Worcester, Massachusetts, on October 23–24, 1850.

Before this convention, Sojourner traveled to many antislavery meetings.[22] In addition to her *Narrative*, she often sold her "home-made songs" at antislavery events. These were her own lyrics, printed on a single sheet of paper, which she sold for five or ten cents each. "I always had something to pay my way with," she recalled years later. "Nobody paid me, for I was a free agent, to go and come when I pleased."[23]

A few years later at an antislavery convention in upstate New York, the abolitionist Aaron Powell observed Truth during an intermission between speakers. Her voice rang out clear and loud as she stood in the aisle and sang of going to Canada, where "colored men are free." Then she called out to the milling crowd, asking them to buy her song sheets, going so cheap at five cents each! "Now Friends, don't be scared," she teased "good-naturedly."[24] To hear Truth sing was unforgettable. She sang hymns, spirituals, and antislavery songs. "They were not usually accompanied by any instrument," writes historian Isabelle Richman, "but the audience might clap or stamp to the music." Her deep contralto voice may have sounded like Odetta or Fannie Lou Hamer,[25] Truth's heirs in the civil rights movement a century later.

Sojourner Truth sang not just to entertain but to change people's hearts and minds. To use a phrase popular among abolitionists, her singing was "whole-souled." With it she united her audience in the shared goal of ending slavery and filled them with militant courage. Truth's leadership in song, whether solo or group singing, no doubt fortified the antislavery movement with spiritual power.

On the Fourth of July 1850, Truth went to an antislavery picnic near Boston. For abolitionists, Independence Day was a time to proclaim that if the nation espoused liberty and justice for all, slavery must be abolished. The usual patriotic songs were given antislavery lyrics—like this version of "My Country, 'Tis of Thee" from a tune book called *Antislavery Picknick.*

My country 'tis of thee,
stronghold of slavery,
Of thee I sing.
Land where my fathers died,
where men man's rights deride,
from every mountainside
Thy deeds shall ring.

My native country! Thee,
where all men are born free,
if white their skin.
I love thy hills and dales,
thy mounts and pleasant vales,
but hate thy Negro sales
as foulest sin.[26]

The picnic Truth attended was held in a pine grove beside a lake, just a short train ride from Boston. The air was sweet and fresh from rains the night before, and the sun broke through the clouds as early arrivals set up their tents and tables. The morning program began at 10 a.m. with a speech by William Lloyd Garrison, followed by a poetry reading and then a testimony from a man who had been enslaved.

At lunchtime, hampers were unpacked and the tables laden with fried chicken, bread and pickles, cakes, and jugs of lemonade. Children played outdoor games while the adults relaxed in the shade of the pine trees. For all their earnestness, the abolitionists enjoyed a good picnic as much as anyone else.

At 2 p.m. the program resumed with Sojourner Truth. She spoke on slavery and families, appealing directly to the parents and children at the picnic. A report in the *Liberator* summed up her questions, to which the audience responded eagerly.

"*Do white women love their babies?*" Truth asked.
Yes, yes! came the response.
"*Are colored women human?*"
Yes, of course! answered the crowd.
"*Do we have human feelings?*" Truth pressed.
Yes, you do, the answer rang out.

"We are human," said Truth. "And we suffer so much when our little ones are torn from us, as you white mothers do."

Separating families was wicked, Truth declared. Perhaps she told them how she herself was sold away from her parents, and grew up without her brothers and sisters.[27]

For the next several months, Truth traveled to events and did not return to her home in Florence. In September of 1850, the Fugitive Slave Bill was signed into law, sparking outrage and civil disobedience. Truth must have startled an audience by saying, "Thank God that the [Fugitive Slave] law was made." Then she explained that "the worst" must happen first, and then "the best must come." Evil must come out into the open so that good people can fight it.[28]

In October, Truth went to Worcester to speak at the first National Women's Rights Convention. It was held in Brinley Hall, a brick building on Main Street often used for large gatherings of antislavery and other reform societies. Of the one thousand or so people attending the convention, only 268 publicly "declared themselves" in favor of women's rights and became voting members; the rest were mostly curiosity seekers and journalists.

Several pioneers of the women's rights movement spoke, including Abby Kelley Foster, Lucy Stone, and Paulina Wright Davis. Well-known abolitionists, including Garrison and Douglass, also spoke. Truth was the only Black woman to speak, but not the only female preacher; Antoinette Brown and Lucretia Mott were also on the program. One reporter expressed surprise that women could speak in public with such eloquence and strength.[29]

However, not everyone was favorably impressed. A writer for the *Southerner* said that the convention claimed to be about women's rights but was really about abolition; after all, one of the speakers was Sojourner Truth. The writer warned that this "fanatical gathering" aimed to reduce "society to the basest and most licentious socialism."[30] The reporter, who signed himself "a Southron," was right about one thing. There *was* an overlap between women's rights and abolition. Not only in the people who attended these meetings but also in their challenge to white men who controlled so much of women's lives.

Sojourner Truth embodied Black and women's rights movements, and could no more separate these than she could divide herself in two. And yet she knew that many white people wanted to keep these two movements separate. White women sometimes compared themselves to slaves, who, like them, lacked basic rights. Yet many assumed that only white women should get their rights. Therefore, in her speech at the first National Women's Rights Convention, Truth "urged that Black women, the real slaves, not be forgotten."[31] In effect, Truth told the convention to start seeing Black women. The convention did pass a resolution to include enslaved women in all demands for the rights of women.

In her speech, Truth used spiritual humor to deflate a pious argument against women's rights. That argument said that men should rule over women because Eve ate the forbidden fruit and brought sin into the world. Truth turned this upside down and made the pocket change fall out. The way she saw it, humanity fell into sin together and "had been going down together" for a long time. Since men have not kept evil out of the world, they have no claim to deny women their rights. A man had no right to "rule women unless he was made anew." Which he clearly was not. "If woman turned over the world, as it was said she did, she was now turning it back again. Men have ruled long enough, they can't rule anymore, for all the evil is done that can be done."[32] The audience loved Truth's theological satire, and their laughter distanced them from old ways of thinking.

One reporter mocked Truth's "smart speech . . . in which man, the tyrant, caught it *some.*" He said that Truth prayed, "God, make me a double woman, so that I might hold out to the end."[33] The writer sought to belittle Truth, yet the prayer he attributed to her captures something. She was truly "a double woman," standing for both women's rights and abolition. As for "holding out to the end," the years would prove that nobody had more staying power than Sojourner Truth.

The first National Women's Rights Convention was mostly white, but "several dark colored sisters were visible in the corners," said the *New York Herald.*[34] Seated on the margins and in the shadows, these "dark sisters" heard resolutions calling for equality in employment, religion, education, property, and voting rights.

Some white women did not want Blacks to be part of the women's rights movement. "In a Woman's Rights Convention," the journalist-reformer Jane Swisshelm wrote, "the question of color [has] no right to a hearing."[35] Swisshelm said that if reformers wanted to change things, they must stop trying to do everything at once. She feared that including Black women would create a backlash, so that no women would get their rights. The *Liberator* replied that few Americans believe *any* woman has rights, and nobody would ever think a Black woman has rights "without a specific declaration."[36] Sojourner Truth boldly called for *everyone* to get their rights.

When Lucretia Mott gave the closing address, she quoted Sojourner Truth's speech from earlier in the meeting. "Goodness [is] from everlasting and will never die," Truth had said, "while evil had a beginning and must come to an end." Change would not be easy. "Mountains of difficulty" stood in the way, but Jesus faced hardships too. "We must be living agents of this work."[37]

9

Between a Hawk and a Buzzard

In November 1850 a British celebrity came to Boston. The Honorable George Thompson, member of Parliament, was an antislavery man known for his compelling oratory. Thompson wore his long hair swept back over a chiseled brow, and, despite his debts, he dressed like a wealthy man. The abolitionists invited him to come to the States and speak out against slavery, promising to "take up a purse" to cover his expenses.

Boston's Faneuil Hall was to be the scene of a grand reception for Thompson. But proslavery operatives seeded the crowd with rabble-rousers and instructed them to stay quiet until the program got under way. Sojourner Truth, Frederick Douglass, and others sat on the speakers' platform as William Lloyd Garrison stood to introduce the honored guest. At that moment, the hall erupted with "shouting, cat-calls, Jim Crow dances, songs, and other annoyances,"[1] reported the *Liberator*. As the crowd swirled out of control, the dignitaries on the platform, including Sojourner Truth, fled for safety.

The meeting reconvened later at the Belknap Street Church, an African American congregation. This time the church was "strongly guarded by the police." An iron chain blocked the doors, and only those "known to be orderly citizens" were admitted. Sojourner Truth was among the mostly Black audience that filled the church to welcome Thompson.[2]

In the late winter of 1851, Thompson went on a speaking tour in New York State.[3] Garrison planned to go, and he invited Truth to come along. He offered to pay her expenses, so that Truth could use all the proceeds from her book sales to pay off her debts. She would also get a chance to do some public speaking. Managing the tour was Abby Kelley Foster, an abolitionist and pioneer of women's rights. She booked halls for Thompson to speak in, arranged lodgings and transportation, and took up collections to pay expenses. George Putnam, a correspondent for the *Liberator*, came along to report on the trip.

The tour would begin in Springfield, New York. When Truth arrived, she looked for Garrison at the Hampden House hotel, but he was nowhere to be found. Asking next for George Thompson, she was shown to his room. "He received & seated me with as much courtesy and cordiality," she recalled, "as if I had been the highest lady in the land." Thompson told Truth that their friend Garrison had taken ill and could not come and said he hoped Truth would still join the tour.

"I have no money & Mr. Garrison offered to pay my passage," Sojourner said.

"I'll bear your expenses, Sojourner," Thompson offered. Truth accepted gladly.

That evening, their hotel was surrounded by a mob of two hundred. The ruffians lit bonfires, shot off firecrackers, and hung Thompson in effigy from a tree in the town square. Unruffled, Thompson said the mob would generate publicity for the tour.[4] Sure enough, newspaper reports of the Springfield riot got the attention of the public and attracted many attendees along the way.

The abolitionists toured central New York for two months. The easiest way to travel was by train; however, many towns could only be reached by wagon or coach. Roads were rough and the weather raw, but the travelers were warmly hosted and fed by supporters at each stop. Antislavery rallies were held in Syracuse, Seneca Falls, Rochester, and many other towns. Local choirs performed at these events, but the singing of an entire assembly was the most thrilling of all. Everywhere they went, Truth's strong voice helped lead the singing.

Thompson was the main attraction, but he gladly shared the podium with others. Frederick Douglass, who lived in Rochester, spoke at several events. Abby Kelley and her husband, Stephen, filled in where needed, and Truth had several opportunities.

"Mr. Thompson," said one report, gave a speech and "was followed by *Sojourner Truth*," formerly a slave in New York. She "made an earnest appeal for the slaveholders." She "felt very much concerned" for them and feared they would be lost for all eternity if they did not change their hearts. "Black people [have] suffered so much in this world,"[5] she said. Yet slavery killed the souls of slaveholders. On the tour with Thompson, Truth spoke several times about the fate of masters. "O friends . . . pity the poor slaveholder and pray for him. It troubles me more than anything else, what will become of the poor slaveholder in all his guilt and his impenitence."[6] As she traveled her home state of New York, she likely called to mind many slave owners she had known personally. The *Liberator* said Truth was living "proof of the natural equality (to say the least) of the negro and the white" and expressed the wish "that all whites were her equals."[7]

George Thompson was impressed by Sojourner Truth. "She possesses a mind of rare power and often, in the course of her short speeches, will throw out gems of thought," he wrote near the end of the tour. "But the truly Christian spirit which pervades all she says, endears her to all who know her . . . and all who become acquainted with her esteem her most highly."[8]

Thompson won Truth's respect too. Years later, she recalled that Thompson accompanied her to the train cars and carried her bag on the first day of the tour. He always treated her as an equal. "At the Hotel tables he seated me beside himself and never seemed to know that I was poor and a Black woman." Wherever they went, Thompson promoted Truth's book. "Sojourner Truth has a *Narrative* of her life," he would say. "Buy largely, friends." Later in her life, as Truth thought back on the tour with George Thompson, she wrote: "My heart is glowing just now with the remembrance of his kindness to me in 1851." Thompson was, she added, "a great-hearted friend of my race."[9]

After the tour, Truth stayed for about three months in the Rochester home of Isaac and Amy Post, white abolitionists who became her lifelong friends.[10] Then Truth traveled by boat on Lake Erie, from Buffalo to Cleveland. She sent a letter to the Posts describing "a beautiful passage up the lake." Arriving in Cleveland, she spoke at an antislavery meeting and stayed "among colored friends" who treated her "with great kindness."[11]

From there she went to Akron, Ohio, to attend the Women's Rights Convention at the end of May. The event was held at the Stone Church (Universalist) on May 28–29, with several hundred people attending. Twelve years later, a revision of Truth's Akron talk was published, featuring the refrain: "Ain't I a woman?" Today it is known as Sojourner Truth's most famous speech, though at the time it was not widely recognized as an important speech.

Women's rights events often attracted ridicule, and an account of the speech published in 1863 described a rowdy convention—until Truth saved the day with her speech. However, real-time reports from 1851 describe the Akron convention as peaceful and free from harassment. The *New York Daily Tribune* reported "an intelligent audience" and "utmost good feeling."[12] The *Liberator* described "all faces beaming with joyous gladness in anticipation of a glorious future." The Hutchinson Singers performed on both days.

The delegates heard speeches, held open discussions, and passed resolutions. One of the featured speakers, Emma Coe, compared wives to slaves: both were held in subjection and denied the rights enjoyed by white men.[13] Women's education was a key issue. Women were often denied an education, since females were said to be mentally inferior to males. Sojourner Truth was one of several women who spoke on "the subject of education and the condition of women,"[14] but her words were not recorded in the "Proceedings of the Akron Convention."

The most detailed account of Truth's speech comes from the *Anti-Slavery Bugle*. Though unsigned, it was written by Marius Robinson, the *Bugle*'s editor, who was also "one of the official secretaries of the convention" and the president of the Western Anti-Slavery Society.[15]

Robinson was a veteran of the antislavery cause. While on the lecture circuit in 1837, he was tarred by a proslavery mob and barely survived.[16] He continued to fight slavery in print, working alongside his wife, Emily, to produce the *Anti-Slavery Bugle*. Their abolitionist paper circulated in Ohio, Indiana, and Michigan. Truth stayed with the Robinsons at their home in Salem, Ohio, around the time of the Akron convention, and later on when she toured Ohio giving antislavery speeches.[17] Much like Truth herself, the Robinsons harnessed religious fervor to the campaign for human rights.[18]

No wonder Marius Robinson had a receptive ear for Truth. He reported on many of the speeches of the convention but found Truth's to be "one of the most unique and interesting." Unlike many journalists, Robinson did not force a dialect on Truth but reported her words in standard English. He acknowledged that words on paper could not do justice to her speech. Only those who "saw her powerful form, her whole-souled, earnest gesture, and listened to her strong and truthful tones" could fully appreciate her message. Truth "came forward to the platform." Speaking with "great simplicity," she asked permission to "say a few words," and it was granted.

Truth's speech, as Robinson reported it, is in italics below, followed by comments in standard type. The speech is available without comment in the appendix of this book.

Sojourner began her speech with this statement: "*I want to say a few words about this matter. I am a woman's rights.*" Truth called herself "a woman's rights." What she was about to say was not an opinion or a set of beliefs. She was speaking forth her own identity: body, mind, and soul. And her speech follows that order.

Of her body, she said: "*I have as much muscle as any man, and can do as much work as any man. I have plowed and reaped and husked and chopped and mowed, and can any man do more than that? I have heard much about the sexes being equal; I can carry as much as any man, and can eat as much too, if I can get it. I am as strong as any man that is now.*"

Her words may have shocked white women who never had to sweat, whose hands were soft and whose fashionable clothing restricted their movements. Nineteenth-century ideals of womanhood did not include "Blacks and certainly not . . . slaves," writes historian Eric Foner. "Slave women regularly worked in the fields, and sometimes comprised a majority of the agricultural labor force."[19] Truth's strong, hardworking body did not conform to white cultural ideals of femininity.

After speaking of her woman's body, she talked of the female mind. "*As for intellect, all I can say is, if woman have a pint and a man a quart—why can't she have her little pint full? You need not be afraid to give us our rights for fear we will take too much—for we won't take more than our pint will hold.*" Many people believed that men's brains had greater capacity than women's, and therefore boys needed more education. If girls did go to school, they should learn domestic arts to prepare them to be homemakers and mothers. Truth made fun of the "man-brain theory," using mock literalism to reduce the theory to pints and quarts. She also shamed the men who would not let women have their rights, implying that these men were fearful and greedy. Her satire "convulsed the audience with laughter," reported the *Liberator*, and produced "roars of laughter," according to the *New York Daily Tribune*.[20] Truth said that if the man-brain theory held water, why were men so scared of letting the women get even a little pint of knowledge?

Then she offered a solution: "*The poor men seem to be all in confusion and don't know what to do. Why children, if you have woman's rights give it to her and you will feel better. You will have your own rights, and they won't be so much trouble."* Truth believed that everyone had the same rights—but some people stole the rights of others. The women and the enslaved people were asking for the return of their stolen rights. If white men returned these rights, they would still have their own rights—and they would no longer have to justify their theft of other folks' rights.

Having now spoken of body and mind, Truth went on to soul. *"I can't read but I can hear. I have heard the bible and have learned that Eve caused man to sin. Well if woman upset the world, do give her a chance to set it right side up again."* The sin of Eve was another excuse that men used to keep women under control. Truth disagreed with that logic. If Eve did bring sin into the world, that didn't mean men could make things right. Truth already said (at the first National Woman's Rights Convention)[21] that since men failed to make things better, they forfeited any claim to superiority.

Then Truth mentioned a "lady" at this convention who spoke *"about Jesus, how he never spurned woman from him, and she was right. When Lazarus died, Mary and Martha came to him with faith and love and besought him to raise their brother. And Jesus wept—and Lazarus came forth."* Jesus did not push women aside as though only men mattered. When Mary and Martha (whose brother Lazarus had died) pleaded with Jesus, he raised Lazarus from the dead—proving that, as one scholar said, "great change could result from the efforts of women."[22]

Now Truth got down to a core claim of Christianity: the incarnation of Jesus as God in the flesh. *"And how came Jesus into the world? Through God who created him and woman who bore him. Man, where is your part?"* God didn't need a man for Jesus to be born. Women who have been pushed aside and told to remain silent are, in fact, at the center of the story.

In closing, Truth said what was happening now: *"But women are coming up blessed be God and a few of the men are coming up with them."* Women were not keeping silent, and there were some men who said that everyone would be better off when women got their rights. But to those who still thought men should run the world, Truth had this to say: *"Man is in a tight place, the poor slave is on him, woman is coming on him, and he is surely between a hawk and a buzzard."*[23]

Truth saw the dilemma: white men were caught between a rock and a hard place. The white man must give back the rights he stole, or the hawk and the buzzard would swoop down on him and take the stolen treasure by force.[24] Truth saw that women and Blacks had already lost their rights, so it was the white men who had the most to lose. Yet the white men also had something to gain. Men will, Truth said, *"feel better when everybody gets their rights"* and men no longer have to pretend to be better than women.

Sojourner had no idea that Akron would go down in history as the place where she gave her most famous speech. After the convention, Truth sent a letter to Amy Post. "I sold a good many books at the Convention and have thus far been greatly prospered," Truth said. Several people at the convention offered to welcome her into their homes if she gave speeches nearby.[25]

She took them up on it. For the next two years, Truth traveled in Ohio, speaking out against slavery and for women's rights. Wherever she went, she sold copies of her *Narrative*. In the summer of 1851, she stayed with Marius and Emily Robinson in Salem. They loaned her a horse and buggy so that she could drive "from town to town, attending conventions and holding meetings of her own."[26] It was said that when Truth and the buggy came to a crossroads, "she laid the lines down and said, 'God, you drive.'" Soon she would arrive at "some good place where she had a successful meeting." While driving from place to place, Truth enjoyed her pipe and tobacco, for in those days she was still "a great smoker."[27]

Driving the country roads in a buggy, speaking to crowds, and selling books might sound pleasant, but it was risky for a Black female abolitionist. Like other Northern states, Ohio had people who wanted to silence abolitionists. Truth knew she was taking chances, but she felt called by God to preach freedom.

She also felt obliged to pay her debts. Much of what she made in book sales was sent to pay her publisher. Truth also sent mortgage payments to Samuel Hill in Florence, and may have sent money to her daughters. Thanks to the friends who hosted her, most of her food and lodging was covered. In return, she gave her hosts the opportunity to support the antislavery movement.

While Truth traveled Ohio in the summer of 1851, a story about slavery ran in weekly installments in the *National Era*, an antislavery paper based in Washington, DC. The author said she wrote to "awaken sympathy for the slave." Harriet Beecher Stowe's fictional story was published in book form in 1852. *Uncle Tom's Cabin; or, Life among the Lowly* opened the hearts and minds of countless readers to the antislavery cause. It was the best seller of the century and made Stowe world famous. Before long, the two women would meet.

Sojourner Truth was working hard to win people to the antislavery cause. "Every few days Sojourner Truth joins us and aids us in our meetings," wrote antislavery activist and educator Sallie Holley. Truth "travels in a buggy by herself. . . . She is quite a strong character and shows what a great intellect slavery has crushed." Holley noted that Truth talked like someone who "did not just hear about slavery, but lived it."[28]

In October 1851 Truth attended an antislavery convention in Salem, Ohio. One of the featured speakers was Parker Pillsbury, a minister who was expelled from his church because of his radical antislavery stance. Pillsbury then went to work for the American Anti-Slavery Society and also spoke for women's rights.

Pillsbury and Truth became friends and sometimes reinforced one another's speeches. In Salem, Pillsbury said the Union was built on the backs of slaves. Political parties made compromises to hold the Union together, but those compromises were paid for by the blood and tears of slaves. Rather than compromise, Pillsbury called for "no union with slaveholders." Better for the North to secede from the Union, Pillsbury said, than to continue in an unholy alliance that supported slavery.

Then Truth stood up to speak. "Sojourner said SHE knew something of the Union—she had felt it; the scars of it were on her back, and she would carry them to her grave," reported the Anti-Slavery Bugle. Truth said that "the Union was not sweet to her, it was very bitter, and if others would taste it in the same way, they would think it was bitter."[29] Who suffered to keep the Union together? Truth asked. The slaves did, and the price they paid was too high.

This call for disunion followed the abolition doctrines of William Lloyd Garrison. The Garrisonians saw dissolving the Union as the only way the North could end its complicity in slavery. Disunion became "a test of ideological loyalty among Garrisonians," writes historian Douglas Blight.[30]

Another test had to do with the Constitution. Garrison said the Constitution lacked moral authority, because it permitted and supported slavery without explicitly naming it. Truth agreed, but she had her own way to make the point. At one meeting, after a speaker praised the Constitution, Truth stood up and spoke in a quiet and calm tone. "I talk to God and God talks to me," she said. One morning she climbed over a fence and walked into a field. "I saw the wheat holding up its head, looking very big." She reached out and plucked a head of wheat, but when she looked inside, she saw that there was no grain. "What *is the matter with this* wheat?" she said to God. "Sojourner, there is a little weasel in it," God said. Then Truth explained: "I hear talk about the Constitution and the rights of men," she said. "I come up and I take hold of this Constitution. It looks *mighty big.* But I feel for *my* rights and there's nothing there. Then I say, 'God, what *ails* this Constitution?'" God said to her, "Sojourner, there is a little *weasel* in it."[31] Slavery was the weasel that ate the heart out of the Constitution.

Truth was deeply committed to Garrison's brand of abolition. And that put her at odds with Frederick Douglass. One of the most iconic scenes of Truth's career was her confrontation with Douglass, when she derailed one of his speeches with a simple question. This moment, which became known as the "Great Interruption," was part of the larger conflict between Garrison and Douglass, and at the same time it illustrated the diversity among Black abolitionists.

———

When Frederick Douglass was a young man recently escaped from slavery, Garrison mentored him and got him started as an antislavery speaker. But Douglass, an independent thinker, did not stay within the bounds of Garrisonian orthodoxy. In 1847 Douglass launched the *North Star* (later renamed *Frederick Douglass' Paper*), which some people saw as competition with Garrison's *Liberator*.

In print and from the lectern, Douglass challenged some of Garrison's core beliefs about abolition, such as Garrison's views that *only* moral suasion could end slavery and that violence was never justified. Douglass's own life taught him otherwise. As a young enslaved man, Douglass was abused by a cruel overseer. Douglass tried to bear it in silence, but one day when the overseer struck him, Douglass fought back. After a bloody brawl lasting nearly two hours, Douglass won. Normally an overseer would get help to punish such resistance. But this overseer didn't want word getting out that a Black man had beaten him. He never laid a hand on Douglass again. "This battle . . . was the turning point in my career as a slave," Douglas wrote. "My long-crushed spirit rose, cowardice departed [and] bold defiance took its place."[32] Later, during the furor over the fugitive slave law, Douglass warned that slave catchers trying to force Blacks into slavery "will be murdered in the streets."[33]

In another departure from Garrison, Douglass embraced politics. Garrison was a perfectionist, and "politics and perfectionism do not easily mix."[34] Douglass saw politics as a potential tool (though surely not a perfect one) to help bring slavery down.[35]

The rift between Garrison and Douglass became public at the American Anti-Slavery Society in Syracuse, New York, in May 1851. Douglass gave a speech in which he said that "his views on the Constitution had changed." After careful study, he now believed that the Constitution (though flawed) was not a tool for evil; in fact, it could be read and used in the antislavery cause. Further, Douglass said it was every American citizen's duty "to use his political as well as his moral power" to "overthrow" slavery.[36] On hearing this from the lips of his erstwhile protégé, Garrison fumed, "There is roguery somewhere."[37]

The break between Douglass and Garrison sent tremors through the antislavery movement. Truth took Garrison's side. It was not just that she was grateful to Garrison for helping get her book published and for opening doors for her to speak on the antislavery circuit. Truth, like Garrison, was a perfectionist and a come-outer. Garrison's brand of activism dovetailed with Truth's quest for holiness.

Truth and Douglass had important things in common: both freed themselves from slavery and created new lives. They met at the Northampton Association, and both won fame in the antislavery movement; both were prophets of social justice. "Douglass focused on political rights," writes historian Kyle Bulthuis, while "Sojourner Truth closely linked personal righteousness, even individual perfection, with her conceptions of reform."[38] Douglass was the man of letters, and Truth the woman of spoken and sung word. It was as though Douglass played the violin and Truth played the fiddle, creating very different kinds of music.

Truth's Great Interruption of Douglass took place in Salem, Ohio, on August 22, 1852. Douglass had been invited to speak at the meetinghouse of the Progressive Friends on a Sunday evening. The hall was packed with people eager to hear "an eloquent and powerful speaker" who could move an audience to tears, said the *Pennsylvania Freeman* (a Garrisonian paper). Douglass was right about the evils of slavery, opined the *Freeman*, but wrong to say that voting was necessary. Douglass said that "the Constitution is free from the taint of slavery," an idea that the *Freeman* called a "failure."

Then Douglass said that "violence . . . in some circumstances [is] far more potent than Moral Suasion." There were times, Douglass said, when only violence could change things, for example, in Russia where the serfs were in thrall to the czar, and only "the shedding of the blood of the tyrants could afford relief."

Douglass had worked his audience into "a high pitch of excitement," and they hung on his every word. Sensing that they were ready, Douglass asked a simple, rhetorical question. It struck a blow against Garrison's doctrine that only moral suasion could end slavery and violence was always wrong. "What is the use of Moral Suasion," Douglass asked, "to a people thus trampled in the dust?" He waited for his challenge to sink in, not expecting anyone to speak. But from the hushed crowd came the lone voice of Sojourner Truth, asking her own question: "Is God gone?" With three little words, she shot down Douglass's oratory in midflight.

Douglass was stunned into silence. Truth's question implied that if God is with us, there is no need for violence. And that those who resort to violence lack faith in God. Douglass tried to respond. "God is present in the mind of the oppressed," he ventured. But according to the *Pennsylvania Freeman*, "Sojourner's arrow . . . pierced with deadly effect the Atheism which teaches that the Sword is mightier than the Truth." So it was that "a simple question from the mouth of an illiterate woman" confounded the great orator.[39] Of course, Frederick Douglass was no atheist. But to Garrisonian abolitionists, he had spoken heresy.

Frederick Douglass' Paper reported this event much differently than did the *Pennsylvania Freeman*. In the Douglass version, the speech was about how the Constitution and politics can be instruments for ending slavery, and Truth was not mentioned by name. However, *Frederick Douglass' Paper* did say that "frequent interruptions" only drew out "his whole strength."[40] Yet Truth's Great Interruption vexed Douglass. Years later he recalled that when Truth lobbed her question into the silent crowd, "We were all for a moment brought to a standstill; just as we should have been if someone had thrown a brick through a window."[41]

William Still, an African American abolitionist, wrote years later that "Frederick Douglass was making one of his most eloquent speeches . . . portraying the situation as though everything was about to go headlong into wreck and ruin when Sojourner interrupted." Her question was "stunning" for Douglass and had an "electric effect upon the entire audience who evidently sympathized with the poor old ignorant woman rather than with the renowned orator. None who were present will ever forget the occasion."[42]

But what did Truth actually say? The *Pennsylvania Freeman* was "more likely to be accurate" than later versions of Truth's question.[43] The *Freeman* had Truth ask: "Is God gone?" That rhetorical question expects the response, "No, God is not gone. God is still here." And since God is still here, violence is unnecessary. But Truth's question was soon quoted as "Is God dead?" perhaps because it had greater shock value. For the rest of her life, Truth was reported as having asked, "Is God dead?" until finally it ended up on her tombstone. Without the context of her dispute with Douglass, it is a misleading epitaph insofar as it implies Truth doubted God's existence.

Truth's question mattered to abolitionists. "Behind Sojourner's simple question lay a larger issue," writes historian Isabelle Richman. "How were they to achieve their goal of ending slavery? And what role might God play in that?" Like William Lloyd Garrison, Truth was a pacifist who believed that slavery could end nonviolently. At the opposite end of the spectrum were the insurrectionists, from Denmark Vesey to Nat Turner to John Brown. Somewhere between those two extremes were those who said violence was justified and at some point necessary (Frederick Douglass, Henry Highland Garnet, Henry Ward Beecher). There were whites *and* Blacks at all points on the spectrum, and people could and did change their minds. Even so, "the public confrontation between Sojourner Truth and Frederick Douglass clarified the division within the abolitionist movement."[44]

In the end, Frederick Douglass was right: it would take both politics and violence to uproot slavery. The election of Lincoln followed by the Civil War proved it. Yet Douglass gave credit where credit was due. In 1870 he wrote an article acknowledging Truth's work for the rights of women and of Black people, adding, "Let him who is foolhardy enough to cross her beware."[45]

10

"Am I Not a Woman and a Sister?"

The abolitionist and women's rights meetings where Sojourner Truth spoke were often harassed and sometimes mobbed. But Truth could usually hold her own against opponents by using her sharp wit. Sometimes other challenges threatened to upend her public speaking—such as meeting the needs of her family.

In the spring of 1853, Truth was in Boston at an antislavery meeting when word came that her daughter Diana was "dangerously ill." Sojourner immediately set out on a journey of one hundred miles by train to Northampton and by foot or wagon to nearby Florence. Reaching her destination, she found Diana sick with "pleurisy and lung fever" that made breathing painful. Sojourner nursed Diana through the crisis, but full recovery would take months, and Diana would also need help taking care of her child. This posed a dilemma for Truth: she had important speaking engagements coming up in New York City, but Diana needed care. If only Truth's daughter Elizabeth could come home to take care of her sister, but Elizabeth worked for a white family in another town, and if a Black woman wanted to keep her job, white people's needs came first.

Not accepting this, Sojourner got someone to write down her words in a letter, which she sent to a friend who knew Elizabeth's employer. The friend presented Truth's letter to the employer. "Diana is very anxious that [Elizabeth] should come," the letter said, stating that Sojourner Truth had "necessary business" to do and could not stay home indefinitely. Truth promised to pay for Elizabeth's transportation.[1] Elizabeth's employer agreed to let her go home. The small victory mattered. Truth could now keep her speaking engagements. After putting her own needs last for so many years, Truth now used her agency to follow her higher calling.

With Diana now under her sister's care, Truth went to Philadelphia in May to attend conventions and do some speaking.[2] September found her in New York City for the annual meetings of reform societies. Since many activists embraced more than one cause, the big annual meetings were scheduled so that people could go from one to another like bees in a honeycomb.

The New York Anti-Slavery Society met on September 4 in a large theater called the Metropolitan Hall. About 1,500 people attended the afternoon session to hear William Lloyd Garrison give the keynote speech. "This Union must be dashed to pieces like a potter's vessel," he declared, "or the Slave Power must be destroyed."[3]

Several speakers followed. When Truth's turn came, she told the crowd that her body was scarred from beatings, but not all scars are the kind you can see. Growing up, she heard white people call Black people "a species of monkeys or baboons." She had heard her mother weep for her children already sold away, knowing that Isabella would be sold too. Her mother told her to ask God to make bad masters good. So young Isabella prayed accordingly. Then, when the whites didn't get any better, she prayed that God would kill them, "for they seemed to die quicker than they got good." This went on for years, Truth said, until "Christ Jesus lighted up my mind, and . . . my soul filled with love."[4] The afternoon session adjourned.

The evening session was sabotaged by men who came to "hiss, hoot, growl, scoff, mock, and howl."[5] The abolitionists made a valiant effort, but the uproar "continued until the lights were put out, and the leaders of the meeting had disappeared."[6]

The following Tuesday evening, Sojourner spoke in a Black church. Truth said she felt thankful to stand "before her own people." According to the *New York Daily Tribune*, Truth said she was so used to speaking to "the race of slaveholders" that she now found it hard to speak "to her own race on the subject of slavery." She was robbed of an education, denied her rights, and separated from her family. "And yet I live! Not only that, but God lives in me." Warm applause filling the church, Truth paused.

"Why is our race so despised?" she continued. "What have we done to be hated? Is it because we are Black? We have not made ourselves Black. If we have done something wrong, why not let us make things right?" She knew that Blacks had done nothing wrong, but her rhetorical strategy was to take away excuses from those who would blame the victims. "Our oppressors bind us hand and foot and ask us why we don't run," she said.

She said that "the filth of the City" shocked her when she came to New York for the first time; she could never get used to it. As a housekeeper, she strove for order and cleanliness and knew that *she* had higher standards than many whites.

Plunging in deeper, Truth insisted that *slavery did not come from God*, as defenders of slavery claimed. It was not God's will that Blacks be robbed of the fruit of their labor, their bodies bruised and their families scattered. Yet many whites felt entitled to take all they could. As a young girl, Truth said, she almost believed the lie that slavery came from God. Truth said she used to wonder why whites had plenty of food and clothes and Blacks did not. When she was young, she used to envy white people—while at the same time hating them. But after God freed her, she "gloried in her color." In fact, she "rejoiced in the color that God had been pleased to give her . . . she was well satisfied with it."

Truth forgave, but she did not forget: her people's blood soaked the nation, and God's judgment must come. She urged her people to fight slavery and not leave the struggle to white abolitionists. No one should accept slavery or unequal treatment. As for herself, Truth said, she "wanted *all* the rights she was entitled to."[7]

The next day Truth spoke to a women's rights convention. The large, mostly white gathering was held on September 6, 1853, at Manhattan's Broadway Tabernacle. Its "great rotunda" had "tiers of pews rising steeply from the central pulpit" and could seat 2,500 people.[8] Broadway Tabernacle was once the church of Charles Finney, the revivalist who preached "holiness unto the Lord." But it was unholy clamor that made this meeting go down in history as "the Mob Convention." On the first day, a mob infiltrated the meeting to harass the speakers and inflame the audience. The invaders were led by Isaiah Rynders, a Tammany Hall operative known for disrupting meetings of reformers. But the women did not give up. The next day, they "reconvened with Lucretia Mott in the chair and managed to get through their day's agenda despite continued heckling."[9]

Elizabeth Cady Stanton described the Mob Convention in *History of Woman's Suffrage*. Truth took the brunt of the mob's abuse, Stanton wrote, because she "was Black, and she was a woman and all the insults that could be cast upon color and sex were together hurled at her."[10]

Truth walked to the podium amidst a "perfect storm of applause, hisses, groans," reported the *New York Daily Times*. Several young men shouted for oyster stew and crackers, their way of saying that a Black woman should wait on them but could never, ever teach them. "It is good for me," Truth began, "to come forth to see what kind of spirit you are made of." Hissing filled the huge circular auditorium. "I see," Truth quipped, "some of you have got the spirit of a goose and a good many of you have got the spirit of snakes."

"Give it to them!" Truth's supporters yelled.

"I feel at home here," Truth said. "I was born in [New York]. I've been a slave, and now I'm a good citizen." Some folk might find it strange to "see a colored woman get up and tell" them about woman's rights, she said, "when we've all been trampled down so nobody thought we'd ever get up again. But we have come up, and I am here."[11]

Then, to prove that men should listen to women, she told a Bible story. The king of Persia listened when Queen Esther warned him of a terrible plot to kill all the Jews of Persia. Believing Esther, the king executed the leader of the plot and armed the Jews to defend themselves. The oppressed rose up and cast out their foes. Truth concluded that, since a king listened to a woman in Bible times, today's rulers should do likewise.

Women are coming forward to ask for their rights, Truth said. *We will have our rights, and you can't stop us.* Truth said it was a shame that men were laughing and pointing at their mothers up on the stage. If they'd been brought up properly, they would know better than to hiss like snakes and geese. "I'm around watching these things," Truth said. "I wanted to come out and tell you about Woman's Rights, and so I came out and said so. I am sitting among you to watch; and every once in a while I will come out and tell you what time of night it is."[12]

Through it all the mob kept shouting and calling for oysters. So great was the din that Lucretia Mott decided to adjourn. The attendees were told to walk out two by two—each woman with a man, and each Black person with a white one. When Mott was "left without an escort she chose [Isaiah] Rynders to lead her out. Nonplussed by this unexpected act of trust, the ring leader complied."[13]

———

Truth went to Andover in October to visit Harriet Beecher Stowe, author of *Uncle Tom's Cabin*. Several abolitionists (including Frederick Douglass and William Lloyd Garrison) had visited Stowe. Truth also wished to pay a call on the author and ask her to write an endorsement for the next edition of *Narrative of Sojourner Truth*. Little did Truth know that Harriet Beecher Stowe would write a great deal more about her.

The Stowes lived in a huge stone house at Andover Seminary, where Harriet's husband, Calvin Stowe, was a professor. Stowe was entertaining a group of clergymen when Truth arrived unannounced. She stood at the door, dressed in "stout, grayish [cloth] neat and clean, though dusty from travel," Stowe later wrote. On her feet Truth wore "heavy traveling shoes," and "on her head a bright Madras handkerchief, arranged as a turban."[14] Accompanying Truth was her grandson James Caldwell, then about eight years old. Stowe brought the visitors inside and made introductions. Then Truth told of her experiences in slavery and sang some hymns. Sojourner and James stayed for a few days as guests of Harriet Beecher Stowe.

Stowe wrote the endorsement for Truth's *Narrative*, praising Truth's character and urging people to buy the book. This appeared in the front of the second edition of Truth's *Narrative* (published in 1855), but Stowe was not done writing about Truth. In her second antislavery novel, *Dred, a Tale of the Great Dismal Swamp* (1856), Stowe based a fictional character on Sojourner Truth. This character, named Milly, was an enslaved woman of deep Christian faith who believed that freedom was coming and pleaded with her fellow slaves to refrain from violence.

December of 1853 found Truth back in New York City for the twentieth anniversary of the American Anti-Slavery Society. She also spoke at a Black church in the area. The pulpit from which Truth spoke was decorated with an antislavery banner well known to abolitionists. It pictured a Black woman, hands chained, kneeling in supplication. The motto on the banner read: "Am I not a woman and a sister?" Similar banners were used at antislavery rallies in Great Britain and the United States. The question—Am I not a woman and a sister?—exposed the harsh truth that Black females "were the only women in America who were sexually exploited with impunity, stripped and whipped with a lash, and worked like oxen." White women were told to stay home and be protected by their menfolk, but enslaved Black women had no protection from men or from the law.[15]

Before she began her speech, Truth asked, "Does someone have the spirit of prayer?" An elderly man stood up to pray, and then Truth sang a hymn.

In her speech, Truth talked about how hard it was for Black people to earn a living in New York City. It used to be, she said, that Black men could get work as barbers, coachmen, and street cleaners. But now even *those* jobs were being taken by whites. It was no use telling people to work harder when they could not get work.

Something must change, Truth said. She could feel change coming, but just what would bring it she did not know. Some said the answer was colonization—sending Blacks away to Africa or perhaps Central America. But Truth rejected colonization because it would deprive Black people of the fruits of their labors in the United States.

"My colored brothers and sisters, there's a remedy for this," Truth said. Blacks must get back to the land. Not some foreign land, but American land. Black farmers might have to rent cropland for a while, Truth allowed, but "in the course of time you will get to be independent." She suggested that New York Blacks go to Pennsylvania, where they could work for white farmers and save money to buy land of their own.

Truth described the big churches she had seen in New York City. These magnificent buildings sat on prime real estate but were "about one-third filled once in the week, and for the other six days allowed to lie unoccupied and a dead loss." And every day, poor people lived in dark cellars or cold attics. So why not let them into the churches?

Truth blamed the clergy for the empty churches. "The parsons went away into Egypt among the bones of dead Pharaohs and mummies," said Truth, "and talked about what happened thousands of years ago." These men knew nothing of real life, Truth scoffed. And now that women are trying to speak out and do good work, the clergy only heap "shame" on them. Truth saw the ministers as too fond of "the fat and easy work of preaching." No wonder it scares them "when women attempt to set matters aright," Truth said.

People say women are made for the home, she continued. If that's true, then men are made for the farm and the plow. So, asked Truth, do those men lose their masculinity by taking to "the pulpit and the platform"? Men should let the women talk in public. Women are criticized for talking too much, said Truth, but that only shows that women are well suited "to fill the talking professions." Women could use more speaking opportunities to help everyone get their rights.[16] Truth's oratory contained many such reversals, which she used to get people to think anew and change society.

———

A few years had now passed since the Fugitive Slave Bill became law. In the North, confrontations flared between slave catchers and resisters. Sometimes the slave catchers won, and the fugitive was dragged back into slavery; at other times fugitives escaped but suffered personal injury and separation from loved ones. These wrenching stories spread via newspapers, sermons, and lectures throughout the North.

A story that lived in infamy was the capture of Anthony Burns, a fugitive slave from Alexandria, Virginia, who had fled to Boston. Burns was arrested on May 24, 1854, and held in the courthouse jail to await his fate. Abolitionists decided to liberate Burns by force. One group began ramming the courthouse door with a huge log, while a second group chopped at another door with their axes. Inside the courthouse, fifty guards stood armed and ready to fight. "One deputy was shot dead, several men wounded, and thirteen arrested. Burns remained in custody." Then came a week or so of hearings, after which the court ordered Burns to be returned to slavery. Burns was marched under heavy guard through the streets of Boston, past "store and office windows . . . [that were] draped in black crepe." American flags hung upside down, and protesters suspended a coffin across State Street, "with the word 'Liberty' painted on its side." Down in Boston Harbor a ship waited to take Burns back to Virginia,[17] while thousands packed the streets, shouting, "Shame, shame!"

Just a few days later, on May 30, Congress passed the Kansas-Nebraska Act. It said that people in the Kansas and Nebraska Territories could now decide for themselves whether or not to allow slavery within their borders. The Missouri Compromise of 1820 had prohibited slavery north of latitude 36°30′. But now, under the new policy of "popular sovereignty," slavery could go anywhere if it had enough popular support. The Kansas-Nebraska Act, together with the Fugitive Slave Law, extended the power of slavery into the North and West.

On the Fourth of July 1854, Sojourner Truth attended the annual picnic of the Massachusetts Anti-Slavery Society. From the speakers' platform hung an upside-down US flag bordered in black. William Lloyd Garrison gave the opening speech. He condemned the nation and its organized religion for the crime of slavery and called on the North to secede: "no union with slaveholders" was the cry. Radical abolitionists would rather secede from the Union than live in a slaveholding nation. Saying that he must make "the testimony of his own soul to all present," Garrison performed three symbolic acts. First, he produced a copy of the Fugitive Slave Law, "set fire to it, and it burnt to ashes" as the crowd cheered. Then he held out a copy of the court verdict that sent Anthony Burns back into slavery. This too was devoured by flames as the crowd cheered its approval.

Finally, Garrison held up a copy of the US Constitution, branding it "the source . . . of all the other atrocities." The Constitution was "a covenant with death, and an agreement with hell," Garrison said. "Perish all compromises with tyranny!" Then, like a preacher, he called out: "Let all the people say, Amen!" Then "a tremendous shout of 'Amen!' went up to heaven" as flames consumed the Constitution. The *Liberator* reported that a few people hissed and booed their disapproval, but their voices were lost in the roar from those who would rather leave the Union than live one more day with slavery.[18]

And the program was just beginning. Other speakers for that day included Lucy Stone, Wendell Phillips, and Henry David Thoreau. Before Sojourner Truth spoke, a Scotsman addressed the crowd. He claimed to carry within himself "a little bit of Scotch thistle, which pricked him up to struggle for liberty . . . as long as he lived."[19] The Scotsman had joined the failed attempt to free Anthony Burns and was jailed for his efforts. Now he told the crowd of his experience in jail—how he was separated from his family and denied basic rights. In this way he said he got a small taste of how Blacks were treated.

When Truth addressed the crowd, she said she agreed with the Scotsman: the evils of slavery cannot merely be spoken—they can "only be *felt*." Then, referencing the thistle, Truth said it was good that white folks should feel the thorn. The audience laughed and cheered, but Sojourner was using humor to open up a space for hard truths. God would judge "white people for their oppression and cruelty," she warned. "Why did the white people hate the Blacks?" she asked. It was because white people owed Blacks "a big debt." But if they "paid it all back, they wouldn't have anything left for seed." All they "could do was to repent, and have the debt forgiven them."

Truth said that Black children were "sold to help educate ministers of the gospel." She did not give a specific example, but in 2019, several prestigious schools, including seminaries, admitted to profiting from slavery and the slave trade. Princeton Seminary and Virginia Seminary promised to pay large sums in reparations.[20] So much wrong, as Sojourner had said, but why did whites keep on hating the very people they had wronged? If whites couldn't answer for it now, Truth said, they must answer before God.

Then she invoked the biblical story of the brothers Cain and Abel: God favored Abel's offerings, and Cain grew so jealous that he murdered his brother. When God questioned him, Cain denied knowing where his brother was, and God punished Cain by sending him into exile. With this story in mind, Truth quoted Genesis 4:10: "Even the blood of one man, Abel, did not call from the ground in vain." That promise was for Black people, Truth said, like all the promises in Scripture.

She had her audience picture "the poor slave in heaven . . . robes washed white in the blood of the Lamb." Yet peace in heaven was not all. God moves on this earth, toward a day of reckoning in history. Right now, she said, Black people are in tribulation—a time of suffering leading to glory. She acknowledged that there are whites who suffer with the Blacks, adding that "white folks [who] don't suffer tribulation" will never know "peace and joy in the kingdom." A mighty change must come soon, Truth preached. "Wait a little longer . . . and I shall hail you where slaveholders do not come, and where bloodhounds cannot enter." Her sermon won loud applause.[21]

But what ever became of Anthony Burns, whose capture and forced re-enslavement roiled the nation? Burns spent several months in a Richmond jail; then he was sold to a North Carolina plantation owner, who allowed him to do some preaching. When sympathizers in Boston found out where Burns was enslaved, they raised money to buy his freedom at a cost of $1,300 (roughly $40,000 today). A public celebration was held when Burns returned to Boston as a free man. Burns attended both college and seminary in Ohio and then became a Baptist minister. He served a congregation in Indiana and then in Ontario, but he died of tuberculosis in 1862. Truth's words seem almost to tell the story of Anthony Burns's life: he went through tribulation, the suffering that leads to glory in this life and the next.

Perhaps Truth got a little taste of glory on November 1, 1854—the day she paid off her mortgage. It was a victory, not merely to own the house outright, but because she earned the money working for freedom.

Her example inspired others. A reporter for *Frederick Douglass' Paper*, who identified as a Black woman, covered an abolitionist meeting in Boston in June 1855. The unnamed reporter "often heard [of Truth's] store of 'mother wit,'" and was curious to hear her. Truth did not get an opportunity to speak that day, but she "did very well with her book, for the abolitionists bought it like fun." It mattered that Truth was selling her books. For a Black woman to be paid for her talents was "of more practical importance to us than ten thousand resolutions," said the reporter. What "*we* need so much" is a chance to "show ourselves competent."[22] Truth did so, as did the Black female journalist.

Truth inspired other women to use their talents. And she also had occasion to deflate men with big egos. Moments when proslavery men felt the sharp edge of scorn became the stuff of legend. The story below was told in many versions. This retelling omits some of the worst racist language, leaving enough to hint at what Truth confronted.

Around the year 1855 Truth was out on a speaking tour with other abolitionists. Her friend Parker Pillsbury stood at the podium, calling out the church and clergy for complicity in slavery. Many of these conventions allowed anyone to speak, the nineteenth-century equivalent of an "open mike." When Pillsbury sat down, a young lawyer (some accounts say minister) stood up to defend slavery. He argued that "Negroes were fit only to be slaves," and if any of them showed intelligence, it was only because they had some "white blood for, as a race, they were but the connecting link between man and animals." As he droned on and on, some people slipped out of the meeting while others slumped in their seats, waiting for "the flea of the convention" to stop biting them.

Outside, a distant thunderstorm came closer. The meeting hall grew dark, save for flashes of lightning. The lawyer (or minister) said the thunder and lightning must be God's wrath. Here they were, on the holy Sabbath day, listening to antislavery heresy. He said he feared being struck by lightning just for attending this unholy gathering.

Sojourner Truth waited for the man to finish. Then she stood up and told the convention moderator not to worry; she would clean up the mess that had just been made. She walked to the podium, tall and straight, "dressed in dark green, a white handkerchief crossed over her breast, a white turban on her head," Parker Pillsbury recalled. "When I was a slave away down there in New York," Truth began, "and there was any particularly bad work to be done, some colored woman was sure to be called on to do it." She spoke in calm, measured tones. "And when I heard that man talking away there as he did, almost a whole hour, I said to myself, 'I have done a great deal of dirty scullion work, but of all the dirty work I ever did, this is the scullionest and the dirtiest.'

"Now, I am the pure African," she proclaimed. "You can all see that plain enough." She stood proudly and repeated: "I am the pure African: none of your white blood runs in my veins." She expressed disgust for "the greedy passions of the white race, which made it almost a marvel that any African person could boast unmixed blood." Everything the lawyer just said about race, she swept away. Having cleaned up that mess, she turned to the next one: the man's religion. So convinced was he that slavery was God's will that he feared God would smite him for attending an antislavery meeting. She looked down at him from the speakers' platform. "Don't be scared," she said. "I don't expect God ever heard tell of you." In one stroke Truth lanced his ego, and one could almost hear the hot air rushing out. "The convention was a success," wrote Pillsbury,[23] and would have been with that moment alone.

Meanwhile, mayhem broke loose out in the Kansas-Nebraska Territories. Proslavery men looted and burned the antislavery town of Lawrence on May 21, 1856. Three days later John Brown and his followers massacred five proslavery settlers, hacking them to pieces with swords.

Back east in Washington, Senator Charles Sumner of Massachusetts gave a scathing antislavery speech, insulting slaveholders. Congressman Preston Brooks vowed to avenge a relative whom Sumner had insulted. Two days later, on May 22, 1856, Brooks entered the United States Senate chamber, where Sumner sat at his desk. Brooks seized Sumner and beat him with a cane until the senator was nearly dead. Northerners were aghast, but Brooks's supporters in the South sent him more canes. Not even Sojourner Truth could have cleaned up the mess.

11

"We Believe You Are a Man"

Sojourner Truth was well established in Florence, Massachusetts. She had many friends in the area, and Boston was not far away. Truth probably meant to stay when she bought the lot next to her home in 1856. In the fall of that year, however, she went to Michigan for a speaking engagement in Battle Creek. She was invited to address the annual meeting of the Michigan Progressive Friends (radical Quakers who promoted "abolitionism, temperance, and women's rights").[1] There she met like-minded people such as Frances Titus, who became Truth's mainstay in old age.

Michigan's natural beauty must have impressed Sojourner, and as a relatively new state with less baggage from slavery, it seemed like a place where her daughters and grandchildren could thrive.[2] Later on, she gave another reason: "old friends of mine from Ulster County, N.Y." had moved there "and wanted me to follow."[3]

Michigan attracted come-outers from back east who sought a place to create new communities and start new institutions. Health reform was part of the culture of the Battle Creek area from early on. Unitarians, Swedenborgians, and spiritualists who settled there took "an intense interest" in alternative medicine and helped to shape "the development of the region." Quaker spiritualist Henry Willis opened "the first successful water cure facility in Battle Creek . . . in 1858."[4]

The Seventh-day Adventist church (SDA) established its headquarters in Battle Creek in 1863, and Truth would soon come to know them. The SDA had roots in the Millerite movement—as did Sojourner. After the Great Disappointment (when Christ did not return as William Miller predicted), Ellen G.

White reinterpreted Miller's prophecies and founded the Seventh-day Adventists. Mrs. White taught that Christians must prepare for the Lord's return by worshiping on Saturday and following strict rules for healthy living.

The SDA became a leader in alternative medicine and diet, and opened the Western Health Reform Institute (later called the Sanitarium) to promote natural healing. This health resort in Battle Creek attracted patients from far and wide. Near the end of her life, Truth received medical treatment from Harvey Kellogg, a leading SDA physician.

Seventh-day Adventists have sometimes claimed that Truth was baptized in their tabernacle in Battle Creek. After Truth's death, some newspapers mistakenly reported that her funeral was held in the Seventh-day Adventist Tabernacle, and it was said that Truth "was a good SDA."[5] She did share some things in common with Seventh-day Adventism. According to historian Carleton Mabee, Truth "occasionally spoke" in the SDA Sanitarium to "patients in their 'great parlor,'" and the SDA printed copies of Truth's *Narrative*. But Mabee found no evidence that Truth ever attended or spoke in the large tabernacle in Battle Creek, or that she was baptized into the SDA.[6]

The Seventh-day Adventists came to Battle Creek just a few years after Truth arrived in Michigan, perhaps because the area welcomed innovators and reformers. Sojourner Truth was drawn to the progressive ethos.

She returned to Massachusetts, but when another speaking engagement brought her back to Battle Creek, Truth bought a building lot plus one acre of land on the outskirts of town, in the small hamlet of Harmonia. She sold her house in Florence and moved to Michigan in 1856, when she was close to sixty years old. Eventually her daughters and their families came to the Battle Creek area too.[7]

Sojourner's first home in Michigan was in Harmonia, a small settlement close to Battle Creek where Progressive Friends who embraced social reform and spiritualism had set up a community. Like Truth, they were deeply religious yet "critical of organized churches and clergy."[8] Harmonia attracted "not only farmers and artisans but educators, newspaper editors, and former statesmen" who embraced spiritualism and social reform.[9] The name Harmonia reflects the spiritualist quest for harmony between the living and the dead and between heaven and earth.

The village of Harmonia had five short streets flanked by farms, with a cemetery on one side. It was home to the Bedford Harmonial Institute, a school open to all regardless of race or gender. Here students could learn classic academic subjects and attend lectures on reform and spiritualism.

A popular religion, spiritualism saw death as a "translation" to another state of being. Devotees believed that a medium could channel messages between the living and the dead. These messages often came in sounds of knocking or rapping that could be translated into letters—much like the clicks from a telegraph. If the telegraph could transmit messages over physical distances, some people reasoned, then perhaps messages could flow between the living and the dead. "The American hunger for contact with the dead gave spiritualism its content . . . transforming [it] into a new religion," writes historian Ann Braude.

American spiritualism drew from many sources. The eighteenth-century Swedish mystic Immanuel Swedenborg was said to have "conversed with a host of enlightening spirits during his lifetime,"[10] and his teachings were spread by his followers. The Quaker belief in the Inner Light was understood by some to include spiritual companions from beyond the grave. Belief in spirits was basic to many African cultures: spirits of ancestors were active and entitled to receive homage from their living kin. It was a common African belief that "the dead can return to the living in spiritual visitations that are not necessarily ill-intentioned or dangerous."[11] Spirits appeared in nature, came through dreams, or were conjured in rituals.

Many nineteenth-century reformers were drawn to spiritualism as an alternative to Christian churches. Among reformers, spiritualism was perceived as "a progressive movement that championed health reform, education reform, temperance and social justice causes such as women's rights and the abolition of slavery."[12] Unlike most churches, spiritualism allowed women, called mediums, to be leaders.

Truth knew spiritualists long before she moved to Harmonia. She had met them at the Northampton Association and in her travels as an antislavery lecturer. Truth's friends Amy and Isaac Post held séances in their Rochester home,[13] where Truth attended a séance in April 1851.

A participant of that séance, one Mr. Lukens, wrote to the *Anti-Slavery Bugle* about his observations at this event. A full circle of people sat around a table, Lukens said. The medium invited the spirits to communicate through raps or knocks that came from under the table, or sometimes from the ceiling. But the sounds were so "faint and low" they could barely be heard. Sojourner Truth rose from her chair, got down on her hands and knees, and put her ear to the floor. She "called out very unceremoniously 'come spirit, hop up here on the table, and see if you can't make a louder noise.'"[14] Lukens said that Truth's "simple minded manner amused them beyond description," but he may have misinterpreted her actions. Truth could have been poking fun at the whole affair. "In séances, as in secular meetings during the 1850s," writes Nell Irvin Painter, "Truth's role was often to interrupt earnest proceedings with irreverence."[15]

Truth may have accepted spiritualism "gradually . . . [as] the practice melded with [her] basic beliefs in the power and reality of the spirit world."[16] If so, spiritualism was not her touchstone. The core of her spirituality was the vision of Jesus she'd had as a young woman.

Truth was open to spiritualism if it did not become all-consuming. The Northampton Association had been a reform commune that dabbled in spiritualism. But Harmonia seems to have become a spiritualist commune that dabbled in reforms. This may explain why "Truth came to dislike Harmonia" and eventually moved to nearby Battle Creek.[17]

A white abolitionist named Lucy Colman (who later became a friend of Truth's) described her alarm about the effect of spiritualism on reform. Colman traveled in Michigan in the 1850s to give antislavery lectures. "When I went to Michigan," she wrote, "Spiritualism was rioting like some outbreak of disease," with séances going on day and night. Colman was open to spiritualism at the time, but she "could not consent to be dictated in [her] work by spirits." She went on, "I went to Battle Creek and vicinity, but everywhere Spiritualism was in the ascendant, no one cared much for the slave."[18] Traveling through Indiana and Ohio, Colman found that where spiritualism was the center of attention, abolition fell by the wayside.

Truth attended a Progressive Friends meeting in Battle Creek in October 1857. Her friend Parker Pillsbury was one of the speakers, and he covered the meeting for the *Liberator*. Spiritualism, antislavery, and women's rights were discussed, Pillsbury wrote, as well as "disunion" (Northern secession from the Union). Pillsbury saw spiritualism encroaching on reform. Spiritualism was a "blight" or "potato-rot . . . working its ruin" on abolition, he wrote.[19] Pillsbury noted that when Truth spoke, she kept her focus on slavery and the suffering it brought to her people.[20]

Eventually Truth disassociated herself from spiritualism. In 1869 the Reverend S. E. Wishard of Battle Creek asked Truth if she had joined the spiritualists—for this had been reported of her "some time ago." She replied, "Bless your soul, child, there's nothing to join." She added, "You may tell all the people Sojourner [be]long to Jesus these many years. She's true to the Master as the anvil to the hammer. I never gave up my faith in Jesus for anything else."[21]

Years later the *Detroit Free Press* reported that Truth, speaking at a meeting of spiritualists, rebuked her audience for "talking so much and doing so little." The spiritualists talked on and on about "Summerland" (the highest sphere of the afterlife) and looked forward to "the good times they were to have when they got there, but forgot to do anything for suffering humanity about them." Truth warned that they would "never get to heaven by lifting themselves up in a basket." Instead "they must lift those up below them, and then they would all go up together."[22]

In 1857, the year after Truth moved to Michigan, the Supreme Court heard the case of Dred Scott, an enslaved man about the same age as Truth. Scott was brought north and lived many years in free states or territories. Yet he was still a slave. His effort to win his freedom in the courts began in 1846, finally ending up in the Supreme Court. The Court handed down its decision on March 6, 1857, with two dissenting votes. In *Dred Scott v. Sandford*, the Court ruled that the Constitution did not guarantee the rights of citizenship to Black people, slave or free. Scott's residence in the North was irrelevant, because Blacks "had no rights which the white man was bound to respect; and that the negro might justly and lawfully be reduced to slavery for his benefit."[23]

This meant that masters could take their slaves anywhere—into the western territories and even into the free states. The *Dred Scott* decision sent "shock waves . . . across American society like nothing before it in the long story of the slavery debate," wrote historian David Blight.[24] Activists warned that slavery, instead of being abolished, was now poised to take over the whole country.

Such was the political climate in the years just before the Civil War. Truth made several trips to Detroit to attend conferences and make speeches against slavery. She also traveled to the nearby states of Indiana and Ohio, which bordered the slave state of Kentucky. In her travels, Truth encountered many whites who either supported slavery or tried to ignore it.

Truth ran into stiff headwinds in Ohio. The Buckeye State had exclusionary laws designed to prevent African American migration to that state and to intimidate Blacks who already lived there.[25] So Truth gave some confrontational speeches. At the end of one meeting a man came up to her and said, "Old woman, do you think that your talk about slavery does any good? Do you suppose people care what you say? I don't care anymore for your talk than I do for the bite of a flea."

"Maybe not," Truth replied. "But the Lord willing, I'll keep you scratching."

Truth was "especially" drawn to "Indiana, which she felt needed her missionary efforts."[26] Indiana was a free state, but its 1851 constitution made it clear that Blacks were not wanted; article 13 said that "no negro or mulatto shall come into, or settle in the State, after the adoption of this Constitution." Violators would be fined, and the money used to help pay the costs of sending Blacks to Liberia. "Additional legislation required all Blacks already living in Indiana to register with the clerk of the circuit court."[27] No wonder Truth thought Indiana needed her missionary efforts.

Antislavery activists faced hostility in many Northern states, Indiana among them. In 1843, Frederick Douglass and other abolitionists gave public lectures in eastern Indiana, where, in Richmond, they were pelted with eggs and rocks. In Pendleton, a mob of thirty men tore down the podium, attacked the speakers, and knocked down several people in the audience. Douglass later wrote that he "attracted the fury of the mob, which laid me prostrate on the ground under a torrent of blows." Douglass's hand was broken, and he was knocked unconscious.[28]

Fifteen years later, in the fall of 1858, Truth was invited to speak in northern Indiana.[29] Even before Truth arrived, her foes were spreading lies about her. They said Sojourner was a man dressed in woman's clothes, or "a mercenary hireling" paid by the antislavery Republican Party,[30] or perhaps both.

During her trip to Indiana, a conflict took place that soon become notorious. A report of it was written by William Hayward and published in the *Northern Indianan*, and much of this account comes from that source.[31]

On October 1, 1858, Truth was giving an antislavery talk in the meetinghouse of the United Brethren in Silver Lake; it was her third appearance on her tour of northern Indiana. "Friends of the slave" gladly welcomed her, but proslavery men planned to spring a trap on her. As Truth finished speaking and the meeting was breaking up, a deep voice boomed, "Hold on!" The voice belonged to T. W. Strain, a medical doctor and supporter of slavery. Dr. Strain said he doubted that Truth was really a woman, and that many people in the room "believed the speaker to be a man." Dr. Strain "demanded that Sojourner submit her breast to the inspection of some of the ladies present," to remove all doubt about Truth's gender.

In those days, many believed women to be incapable of public speaking. Female orators were deemed "unnatural" or were accused of being men in disguise. "Hostile audiences questioned the sexual identity of American women preachers . . . lecturers . . . and of actresses," wrote historian Nell Irvin Painter. And since Truth was Black, "the charge that [she] was a man polarized the meeting between pro- and anti-slavery factions."[32]

Dr. Strain's demand offended Truth's friends, especially the women. But Strain and his cronies called for Truth's gender to be proved once and for all. "Confusion and uproar ensued. A gun or pistol was fired near the door," said the *Northern Indianan*. Then Sojourner stood up, "rising in all the dignity of womanhood."[33] Truth waited for the crowd to hush, then asked Strain why he said she was a man.

"Your voice is not the voice of a woman," he replied. "It is the voice of a man, and we believe you are a man."

Then Strain asked if Truth should be "examined" and called for a vote.

"Aye," shouted many (though a negative vote was not called for).

Truth told the audience that her breasts suckled many a white babe while her own children went hungry. Now some of those white babies have grown to manhood, she said. And although they "had sucked her colored breasts, they were, in her estimation, *far more* manly" than Strain and his friends.

Sojourner refused the private exam by other women, choosing instead to "show her breast to the whole congregation." This was no shame to her, she said, but it was a shame on her accusers. As she disrobed her bosom, two young men stepped forward—perhaps to shield her, or to get a closer look. *Do you too wish to suck?* Sojourner quietly asked them. And someone jeered, "Why, it does look like an old sow's teat."

That crude taunt only proved Truth's point. Her enemies were not brave men but cowards. They were infantile; she was the adult. In proving her own womanhood, Truth "unmanned them."[34]

People swarmed from the meetinghouse as though from a hornet's nest. The reporter William Hayward, on his way out, heard someone say that Dr. Strain had "offered to bet forty dollars that Sojourner was a man!"[35] So much for his competence as a physician.

The confrontation at Silver Lake raises the question whether enslaved Isabella actually nursed white babies. It is possible, but there is no mention of it in her *Narrative*. The practice of using slaves for wet nursing "was far more prevalent in the plantation South than Dutch New York." When Truth said she had "suckled many a white babe, to the exclusion of her own offspring," she "evoked her symbolic history as a slave mother rather than her own actual experience."[36] She spoke for Black women and defied the attempts of proslavery whites to shame and manipulate her.

After this Truth returned to Michigan and divided her time between Battle Creek and Detroit in 1859. That was the year John Brown brought his war against slavery into the Old South. With financial backing from Boston abolitionists, he laid plans to instigate a slave revolt. In mid-October, Brown and his band of twenty-one men captured the federal arsenal at Harpers Ferry, Virginia. But no slaves rose up. Instead, US Marines stormed the arsenal, killing or capturing Brown and his followers.

Brown's raid on Harpers Ferry inflamed Southern fears of slave rebellion and confirmed their suspicions of Northern treachery. In the North, many hailed John Brown as a martyr. Henry David Thoreau, addressing a crowd just days before Brown's execution, compared Brown to Jesus Christ and called him an "angel of light." Brown was tried and found guilty of murder, treason, and conspiracy to incite insurrection. On December 2, the day of his hanging, he wrote, "I John Brown am now quite certain that the crimes of this guilty land will never be purged away; but with Blood."[37]

Several months later Truth attended a Michigan State Anti-Slavery Convention, where she doubtless heard much talk about the presidential election. Many abolitionists objected to Abraham Lincoln because the Republican Party, though antislavery, was too moderate: it stood for containing slavery within its present borders rather than abolishing it immediately. And yet Lincoln's moderation may have helped him to win the election.

Fearing that Lincoln meant to abolish slavery in the South, several Southern states prepared to leave the Union. In December the lame duck president

Buchanan gave a speech, blaming everything on the abolitionists. Harriet
Beecher Stowe responded to Buchanan with a scathing editorial that ran in
the *New York Independent* on December 20—the same day South Carolina
seceded from the Union. Rejecting all attempts to appease the South, Stowe
said that to save the Union by allowing slavery to continue was "a covenant
with death, and an agreement with hell." Her article told "of an old Black
slave-woman calling herself '*Sojourner Truth*'" who dared to interrupt the
mighty with a question. Stowe cast Truth as a symbol of "Old Africa . . . raising her poor maimed, scarred hand to heaven, ask[ing]—'IS GOD DEAD?'"[38]
Thus, on the eve of the Civil War, America's most famous writer invoked
the name of Sojourner Truth.

12

Showdown at the Angola Courthouse

When Abraham Lincoln became the sixteenth president of the United States on March 4, 1861, his inaugural address expressed his desire for peace. Yet he warned that if the South started a war, the North would fight to preserve the Union. "Though passion may have strained, it must not break our bonds of affection." Lincoln said mystic chords of memory that stretched "from every battle-field, and patriot grave, to every living heart and hearthstone, all over this broad land, will yet swell the chorus of the Union, when again touched, as surely they will be, by the better angels of our nature."[1]

Three weeks later, different angels were summoned in a speech by Alexander Stephens, vice president of the newly formed Confederate States of America. The Confederacy was based on slavery and white superiority, Stephens said. "Its foundations are laid, its cornerstone rests, upon the great truth that the negro is not equal to the white man." He extolled the Confederate government as "the first, in the history of the world, based upon this great physical, philosophical, and moral truth" of racial inequality.[2]

Confederate guns bombarded Fort Sumter in Charleston Harbor early in the morning of April 12, 1861, and the following day the Union commander surrendered the fort. On April 15, Lincoln issued a call for troops to put down the rebellion. Seven seceded states were soon joined by four more, leaving only four slave states remaining tenuously in the Union—Kentucky, Maryland, Delaware, and Missouri.

Throughout the North was heard the cry "Save the Union!" Yet many Northern whites said they "didn't care a damn about slavery." Sojourner Truth knew that only by ending slavery could the Union be saved. Early in

1861, Truth told a mostly white audience in Michigan, "Slavery will have you all if you don't look out." Being white did not make one safe from slavery. "If you want to save yourselves from meaner slavery than mine ever was, you've got to put *down* Slavery. You or slavery, one or the other's going to be thrown [down] pretty soon."[3] Truth had been a pacifist, but now Union victory was the way to free the slaves. Although many Northerners wanted to keep slavery in the background of the conflict, Truth saw its centrality and believed that the war would bring "the emancipation of her race."[4]

Truth brought this message to Indiana in May 1861. Local abolitionists invited her to make a speaking tour of Steuben County (in the northeast corner of the state, about sixty miles south of Battle Creek, Michigan). On her first visit to Indiana, Truth was scorned as an imposter in women's clothing, and her enemies tried and failed to degrade her by demanding proof of her womanhood. Despite all that (or perhaps because of it), Truth accepted the invitation.

Just to cross the state line, Truth had to break the law. The Indiana Constitution, article 13, stated that "any person who encouraged a Negro or mulatto to remain in the state could be fined as much as $500." Of course, Black people already lived in Indiana, so the new law was meant to keep their population small and to stifle participation in the Underground Railroad.

"Most Hoosiers were enthusiastically in favor of preserving the Union," writes Indiana historian Patrick Furlong, but "far fewer favored the abolition of slavery." And few of those who favored abolition "would have welcomed freed slaves to live in Indiana."[5]

Like all Northern states, Indiana had Southern sympathizers. They were called "copperheads" because, like poisonous snakes, they could strike without warning even in one's own back yard. Sojourner Truth did not fear copperheads. She said she liked to flush them out into the open for everyone to see.

On this, her second trip to Indiana, Truth's traveling companion was Josephine Griffing, a white reformer and writer. An abolitionist and women's rights advocate, she was a fearless and powerful ally. She was once described as "a moralist in the Yankee tradition, a *furious*, uncompromising woman."[6] Writing to the *Liberator*, Griffing said she and Truth were on a mission to challenge the "Black Laws of Indiana."[7] When Truth was arrested shortly after crossing into Indiana, Griffing argued with local authorities and got them to drop the charges. She told the *Liberator* that Truth "was first arrested" for entering Indiana while "being Black; next as a mulatto; then, for coming in; then, for remaining in the State! In every case, we have outwitted and beaten them."[8] All told, Truth was arrested six times.[9] Thanks to Griffing and local allies (including lawyers and one or two sympathetic judges), Truth was never convicted.

Truth's friends ran interference for her. Early in the tour the Union Home Guard (a local militia) took Truth "into custody to protect her from being thrown into jail."[10] During her trip some friends attempted to settle the question by having Truth arrested, "tried before a friendly justice of the peace, and then set free." They even held a mock trial to dramatize the absurdity and injustice of exclusionary laws. Truth's foes retaliated by having her arrested again and taken before an unfriendly judge. Then Truth's friends got the venue changed to another court ten miles distant, where they knew the judge would dismiss the case.[11]

Together, Truth and her friends exposed the anti-Black laws as both absurd and unenforceable. This must have been an ordeal for Truth, who could never walk about freely and may at times have felt like a prisoner of those who protected her.[12] But the local abolitionists provided lodging, meals, and transportation for Truth and Griffing. They arranged Truth's speaking engagements and held picnics and dinners in her honor. On at least one occasion Sojourner was greeted by the music of a marching band.

Griffing wrote to the *Liberator* that many respectable folk in Indiana were on Truth's side. "Several of the most wealthy and influential white families" came to hear Truth speak, as well as "noble-hearted women" of high character. Griffing said Sojourner's opponents were ruffians who shouted "stop your mouth" whenever Truth spoke. These men threatened to whip Truth, or even tar and feather her.[13] "Armed men were in our midst and had declared they would blow out our brains."[14]

Truth's visit revealed deep conflicts over race and the Union in northern Indiana. The *Steuben Republican* nearly twisted itself into a pretzel trying to please everyone. "The policy of the Government," the newspaper declared, was to put "down the rebellion in the South." But "a flaming anti-slavery speech" from Truth "ought not to be allowed." Silence was better than strife, so "the negro question ought not to be raised again by anyone in the north, either Black or white." On the other hand, the paper equivocated, "free speech" should never be suppressed.[15]

The climax of Truth's tour was her speech at the Angola County Court-house on June 2, 1861. It was "unheard of in Angola" for a Black woman to give a speech, the *Steuben Republican* said later, "and the simple announce-ment fanned some people of the town into a white heat of opposition."[16] It was indeed white heat.

Those who stood for the Union, free speech, and abolition supported Truth. "The pro-Union ladies" sewed an elaborate costume for Truth to wear when she gave her speech at the courthouse. They "put upon me a red, white, and blue shawl, a sash and apron to match, a cap on my head with a star in front, and a star on each shoulder," Truth later recalled. She joked that she was "frightened" when she saw herself in the mirror. "It seems I am going into Battle."[17] Sojourner agreed to wear the costume, but she refused to carry a sword or a pistol. "The Lord will preserve me without weapons," she said. "I feel safe even in the midst of my enemies; for the truth is powerful and will prevail." That took courage, since some "rebel sympathizers" wanted Truth silenced by any means necessary.[18]

Truth's foes tried to get the local Union militia ("Home Guards") on their side. They sent a letter to the militia's commander, saying that his troops should come to the courthouse heavily armed, prepared "to suppress negro lecturing" as something "injurious to the peace and good of the country." The militia's commander replied that his duty was to "aid in enforcing the laws and protecting the freedom of speech" rather than "aid in the mob and secession."[19] Snubbed by the Home Guards, the copperheads stashed guns at a nearby grocery store, to be used by anyone who wanted to "suppress the meeting of Sojourner Truth in the Court House on Sunday."[20]

The rebel sympathizers (as Griffing called them) barred the courthouse doors and windows and flew a black flag from the roof. Finally, they made a decoy cannon from wood, painted it, and mounted it on a two-wheeled cart. (These decoys, called "Quaker guns," were sometimes used during the Civil War to feign military strength and deceive an opposing army.) Positioned in front of the courthouse, the wooden cannon looked from a distance like real artillery. On the Sunday morning Truth was to speak, the Home Guards marched into town, taking care to stay out of range of the cannon; but when the gun was found to be fake, the Home Guards took up a position in front of the courthouse.

Early that afternoon, "a large, beautiful carriage" brought Sojourner Truth toward the courthouse. Mounted guardsmen rode alongside, and from the carriage window Truth could see that a large crowd waited around the courthouse.

The sheriff opened the courthouse door. Double files of soldiers stood with their guns held upright, bayonets fixed. A band played the "Star-Spangled Banner," and Truth marched in singing,[21] flanked by the Home Guards, who then took their seats "in the jury box with loaded rifles in hand." Truth was unarmed, but some of her friends "were said to have carried hickory clubs, expecting to see trouble before the day should end."[22]

Truth stood and faced the crowd. "With more zeal than ever before" she preached free speech and called on every loyal Unionist to denounce slavery.[23] If you are *for* the Union, you must be *against* slavery, she said. If only she were ten years younger, Truth said, she would hurry "to the battlefield and nurse and cook for the Massachusetts troops." And if it came to that, Truth said she would fight the Confederate troops herself!

At this, the proslavery whites hissed and jeered. "It seems that it takes my Black face to bring out your black hearts," Truth said, "so it's well I came. You are afraid of my Black face, because it is a looking-glass in which you see yourselves." Like Jesus, Truth "revealed the hearts of many" (Luke 2:35). Her foes rushed forward "like a pack of hounds," Griffing reported. But when the soldiers blocked the mob, all they could do was shout and threaten "this patriotic, noble woman."[24] Truth ended her speech and was "hurried away under guard to the carriage, and out of town."[25]

This was "the Battle of Sojourner Truth," Griffing told the *Liberator*. While Union soldiers fought with guns, Truth used words. Her message was that to save the Union, slavery must go. There was no separating these two issues, for they were like two sides of one coin. In this battle for Northern public opinion, the tide turned in Truth's favor as the war went on.

After the showdown at the Angola Courthouse, Sojourner spent several days with the Roby family, abolitionists who lived five miles south of Angola at Pleasant Lake. Friends came to warn her that "the rebels" (proslavery Democrats) were coming for her and she must flee. Truth refused to run, declaring that she would rather go to jail.

Sure enough, a "rebel constable" came to arrest Truth. No sooner had he stated his business, than a Union officer appeared. To keep the constable from arresting Truth, the Union officer declared Truth "his prisoner." The rebel constable went away "very much disgusted." The local militia "marched up to [Mr. Roby's] house, playing upon the fife and drum." They cheered for

"Sojourner, Free Speech, and the Union." Mr. Roby was later arrested and bound over to the circuit court "for harboring a negro." He was released on bail for $500, but there is no record that he was ever brought to trial.[26]

Sojourner Truth was in Indiana for about a month. Near the end of that time, she was arrested again. She was not put in jail because her friends vouched for her appearance in court. On the appointed day, Truth and her friends came to the "shabby room" where her trial was to be held. There they waited until "two half-drunk lawyers" entered the room. The lawyers stared at Truth for a few minutes. She must have stared them down. They left the building, crossed the street, and entered a tavern, from which they did not return. Then Truth and her friends held "a grand picnic" nearby.[27]

Truth returned to Michigan, and little is known of her activities in the following months. Sojourner later became very ill; the Indiana trip may well have taken a toll on her health.

Meanwhile, the North moved slowly toward emancipation. Slavery was abolished in the District of Columbia on April 16, 1862. A few months later Congress passed the Second Confiscation Act, stating that the United States Army was under no obligation to return runaway slaves. Slaves taking refuge "within the lines of the army" and all those captured from rebels or deserted by them "shall be deemed captives of war, and shall be forever free of their servitude, and not again held as slaves." The Second Confiscation Act further authorized the president of the United States to employ "as many persons of African descent as he may deem necessary" to help put down the rebellion.[28]

Lincoln took office knowing that slavery was wrong, yet also believing that the Constitution did not give him the power to end it. But now, the Second Confiscation Act opened a way for Lincoln to use emancipation as a war measure. Since slave labor propped up the Confederacy, emancipation would weaken the South and shorten the war. Lincoln's role as commander in chief in wartime gave him the authority he needed, but his cabinet advised him to wait for a major Union victory, so as to declare emancipation from a position of strength.

On September 16, 1862, that victory came at Antietam, the bloodiest battle of the war up to that point. Lincoln made his Emancipation Proclamation public on September 22, 1862, promising to sign it into law on New Year's Day 1863. The proclamation applied only to those parts of the South still in active rebellion against the Union. Only a constitutional amendment could outlaw slavery throughout the whole country. The Emancipation Proclamation struck a mighty blow at slavery, but the monster still lived. "We are like whalers who have been long on the chase," Lincoln said. "We have at last got the harpoon into the monster, but we must now look how we steer, or with one 'flop' of his tail he will send us all into eternity."[29]

As the war with slavery raged on, Truth lay gravely ill in Battle Creek, nursed by friends and by her daughter Diana.[30] Truth hoped she would live to see the day when Lincoln signed the Emancipation Proclamation. But she made arrangements for a Dutch Reformed pastor to preach at her funeral if she did not recover.[31]

Too sick to go out and sell her books, Truth ran out of money. Her friend Phebe Stickney wrote to people who might contribute to a relief fund for Truth, and some of these letters were printed in the *National Anti-Slavery Standard*. Truth "is very poorly and probably won't live long," Stickney wrote. She quoted Truth as saying that God sent ravens to feed the prophet Elijah in the wilderness, so Truth asked God to send "good angels" to feed her too. Among those who sent money for Truth's relief was Harriet Beecher Stowe. When one donation came all the way from Ireland, Truth exclaimed that not even for Elijah did the Lord send "angels from so great a distance."[32]

Phebe sat at Sojourner's bedside, reading aloud to her the letters from friends and well-wishers. "Quite overcome with joy," Truth said that the love of these friends was helping her to get well. "Lord, I knew your ways were sure," Sojourner prayed, "but I didn't think they would work so quick." She kept the war in mind and prayed for the nation to be healed from the curse of slavery.

Sojourner rejoiced that she lived to see Emancipation Day. She told her friend Phebe that she wanted to "live a little longer to praise God and speak to the people a few more times in this glorious day of emancipation."[33] Truth vowed to live until all her people were free.

She was still recovering in March 1863 when an anti-Black riot swept Detroit. The flash point was the rape of a white girl by a man said to be a "negro" (though he was in fact biracial Spanish and Native American). He was put on trial as a crowd gathered outside the courthouse. A mob formed and attacked Blacks in the streets, then set fire to at least thirty homes of Black people. Order had to be restored by military force. What happened in Detroit was one of several anti-Black riots to sweep Northern cities during the war.

Truth would have heard this news, and it probably informed a speech she was soon to make.[34]

By April 1863, Sojourner could walk with a cane and was able to leave her house. Mrs. Stickney told the *National Anti-Slavery Standard* that Truth's "heart is full of praises and prayer." Her "cup of happiness is about to run over, and she prays the Lord to pour it on to some of her friends."[35]

By early June of 1863, Truth was strong enough to speak in public. She attended a Sunday school convention held in a Battle Creek Methodist church. The two-day event closed with an assembly of about five hundred children, parents, and teachers. Truth wanted to teach the equality of the races, and what better place to give that message than a state Sunday school convention?

Truth was not on the program, so she waited for a pause between speakers, stood up, and in a clear, strong voice asked if there was an opportunity for her to say a few words. The moderator hesitated, unsure what to do. Then one of the organizers, a Rev. T. W. Jones, explained that this was Sojourner Truth who wished to speak. That got everyone's attention, reported the *National Anti-Slavery Standard*, and Truth was allowed to speak.

Sojourner said that the Spirit of the Lord told her to speak about "the great sin of prejudice against color." She asked the children: "Who made your skin white? Was it not God? Who made mine Black? Was it not the same God? Am I to blame, therefore, because my skin is Black?" If we despise some of God's children because it pleased God to create them Black, she told the children, then we despise God. "Your teachers ought to tell you so, and root up, if possible, the great sin of prejudice against color from your minds." Sunday school teachers know prejudice is a sin, Truth said; yet they do not teach children that it is bad. When teachers hold prejudice in themselves, Truth continued, they cannot expect God to bless them or the children. Jesus died to save the Blacks as well as the whites, and in heaven Black and white are one in the love of Jesus. We don't take sin with us to heaven, Truth said, so if white children go to heaven, they will go there without their prejudice against color. "Now children," she concluded, "remember what Sojourner Truth has told you, and thus get rid of your prejudice and learn to love colored children, that you may all be the children of your Father who is in heaven."[36]

Many in the audience were moved to tears, perhaps even tears of repentance, reported the *National Anti-Slavery Standard*. In these few words at the Sunday school convention, Truth loved children and called adults to change.

Lincoln's Emancipation Proclamation opened the way for Black men to en-
list in the US Army to fight for their freedom. By war's end, over 206,000
Black men—most of them former slaves—served as Union soldiers or sailors.
They helped to defeat the Confederacy and to make the Civil War a contest
against slavery. *"Once let the Black man get upon his person the brass letter,
U.S.,"* said Frederick Douglass, *"let him get an eagle on his button, and a musket
on his shoulder and bullets in his pocket, there is no power on earth that can deny
that he has earned the right to citizenship."*[37]

Some Northern whites feared that "Negro soldiers" would encourage
Blacks to think themselves equal to whites, and perhaps even ignite a race
war. This may partly explain why Michigan did not get a Black regiment
into action until February 1864.[38]

Blacks faced discrimination at every turn in the military. Whites were
given their uniforms; Blacks had to buy theirs. Black soldiers could not rise
in the ranks through promotion. Thousands of Black soldiers fought Southern whites on the battlefield, but a great many who wanted to fight found
themselves instead digging fortifications, loading and unloading supply
trains, or removing corpses from battlefields. Black soldiers were paid less
than whites. In protest, they continued their duties but refused to accept
lower pay, "thereby humbling the U.S. Government into pay equity."[39]

Despite the discrimination they faced, Black men enlisted in the Union
army by the thousands. "Now is the time to prove that we are men," Truth's
grandson James Caldwell said.[40] Rather than wait for Michigan to raise a
Black regiment, nineteen-year-old James enlisted with the Fifty-Fourth
Massachusetts on April 17, 1863. Two sons of Frederick Douglass joined that
same regiment.

James was now a "tall, able-bodied lad," Sojourner said, and he joined
the Fifty-Fourth with her prayers and blessings. He was going to redeem the
white people from the curse that God had sent upon them, Truth said. "For
now is the day and now the hour" when Black men would save the nation,
for the white man's "sin has been so great that they don't know God, and God
doesn't know them." Truth said if she were ten years younger, she would go
"as the Joan of Arc to lead the army of the Lord."[41]

On July 18, 1863, the Fifty-Fourth Massachusetts attacked Confederate
defenses in and around Charleston Harbor. Fort Wagner on Morris Island
was their main target. To reach it, the Fifty-Fourth had to charge uphill

while being fired on from above. They broke through the fort's defenses and briefly entered it, then were pushed back. The cost was great: 246 killed, 880 wounded, and 389 missing or captured—more than eight times the losses on the Confederate side. Although they lost the battle, the bravery and discipline of the Fifty-Fourth showed the nation that Black soldiers could fight just as well as white ones.

When word reached Truth of the Union defeat at Fort Wagner, she feared that James was dead. "Poor dear boy!" she wrote to a friend seven months after the battle. "He fought bravely at Fort Wagner but was not found among the killed or wounded. He must have been taken prisoner or drowned. I can only trust him in the hand of the good God."[42]

Sojourner did not know that James was captured two days *before* the assault on Fort Wagner. His regiment held off a Confederate assault so that the Tenth Connecticut (a white regiment) could withdraw from an exposed position. According to researcher Tim Talbot, James Caldwell was imprisoned by the Confederates for almost two years. Part of this time was spent in Florence, South Carolina, in a "rebel prison pen." James must have been moved around, for records show that "he was finally released at Goldsboro, North Carolina, on March 4, 1865." From there James was sent on to Annapolis for recovery. He received his discharge on May 12, 1865, along with three months extra pay "due to hardships endured at Rebel prisons" by order of Secretary of War Edwin Stanton.[43] And all that time, James's grandmother knew nothing of his fate.

Knowing that Confederates were savage in their treatment of Black prisoners of war, Truth once said her beloved grandson might be better off killed than captured.[44]

What happened to James after the war, or if he ever saw his grandmother again, is unclear. After the war the *National Anti-Slavery Standard* printed a letter from Truth. "I had a grandson who was a prisoner in South Carolina, with some of Massachusetts' darling sons," she said. They "suffered untold misery—Captains and other officers the same. I am ashamed to put on paper the horrible things they were obliged to submit to, under these rebel fiends."[45]

Surely Truth grieved and worried about her grandson, just as she had for her son Peter, who long before went to sea and never came back. Something of how she coped may be discerned from a letter she sent to a friend, whose daughter had died shortly before her son was killed in battle. Sojourner advised this friend to "go to work . . . you can't help anything that is past." Truth counseled her friend to give thanks that "the good Lord . . . lent you these children—do ye suppose they are dead? Not at all." The goodness of these children would live on. "Take hold and do what you can just as you think they would do. Don't cry no more—but find work. Oh! Lord there's plenty of it all over."[46]

Truth's grandson James had already fought and been taken prisoner by the Confederates before the First Michigan Colored Regiment was ready to join the fight. The new Black regiment began to muster at Camp Ward just outside of Detroit in February 1863, and would not see action until the following year. Sojourner Truth was one of several Black leaders who recruited men. Some fourteen hundred enlisted; roughly two-thirds of them from slave states.[47]

The new recruits were poorly supplied by the army. There were never enough blankets and clothing, but "the most serious problem was their barracks at Camp Ward . . . leaky roofs and walls, no flooring, and straw-stuffed bed sacks instead of bunks." Many of the men became sick, and, before the harsh winter of 1863–1864 was over, twenty-five had died.[48]

Truth gathered food, clothing, and other supplies for the new recruits. In November 1863 the *Detroit Advertiser and Tribune* reported that soldiers at Camp Ward had "a regular jubilee" when a carriage arrived full of "boxes and packages containing all manner of delicacies . . . from Battle Creek." These were delivered by Sojourner Truth, "who carries not only a tongue of fire but a heart of love." The colonel ordered the regiment into line "in their best" for the presentation. Along with these much-needed supplies, Truth delivered "a speech glowing with patriotism, exhortation, and good wishes." The men gave back "rounds of enthusiastic cheers." After the ceremony, Sojourner lingered to speak with the soldiers "in motherly conversation." To the delight of the soldiers, she helped to open the boxes and distribute the contents.

Truth returned to Camp Ward two days later to speak to the Black recruits again. A very large crowd of white citizens were there, thanks to this advertisement in the *Detroit Free Press*: "Sojourner Truth, a colored prophetess, will address the members of the First Michigan Colored Regiment at Camp Ward this afternoon at two o'clock."[49] Truth, perhaps seeing this as an opportunity to convince white people that Black men would make fine soldiers, spoke to the civilians and promised to come back another time for the soldiers. After the lecture, a collection was taken up for Truth, who received no pay for her work as a recruiter and supplier of the army.

That winter Truth stayed in Detroit, where she could hold meetings and visit nearby Camp Ward regularly. In a letter, she told a friend that her health was good and her mind sharp. "I mean to live till I am a hundred years old, if it pleases God, and see my people all free." She was feeling good enough to travel too. "Maybe I will see you in New York City yet."[50]

The First Michigan Colored Regiment was mustered into the Union army on February 17, 1864. It fought in the Battle of Honey Hill and other conflicts in South Carolina and served two years before being mustered out. The regiment fulfilled the "long-held desire" of Michigan's Black community "to contribute to the war effort, demonstrate loyalty to the Union, and earn a full measure of equality," wrote historian Michael O. Smith.[51] Sojourner Truth helped to recruit and supply them. And especially for Black soldiers, she wrote new words to be sung to the tune of the Battle Hymn of the Republic.

The Valiant Soldier, by Sojourner Truth
We are the valiant soldiers who've 'listed for the war;
We are fighting for the Union, we are fighting for the law;
We can shoot a rebel farther than a white man ever saw,
As we go marching on.

Chorus
Glory, glory, hallelujah! Glory, glory, hallelujah!
Glory, glory, hallelujah, as we go marching on.

Look there above the center, where the flag is waving bright;
We are going out of slavery, we are bound for freedom's light;
We mean to show Jeff Davis how the Africans can fight,
As we go marching on.

Father Abraham has spoken, and the message has been sent;
The prison doors have opened, and out the prisoners went
To join the sable army of African descent,
As we go marching on.[52]

While Sojourner wintered in Detroit, her mail piled up in Battle Creek. She asked to have it forwarded to her, and soon a large package of letters came, with requests for photographs and copies of her *Narrative*. Truth could not answer all the letters individually, so she asked a friend, Oliver Johnson, to write a general message to be printed in the *Anti-Slavery Standard*. In it, Truth apologized for the delay in her response. Promising to fulfill all the requests as soon as she could, she said that "her heart overflows with love and gratitude to [her friends]." To those who asked for her prayers, she said, "I *do pray* and will continue to pray that God will fill their cup of blessing full and *running over*; as I would if I had the power."

By now Truth could almost walk without her cane. She took this as a sign: "The Lord means me to do what I want to do . . . to go east in the Spring, to Ohio and New York, to New Jersey, and finally to see the freedmen of my race" in Washington, DC. If her friends kept on praying for her health, she said, "I shall be able to accomplish my desire."[53] Around this time Truth sent a personal letter to her friend Mary Gale. "This is a great and glorious day! It is good to live in it & behold the shackles fall from the manacled limbs. Oh, if I were ten years younger, I would go down with these soldiers here & be the Mother of the Regiment!"[54]

13

"I Sell the Shadow"

Abraham Lincoln proclaimed freedom with pen and ink, but an American sculptor used marble. William Story created a majestic figure to be his "anti-slavery sermon in stone." Story combined classical and African themes in his art, showing the dignity and nobility of Africans through the ages, debunking the myth of white superiority.[1]

Story was working abroad in Rome when he sculpted an African-themed work that won critical acclaim at the International Exposition in London in 1862. The *Liberator* hailed it as a sign that white people were beginning to see their crimes against Africans.[2] Story (for reasons soon to be explained) titled his work *The Libyan Sibyl*. Sojourner Truth may not have heard of the statue until an article by Harriet Beecher Stowe appeared in the *Atlantic Monthly*.

Truth had made a deep and lasting impression on Stowe when the two women met in 1853. However, a decade passed before Stowe picked up her pen to write about that meeting. Meanwhile (before the Civil War started) Stowe went to Europe three times. She loved hobnobbing with writers and artists abroad, including the American sculptor William Story.

When Stowe visited Story at his studio in Rome, she told him about Sojourner Truth. The artist had never seen Truth and did not sculpt her likeness, but Stowe's tales of Truth may have affirmed Story's artistic vision. Three years later when Stowe again visited Story in Rome, she was thrilled to see Story's plans for a sculpture to be called *The Libyan Sibyl*.

In ancient mythology, a sibyl was a female oracle who saw the future. Tradition held that one such sibyl lived in a desert oasis west of Egypt;

this gave Story a classical figure based in Africa. He sculpted a large, noble woman who sat pensively with head in hand, as though "contemplating the terrible fate of her race"—slavery and the slave trade.[3]

Story wanted the sculpture to show Africans as noble people who should never have been enslaved. Although he used white marble, he gave the figure the "full lips, a wide nose with flared nostrils, flat broad cheek planes and wavy braided hair." Like a classical Greek statue, this sculpture was draped only below the waist. Story adorned the figure "with a talismanic hexagram pendant and an ammonite shell headdress that symbolically links her to the ancient Egyptian sun god, Amun," to show the antiquity of African civilizations.[4]

Around the time Story's statue was on view in London, Sojourner Truth was seriously ill. As the reader will recall, rumors of Truth's death spread in the abolitionist community. Stowe assumed that Truth had died and decided to write a tribute to her for the *Atlantic Monthly*. She drew on memories of Truth's visit to her home years earlier; she may have sprinkled in some bits from the antislavery grapevine and perhaps even consulted Truth's *Narrative*. In her article, Stowe also dwelt on her visits to the sculptor William Story in Rome, relishing the thought that her tales of Truth had helped inspire Story's work of art. Stowe titled her piece for the *Atlantic* "Sojourner Truth the Libyan Sibyl." It was a stretch, but then, Stowe had a lively imagination.

Stowe was a novelist, and Truth, as she portrayed her for the *Atlantic*, was a partly fictional character who spoke a plantation dialect. "Laws, you did n't think o' sech a thing as my sleepi' in dat 'ar' *bed*, did you?" Stowe made Truth say. "I never heared o' sech a thing in my life." Stowe romanticized Africa, writing that Truth sang "with the strong barbaric accent of the native African . . . [with] a wild, peculiar power . . . burning after God in her tropic heart."[5] Using stereotypes common in that era, Stowe described Truth's grandson James as "the fattest, jolliest, wooly-headed little specimen of Africa . . . showing his glistening white teeth in a state of perpetual merriment." A modern African American scholar said that Stowe painted Truth "in blackface."[6]

When Stowe's article came out in 1863, it boosted Truth's fame. Olive Gilbert (who collaborated on the *Narrative*), wrote to Sojourner, "I was much pleased with Mrs. Stowe's enthusiasm over you. You really almost received your apotheosis from her."[7] After all, Stowe was the best-selling author of the era. Her *Atlantic Monthly* article quickly became the most widely read piece about Truth, and remained so for decades.

The *Atlantic Monthly* article boosted Truth's fame—but at a price. She became known as "Sojourner Truth the Libyan Sibyl." Or even "Mrs. Stowe's Libyan Sibyl." The moniker stuck for the rest of Truth's life. But Truth "would never listen to Mrs. Stowe's Libyan Sibyl," a friend wrote. "'Oh!' [Truth] would say, 'I don't want to hear about that old symbol; read me something that is going on now, something about this great war.'"[8]

Sojourner tried to correct some of the factual errors in Stowe's piece. In a letter to the *Boston Commonwealth*, Truth said, "The history which Mrs. Stowe wrote about me, is not quite correct. There is one place where she speaks of me as coming from Africa. My grandmother and my husband's mother came from Africa, but I did not; she must have misunderstood me, but you will find my book a correct history." It rankled Truth that Stowe's article had her calling everyone "honey." "She has put it on me," Truth objected, "for I never make use of the word honey." Truth sent the *Commonwealth* editor six copies of her *Narrative*. "You will find them correct, for they are Sojourner herself."[9]

The worst mistake in Stowe's article was her statement that Truth had "passed away from among us as a wave of the sea." The *National Anti-Slavery Standard* quickly printed a correction: Truth "is living at Battle Creek, Michigan," and remains "deeply interested [in] . . . the welfare of the oppressed."[10]

Stowe got some things right when it came to Truth's Christian faith. She quoted Truth as saying "Jesus loved me . . . and would love me always." Stowe was right when she said that Truth had "a faith in the power of truth, a devotion in the cause of humanity, and a perseverance . . . which command[ed] attention and respect."[11]

Stowe's article fanned public interest in Truth, and soon another white female author penned an article about Sojourner. This was the abolitionist and woman's rights advocate Frances Dana Gage, who "often published commentary and fiction under the pen name of Aunt Fanny."[12] She had heard Truth speak at the Akron woman's rights convention back in 1851. Twelve years later, Gage recast Truth's hawk-and-buzzard speech into "Ain't I a Woman?" Gage's article ran in the *New York Independent* on April 23, 1863.[13] It was later printed in *History of Woman Suffrage* under the heading "Mrs. Stowe's Libyan Sybil."[14] In 1972, feminist scholar Miriam Schneir updated the language, and this modern version endures as a touchstone of Black history and American feminism.[15]

Since Frances Gage chaired the 1851 Akron Convention, she could speak with authority about what happened there. However, Gage wrote a dozen years after the fact, and her article about Truth contradicted earlier accounts, including the most authentic version of Truth's speech, which was printed in the *Anti-Slavery Bugle* in 1851. And yet the "Ain't I a Woman?" speech from Gage's article is part of Sojourner Truth's legacy (see the appendix for three versions of the speech). If people know just one thing about Truth, it is the modern version of that speech.

Gage began her article about Truth with a nod to Stowe's *Atlantic Monthly* piece, going on to explain that Stowe's article called to mind "a scene in Ohio" at the 1851 Akron Women's Rights Convention, "never to be forgotten by those who witnessed it."[16]

The leaders of that meeting were in a "panic," Gage said, fearing that they would be mobbed. To avoid that fate, some of the leaders wanted their convention to strictly avoid the topic of abolition. Therefore they were dismayed to see "a tall, gaunt black woman in a gray dress and white turban . . . march deliberately into the church, walk with the air of a queen up the aisle, and take her seat upon the pulpit steps." A buzz of disapproval swept the crowd. But "Sojourner, quiet and reticent as the 'Libyan Statue,' sat crouched against the wall on a corner of the pulpit stairs, her sun-bonnet shading her eyes, her elbow on her knee, and her chin resting on her broad, hard palm" (like the marble Sybil's posture in Story's statue).

During breaks in the program, Truth went out to sell copies of her *Narrative*. Leaders of the convention warned Gage not to let Truth speak. "Every newspaper in the land will have our cause mixed with abolition . . . we shall be utterly denounced."

On the second day of the convention, ministers from several denominations came "to hear and discuss the resolutions." One of them claimed that the male intellect excelled that of the female; another declared that since Christ was a man, men were superior. Still another said that women must remain subject to men because of the sin of Eve. As the ministers held forth "with long-winded bombast," the "boys in the galleries and sneerers among the pews" enjoyed the show. The convention leaders were distraught to "the point of losing dignity," Gage said.

At this moment (as Gage told it), Sojourner Truth rose from the corner where she sat. "Don't let her speak," gasped several women. But Truth "moved slowly and solemnly to the front . . . and turned her great speaking eyes" to Gage.

Hissing filled the hall as Gage rose and announced Sojourner Truth. Gage called for silence, and a hush descended. "Every eye was fixed on this almost Amazon form, which stood almost six feet high, head erect, and eye piercing the upper air like one in a dream." Truth spoke in her deep clear voice for all to hear—even the overflow crowd listening at the door and windows.

Truth refuted every objection to women's rights that the ministers had raised and returned to her seat amid "roars of applause." Many people had tears streaming down their faces because, as Gage put it, Truth "had taken us up in her great, strong arms and carried us safely over the slough of difficulty, turning the whole tide in our favor." (As for Truth saving the Women's Rights Convention from ruin, the *Proceedings* of the Akron Convention did not even hint of it.[17] Newspaper reports from 1851 describe the Akron convention as harmonious and peaceful.)[18]

Even if Frances Gage misrepresented the mood at the Akron convention, Truth *did* face down mobs and silence hecklers at many women's rights and antislavery meetings. Gage may have heard Truth speak at another time to a hostile crowd (or read reports) and folded these accounts into her story. Gage said she found it hard to describe Truth's "magical influence" that turned "jibes and sneers . . . into . . . respect and admiration." Hundreds of people rushed forward "to shake hands and congratulate the glorious old mother, and bid her 'God speed' on her mission of 'testifying again concerning' the wickedness of this here people."[19]

Whatever the historical errors in Gage's article, she was reinterpreting the story for a wartime context. At the 1851 convention, some whites feared having women's rights get mixed up with abolition. And during the Civil War, some Northerners did not want the war to be about abolition. Although some did not want Truth to speak, she did—and saved the convention. And although some did not want Black soldiers, they fought anyway and helped save the Union. Each time, the very thing some whites feared was what they most needed.

What of Truth's argument with clergymen in Gage's article? Truth some-times confronted ministers, and the 1851 version of Truth's Akron speech carries similar arguments about women's intellect, the sin of Eve, and Christ coming from God and a woman. There is considerable overlap between the theology in the 1851 and 1863 versions of Truth's speech.

Although Gage's account of the Akron convention contains some embel-lishment, it should not be dismissed as folklore. Like Stowe, Gage got some things right. Sojourner could indeed change the mood of a crowd. She was confrontational and witty and proud of her strength. And when men tried to use religion against her, Truth always proved to be the better theologian.

The key thing Gage did for Truth's legacy was to make "ain't I a woman?" into Truth's refrain. The question does not appear in early accounts of her Akron speech, yet it is classic Truth. She always insisted that "the category of 'woman' include those who are poor or not white."[20] Women's rights were not just for white, affluent, and well-educated ladies. Truth stood for the rights of all women, no matter their race or class.

Very soon after Stowe's "Libyan Sibyl" article appeared,[21] Truth took steps to get control of her public image. In the late spring of 1863, she started using a new form of photography called the *carte de visite* (visiting card). When she spoke at events, she could sell these pictures along with her *Narrative*; the pro-ceeds helped to pay her expenses and to define her persona. Truth began using pictures professionally as of May 1863, and did so for the rest of her life.

The first photograph was made in France in 1826. By the 1850s, photogra-phy had become both affordable and practical. The *carte de visite* was a thin photograph made in sets of four or more images at one time. These were glued to card stock and cut into single pictures about 2¼ by 3½ inches in size. They typically cost about ten cents per image (or forty cents per set) and could be reproduced without having to create a new negative. A larger version (4 × 6 ½) called the "cabinet card" also became popular.

More people than ever before could now afford to get their pictures taken. They could trade with friends and even collect pictures of famous people. With pictures cheap to make and easy to mail, "carto mania" was sweep-ing the United States by the 1860s. Photographs were used for fund-raising and propaganda during the war. "Images of starved prisoners of war . . . the whip-scarred back of the fugitive slave . . . and white-looking children" whose skin color did not save them from slavery circulated widely. Truth's own "portraits also reminded purchasers that she symbolized the woman who had been a slave."[22]

Truth's friend Amy Post of Rochester paid for the first set of pictures, and another friend, Frances Titus, may have helped make arrangements with the photographer in Battle Creek.[23] By 1864 her pictures bore the caption "I sell the shadow to support the substance." The pictures were the shadows, and the substance was the living person. Although she called them "shadows," these *cartes de visite* showed what Truth really looked like. She could not control what people wrote about her, but a photographer could get an accurate image through the lens of a camera.

Over the years, Truth had many photographs taken. When her supply ran out, she could get more copies made, or she could pose for a new set of pictures. The photographer could have Truth pose standing or sitting, and when the images were developed, Sojourner could choose what she wanted and how many. She sold them at her lectures and took orders by mail. For *cartes de visite* she typically charged thirty-five cents each or three pictures for a dollar; but cabinet cards (which were larger) cost fifty cents each, plus postage if she had to mail the cards.[24] By selling her pictures and her *Narrative*, Truth could "sustain herself and finance her activism," writes Darcy Grimaldo Grigsby. "To buy one of Truth's photographs was to invest in her work."[25]

The details mattered. In most pictures Truth wore small rectangular glasses and a white wrap on her head. Her clothing said she was a lady, worthy of respect. Black-and-white photographs could not show the colors Truth wore. But over the years she posed in dresses that were plain or striped, plaid or even polka dotted. Over her full skirts she sometimes wore a long apron, perhaps to signify hard work. Or she might choose a white blouse topped by a vest or jacket that buttoned up the front. Some pictures show her wearing a fringed shawl—probably one that she knitted herself.

In some of her seated poses, Truth holds her knitting in one hand, letting the yarn curl out on her lap as if to spell thrift and industry. In one seated pose, Truth holds a photograph of her grandson James in his uniform—a picture within a picture. Sometimes she posed standing, her hand on a cane. Her old injury (she lost an index finger in a farming accident while she was enslaved) can be seen where she grasps her cane.

These images were antislavery because they showed a strong, free, and intelligent Black woman. Frederick Douglass also used photographs to present the "intelligent, dignified black man," beginning in the 1840s and throughout his long life. These pictures made Douglass "one of the most recognizable Americans," writes his biographer David Blight, and "the dissemination of photographs of him became, therefore, a richly political act."[26] The same can be said of Sojourner Truth.

Early in 1864, Truth had new *cartes de visite* made in Detroit. "I have had three photographs taken of me here in as many different positions, and which are considered much better likenesses than the old ones," she told the *Anti-Slavery Standard*. She bought the copyright so she could control the use of these images and reproduce them at a lower cost. She likewise had more of her books and songs printed, to sell them "on my way to see the Freedmen, and thus bear the expenses of the journey."[27] This letter was written in April 1864, and she said she hoped to be in New York in June. From there she would go to Washington, where she would see the freedpeople and meet President Lincoln in the White House.

14

Truth Goes to Washington

Truth left Michigan in June 1864, headed by train for Washington. Her traveling companion was her fourteen-year-old grandson, Sammy Banks. He could read and write for Truth and help in other ways as needed, but most important, she had the company of family. Traveling east by train, they made many stops where Truth could see friends and hold meetings.

In Toledo, Ohio, she was at a meeting along with Frederick Douglass, who spoke first. Then Truth "made an extremely effective address," a newspaper reported. She preached "the duty of her own race to redeem the whites from the doom that was upon them because of their treatment of the African."[1]

Truth also spoke in Rochester, New York, where Frederick Douglass lived. The two veteran abolitionists again addressed a large audience. This time Truth went first, saying she had "pity" for whites in "degradation." She did not envy white people, she said. Their crimes against Blacks made her glad not to be white. She had harsh words for "the Northern Churches that had welcomed slaveholders to the communion table." She would rather eat with hogs from a trough than share the Lord's Supper with "slaveholder devils that had been whipping, burning, hunting and tearing with bloodhounds, her own brothers and sisters." Even so, she hoped that "this country will be beautiful with justice and freedom" after the war. The *Anti-Slavery Standard* said Truth was full of vigor, her voice as "deep and strong and rich" as ever.

Then Frederick Douglass spoke, saying that freedpeople must become self-reliant and do all they could to advance themselves—and not assume that whites would help them. He then turned to Sojourner Truth and reminded her of the time when he had declared that "the slaves with their own right arms [must] take their freedom in blood." And Sojourner famously interrupted him with the question, "Is God gone?" A dozen years later, the nation was torn by Civil War and Black soldiers were fighting for freedom. Douglass looked straight at Truth and asked her what she thought now. "*Wasn't I right then, when I said the slaves must fight for their freedom?*"[2] If Truth responded, her words were not recorded.

Sojourner and Sammy traveled on to Boston. There Truth met Harriet Tubman, the famed "Moses of her people," who risked her life to lead captives out of slavery. Truth and Tubman were the most famous Black women of their time. Both were born into slavery, and each had freed herself from it.

These women fought slavery on different battle fronts. In the North, Truth was a public speaker who faced the wrath of proslavery mobs. Until the war started, Truth embraced nonviolence. Tubman, on the other hand, worked in the South, secretly bringing people out of slavery. After freeing herself from slavery in 1849, she returned to her home state of Maryland thirteen times to rescue people from slavery. She raided plantations by night to "steal away" human property, and she carried a gun. "Wanted" posters offered cash for her capture. When the war came, Tubman went south as a spy for the Union army. In the summer of 1863, she led Black Union soldiers in a raid in South Carolina's Combahee River valley, in which more than seven hundred slaves were freed and many plantations burned to the ground.

When Truth and Tubman met in Boston, they are said to have discussed the war and Abraham Lincoln. Tubman told Truth that she did not trust Lincoln. How could she, when Black soldiers were paid less than half of what white soldiers got? Tubman may also have pointed out that her home state of Maryland was not included in the Emancipation Proclamation because Maryland had not joined the Confederacy.

Truth, however, saw Lincoln as a friend of Black people and believed the president was moving in the right direction. On hearing complaints that Lincoln was taking too long to free *all* the slaves, Truth said, "Have patience! It takes a great while to turn around this great ship of state." Truth may have expressed this view to Tubman.[3]

Leaving Boston, Sojourner and Sammy went to New York City, where Truth gave some lectures. "Give [Truth] a full house," one newspaper advised, and make "a generous contribution"—not for charity but for justice. After all, it was "in the North, in the State of New York," that "our race and our laws" robbed Truth of decades of her life. "Do we not owe her, from abundant fullness, some compensation for those years with their entailed sorrow?"[4] Reparations were due.

From Manhattan Truth and Sammy took the ferry to Long Island, where, twenty years before, Sojourner had become an itinerant preacher. This time she had an invitation to speak at Brooklyn's Plymouth Church, led by the famous Rev. Henry Ward Beecher, brother of Harriet Beecher Stowe. Moving on to New Jersey, Truth gave a few speeches calling for the reelection of Lincoln.[5]

When August came and Truth had yet to arrive in Washington, the *Anti-Slavery Standard* supposed that her "advanced age" required her to travel slowly.[6] Far from it. She took her time because she had so much to do along the way.

When Sojourner reached Washington in the fall of 1864, forts surrounded a city teeming with soldiers. An estimated eighty-five different hospitals received the war wounded. Hotels were full and rents high. Taverns and brothels thrived. "The population surge combined with wartime inflation to strain the community in every way."[7] And the biggest leap in population came from Black people fleeing war and slavery.

Washington was a culturally Southern city, bordered by slave states and largely built by slave labor. The Compromise of 1850 abolished the slave trade in the District of Columbia but did not end slavery there. In 1860 more than three thousand people were enslaved in the nation's capital; there was also a growing population of free Blacks who ran their own businesses and churches. When slavery was abolished in the District of Columbia in 1862, some whites feared that a free city would attract fugitives from slavery. "Most wealthy local whites saw freedpeople as a social and financial burden" that would bring disorder and make property values decline.[8]

As Union forces pushed their way into the South, slaves fled to Union lines seeking freedom. Early in the war their status was unclear. No longer slaves, they were not legally free either. In 1861 the army called them "contrabands of war." (Contraband meant "confiscated property not to be returned to the enemy.") "Contraband camps" sprang up where Union armies prevailed, and Black freedom seekers left the plantations in droves.

Washington was a magnet for contrabands, especially those coming from nearby Virginia and Maryland. By 1863 about ten thousand had made their way to the capital; by 1865 there were about forty thousand.[9] As the war progressed, the terms "freedmen and freedpeople" came into use, signaling a permanent change from slave to free; even so, the term "contraband" remained in use.

Most new arrivals from the South lived in ramshackle slums or make-shift refugee camps. "The atmosphere within these hovels [was] stifling and sickening in the extreme," wrote one observer. The shanty towns "can be considered as nothing better than propagating grounds of crime, disease, and death; and in the case of a prevailing epidemic, the condition of these localities would be horrible to contemplate."[10] Some shacks were so crowded that people had to take turns sleeping because there was no room to lie down. When it rained, water pooled on the dirt floors and sewage came into the houses. Hundreds died from disease and exposure. As if all this were not bad enough, "unprovoked attacks" by whites "became all too common."[11] One of the most dangerous slums was called Murder Bay.

The federal government eventually built several freedmen's camps in and around the city. These quickly became overcrowded. At least one (Camp Barker) was permanently closed due to a cholera outbreak.

Black Washingtonians organized societies to gather food and clothing and to teach basic skills to freedpeople. White and Black volunteers came from the North to help. Truth joined this benevolent army, which included old friends from Truth's abolitionist and women's rights circles. When she arrived in Washington, people offered hospitality and invited her to speak at events in town. She would choose a place to focus her relief work, but first she wanted to meet the president.

———

Abraham Lincoln set aside time for "public opinion baths" to immerse himself in conversation with citizens.[12] He was the first president to receive Black visitors.[13] In August 1863 Frederick Douglass came to the White House—without appointment—to speak to Lincoln about the cruelty of Confederates toward captured Black soldiers. Douglass sent his calling card directly to Lincoln's office. Whites already waiting to see Lincoln were shocked when Douglass was sent immediately to see the president—in effect jumping the line.[14]

Truth's visit to Lincoln was arranged by Lucy Colman, a white abolitionist from Rochester whom Truth had known for many years.[15] Colman, who was in Washington to work among the freedpeople, accompanied Truth to the White House. Like many abolitionists, Colman was critical of Lincoln for moving too slowly on abolition. (Her later acerbic comments about Lincoln suggest that she could never forgive him for being a politician.)

Lincoln's public visiting hours were in high demand, so it was helpful to get an appointment. This was done for Colman by Elizabeth Keckley,[16] a Black woman who was Mrs. Lincoln's dressmaker. In her other life, Keckley ran her own dressmaking business. A leader in Washington's Black community, she founded the Contraband Relief Association in 1862 to "work for the benefit of the unfortunate freedmen."[17] These connections—from Truth to Colman to Keckley to Lincoln—made the White House visit happen.

At eight in the morning on Saturday, October 29, Truth and Colman arrived at the White House. At the entry hall they were directed into the Blue Room, named for its blue-and-gold flocked wallpaper.[18] The circular-domed ceiling, gilt-framed mirrors, and gilded furniture made the Blue Room an elegant space for public receptions and an impressive "waiting room for visitors seeking to see the President."[19] When a visitor's turn came, he or she went to an adjoining room to be received by Lincoln himself.

Truth and Colman waited in the Blue Room for a long time, Colman recalled. Meanwhile, another Black woman entered. She told Truth and Colman that she had a letter for the president; it concerned her husband, a Black soldier who had gone for many months without pay. In the meantime, this woman had suffered illness and was about to be evicted because she could not pay her rent. Her last resort was to appeal to the president. However, she had no appointment. "You may go in with me," Colman said, indicating that the soldier's wife could state her business *after* Sojourner completed hers.

When Colman's name was called, she took Truth and their new friend into the next room to meet Lincoln. The president sat behind a desk, separated from his visitors by a railing with a gate.[20] This may have been an attempt to protect him from "threats of violence [that] swirled about Lincoln . . . especially toward the close of the war in 1864."[21]

"This is Sojourner Truth, who has come all the way from Michigan to see you,"[22] said Colman. Lincoln stood up, shook Truth's hand, and said he was pleased to see her (according to Truth's account of the meeting, published in the *National Anti-Slavery Standard*).

"Mr. President," Truth said, "when you first took [office] I feared you would be torn to pieces," like Daniel in the lions' den. "And if the lions did not tear you into pieces, I knew that it would be God that had saved you."

Truth told Lincoln of her vow that if God spared her (from her illness the previous winter), she would go and see the president. "And now I am here to see you for myself." Lincoln congratulated Truth "on having been spared."

Then Truth told Lincoln he was "the best President who has ever taken the seat." Lincoln said she must be referring to his Emancipation Proclamation, but he refused to take credit for it. He said several of his predecessors would have done the same thing, "if the time had come." Gesturing toward the Potomac River, Lincoln said, "If the people over the river . . . had behaved themselves, I could not have done what I have; but they did not, and I was compelled to do these things." Lincoln deflected any credit or praise. But Truth insisted: "I thank God that you were the instrument selected by Him and the people to do it." According to the *Anti-Slavery Reporter*, Truth "presented him with one of [her] shadows and songs, for which he thanked [her], and said he would keep them as a remembrance."[23]

Lincoln then showed Truth a Bible recently presented to him by a delegation of Black ministers on behalf of "the colored people of Baltimore." Truth did not describe the Bible herself, but it was a large tome bound "in royal purple velvet." The upper part of the cover held "a solid 18 carat gold plate" medallion, depicting "the President in the act of removing the shackles from a slave." Below this was a smaller gold medallion, inscribed "to Abraham Lincoln, President of the United States, from the loyal colored people of Baltimore, as a token of respect and gratitude." The Bible was kept in a solid black walnut case with a silver plate on the lid, on which is engraved a picture of the capitol and the words "Holy Bible."[24] This gift was said to have cost $5,800,[25] an astronomical sum.

The Bible "the colored people [gave] to the Head of the government" was beautiful, Truth later told the *Anti-Slavery Standard*. Yet this same government had long forbidden Blacks "to learn enough to read this Book. And for what? Let them answer who can."

Truth had brought with her a small autograph book, and she gave it to Lincoln for him to sign. He wrote: "*For Aunty Sojourner Truth October 29, 1864. A. Lincoln.*" Lucy Colman, many years later (1891), objected that Lincoln "called [Truth] aunty, as he would his washer-woman."[26] If it bothered Truth that Lincoln addressed her as "Aunty," she did not say so. It was a common usage in 1864. What deeply impressed Truth was that Lincoln signed her book "with the same hand that signed the death-warrant of slavery."

It was now time for the Black soldier's wife to make her appeal. She gave her letter to Lincoln and told him her story. Truth said that Lincoln listened and "spoke to her with kindness and tenderness. He . . . told her where to go and get the money, and asked [Mrs. Colman] to assist her, which she did." Truth thought Lincoln "showed as much kindness and consideration to the colored persons as to the whites, if not more."

As the visit ended, Lincoln stood up and took Truth's hand, saying she was welcome to call again. "I felt that I was in the presence of a friend," Truth recalled. "I now thank God from the bottom of my heart that I always have advocated his cause, and have done it openly and boldly. I shall feel still more in duty bound to do so in time to come. May God assist me."

Ten days after Truth's visit, Lincoln was reelected to a second term in office. Soon after that, Truth's letter about her visit to Lincoln appeared in the *National Anti-Slavery Standard*. "I never was treated by any one with more kindness and cordiality than were shown to me by that great and good man, Abraham Lincoln." Sojourner rejoiced that "by the grace of God" Lincoln was elected "President of the United States for four years more."[27]

Lucy Colman took a different view of Truth's visit with Lincoln. A letter from Colman appeared in the *Rochester Express*, the *National Anti-Slavery Standard*, and the *Liberator* in late November 1864. Colman said that even if women had the vote, she would not have voted for Lincoln (probably because his approach to abolition seemed to her "too little and too late"). Even so, "whatever may have been the former delinquencies of the President, *he has now come to the conclusion to act*." Admitting that "our President received [us] . . . with real politeness and a pleasing cordiality," she rated the visit "quite satisfactory."[28]

———

After meeting President Lincoln, Truth stayed for three weeks with Jane Swisshelm. The white editor and reformer had come to Washington to work on behalf of freedpeople.[29] These two women had met at the Akron women's rights convention back in 1851. At that time, Swisshelm did not welcome Black women into the women's rights movement and did not want Truth to speak.[30] Yet now here was Truth, staying with Swisshelm in Washington. Perhaps Swisshelm had a change of heart, or at least saw Truth as someone who could help the freedpeople.

Truth held many meetings in Washington to raise funds for freedpeople and for the Colored Soldiers' Aid Society. She spoke twice at the Fifteenth Street Presbyterian Church, which was led by Rev. Henry Highland Garnet. Born into slavery, Garnet escaped with his family to New York and in time became an abolitionist minister. In Garnet's famous 1843 speech, "Call to Rebellion," he said violence was necessary to end slavery. Truth had long embraced moral suasion as the best way to end slavery, but the war changed everything—and now here she was in Garnet's church helping to raise money for Black troops. Admission of twenty-five cents was taken at the door, and a portion of this went to support Truth in her work. "These meetings were successful in raising funds," she told the *National Anti-Slavery Standard.*[31]

Early in November 1864, Truth went to Mason's Island (now Roosevelt Island). It had been a training ground for Black soldiers and then was re-purposed as a refugee camp. A thousand former slaves now occupied army barracks. Mason's Island also had a hospital, a dining hall and stables—and a "lunatic asylum" for the mentally and emotionally ill.

While at Mason's Island, Truth stayed with Rev. D. B. Nichols, the super-intendent of the camp. Rev. and Mrs. Nichols told Truth that the clothing sent to the camp was meant to be given away, but government workers and contractors were trying to make freedpeople pay for it. "I am going around among the colored folks and find out who it is sells the clothing . . . that is sent to them from the North," Truth said in a letter to a friend. Some whites "are only here for the loaves and fishes, while the freedmen get the scales and crusts." Truth said her mission was to "elevate these people and make them know they are free," which brought her into conflict with whites who tried to keep Blacks down. Truth told the refugees to learn new skills and embrace their freedom. "The people are delighted to hear me talk," her letter said. "I think I am doing good. I am needed here."

Many of the Black people on Mason's Island came from nearby Maryland, a slave state that had remained in the Union. Since Maryland was not in "active rebellion," Lincoln's Emancipation Proclamation did not apply there. The state of Maryland finally abolished slavery on November 1, 1864, but the people on Mason's Island didn't hear this news. "They never knew that Maryland was free until I told them," Truth told a friend. "One old woman clung around my neck and almost choked me she was so *glad.*"

Truth spoke at the celebration and said she "had a good chance to tell the colored people things that they had never heard."

In the same letter, Truth said she hoped "to go and see President Lincoln again." She did not want any pay for her work, but "only the food I eat, for the colored people must be raised out of bondage. I believe I am on the best place on the planet."[32]

Truth thought she would remain on Mason's Island, but an invitation to speak at Freedmen's Village drew her across the Potomac River to Arlington. Freedmen's Village was built on the former estate of Confederate general Robert E. Lee and dedicated on December 4, 1863. Former slaves were "cultivating the Arlington estate for themselves, and not for its former owner, Gen. Lee, the leader of the rebel army," said the *New York Times*.[33] Freedmen's Village was meant to be a temporary refuge, but Black people set down roots there. They built their own businesses and churches but were forced to leave in 1886. Today Arlington Cemetery completely covers the site where Freedmen's Village once stood.

In November 1864, when Truth arrived at Freedmen's Village, she would have seen rows of duplex houses built along a road that curved around a large central pond.[34] Water had to be carried to the houses from a spring or a well, but the water may have been unsafe to drink. When Sojourner was in residence, the schools had to close due to an outbreak of disease.[35] An average of two people a day died at the overcrowded Freedmen's Village, which lodged about three thousand people.[36]

Offset from the housing area were the administrative buildings: a hospital, a commissary, a guardhouse (jail), and a carpenter shop. Freedmen's Village also had a chapel, a blacksmith shop, a laundry, a dining hall, school buildings, and houses for some of the staff. There was even a residence called "the Home" for the elderly and others who could not work.

Freedmen's Village was run by the War Department and came under military discipline. Able-bodied men were "employed on farm land and in workshops on the former Lee estate."[37] They earned roughly ten dollars a week, but about half of that went to pay for rent and food. Any who refused these terms were to be sent to Mason's Island, reported the *Washington Evening Star*.[38]

Freedmen's Village attracted volunteers (both Black and white) who came to help the people make a transition to freedom. And then there were the "office seekers" who cared nothing for the people and only wanted a paying job. Truth later said "that the government hired people . . . who were not fit . . . ministers that never preached a sermon in their life, doctors who felt the pulse with gloves on."[39]

The superintendent of the village was Captain George B. Carse, a Union officer honorably discharged for battlefield injuries. "I heard there was a woman coming here to speak to the people," Captain Carse wrote to the *National Anti-Slavery Standard*, "and I went to hear her." Carse arrived late to the crowded house where Truth was speaking. He heard her say "be clean, be clean, for cleanliness is part of godliness." Truth told the people they must learn to be independent, work hard, and be thrifty. They should seek education for their children and strive to "*be something.*" Perhaps hardest of all, she said, they "must learn to love white people." She told them that many whites in the North had been working a long time to end slavery. Truth "talked to them as a white person could not," Captain Carse said, because "she is one of them—she can call them her people."[40]

On Sundays, Truth preached to large gatherings at Freedmen's Village.[41] During the week she made many house calls. She used to knit while she visited with the people and probably taught this useful craft. Truth was well aware that some enslaved women were highly skilled, but her concern at the moment was the women who spent all their lives working the fields. These did not know "how to knit . . . few [knew] how to make a loaf of bread, or anything of the kind," she told the *National Anti-Slavery Standard*. "I find many of the women very ignorant in relation to house-keeping," she said. "Most of them were instructed in field labor, but not in household duties."[42] Learning how to care for one's own family was part of the transition to freedom.

Truth's work was part of a greater effort, called "freedmen's relief," that began during the war and continued for some years after it. Teachers and nurses, missionaries and ministers and reformers came down from the North to help former slaves adjust to freedom. These reformers were Black and white, men and women. Collecting and distributing food and clothing was short-term aid; to be prepared for their long-term future, freedpeople also needed to learn how to read and write. The goal of freedmen's education was to "equip" the people "to take full advantage of citizenship," writes historian Eric Foner, "and to remake the culture that Blacks had inherited from slavery, by inculcating qualities of self-reliance and self-discipline."[43]

The freedmen's relief movement was not just whites telling Blacks how to live. Black leaders like Sojourner Truth and Frederick Douglass exhorted the freedpeople to work hard and strive for self-improvement. "African Americans involved in freedmen's relief work also scrutinized the personal habits of freedpeople," writes historian Kate Masur. They taught skills like housekeeping, thrift, and cleanliness to the former slaves. "The women of the Contraband Relief Association, for example, felt it was their 'duty' to assist [freedpeople] towards a higher plane of civilization." And yet (as Truth found out), the freedpeople did not always welcome being told what to do.[44]

Captain Carse could see that Sojourner Truth understood the goals of freedmen's relief, and that she was uncommonly gifted. She made such a favorable impression that Carse asked her to stay. Freedmen's Village became the fourth commune in which Truth lived. She would have "a house rent free . . . to call her own" and permission to speak to large groups whenever she wanted to. "She came amongst us as a stranger," Carse told the *National Anti-Slavery Standard*, but soon everyone knew her. No one else in the camp had her talents or her moral stature. Superintendent Carse was eager and "willing to assist her in her good work."[45]

Soon Truth got an official letter of commission from the New York National Freedmen's Relief Association, a "private, non-sectarian agency [that] worked in cooperation with the Freedmen's Bureau and other agencies of the government."[46] The letter of commission officially made Truth "a counselor to the freedpeople at Arlington Heights, VA." She played an important role in a wider effort to relieve the condition of the freedpeople and to promote "their intellectual, moral, and religious instruction."[47]

Truth received a small stipend from the New York National Freedmen's Relief Association, but "she spent it all in aiding the freed people," a friend wrote.[48] She worked "with the approval of the government" but was "not a government employee."[49] Truth said she had promised Abraham Lincoln to "take care of her people," and that was a personal conviction, not a government job. She moved into the little house Captain Carse secured for her at Freedmen's Village. "I can be useful and will stay," Truth told a friend. She said she would "appreciate any food her friends might send" and asked if someone could send her some sheets and a pillow. Money sent to her for pictures had arrived safely, she said. She asked to have the *National Anti-Slavery Standard* sent to her at Freedmen's Village. "Many of the colored people like to hear what is going on, and to know what is being done for them. Sammy, my grandson, reads for them." Sojourner said she and Sammy were both well and doing good work. "I find plenty of friends."[50]

The freedpeople were curious about Truth, perhaps never having seen a Black woman in a position of public leadership. They wanted to know how Sojourner had lived in the North, and many sought to follow her example. "I am listened to with attention and respect," Truth said.

Not by everyone, for it turned out that some saw Truth as too bossy. After taking orders all their lives, the *last* thing some folks wanted was to have a Yankee woman telling them how to live, whether that Yankee happened to be Black or white. "Truth's identity as a Black woman did not automatically make her an exception"[51] as far as some freedpeople were concerned. Truth hit a raw nerve in one speech when she said it was a "disgrace" that they were "content to live off the government." Many felt entitled to government relief since their whole lives had been stolen. Her "insulted listeners" then rose up and "drove [her] from the building," and she accused them of "being content to live by the 'vilest of habits.'"[52]

Internal tensions were one thing, but Freedmen's Village was also attacked from the outside. Some Marylanders tried to keep a form of slavery by taking "advantage of racially discriminatory state laws that allowed for the involuntary apprenticeship of free Black children."[53] Thus white men from Maryland snuck into Freedmen's Village to "seize and carry away" little children. Truth later said these "low, savage and unfeeling" kidnappers treated her people "worse than beasts."[54] When the mothers cried out for help, they were "thrust into the guard-house" for disturbing the peace. Truth told the mothers to stand up for their rights. "You are free," she said. "You have rights that will be recognized and maintained by the laws. You can bring these robbers to justice."

When the mothers demanded the return of their children, the kidnappers "threatened to put Sojourner in the guard house." She retorted that if they tried it, she would make the nation "rock like a cradle."[55] The Marylanders retreated when they saw they could not intimidate Truth, who could easily expose them in the press.

The *Cleveland Daily Leader* proclaimed that "all lovers of justice to the Blacks may be assured that [Truth] is doing necessary Christian work" at Freedmen's Village, as no other person could do.[56] Truth was reforming abuses and suggesting new methods, the article said. It was no secret that freedpeople were being exploited in the freedpeople's camps. After having worked all their lives for nothing, they were expected to pay rent. Kidnappers stole children. Scammers tried to sell clothing that was supposed to be free. Black females were subjected to sexual abuse, resulting in "a cluster of half white 'contraband babies' in each of the camps."[57] Sojourner Truth, in addition to all her other duties, became a whistleblower too.

One Saturday in February 1865, Truth and Captain Carse left Freedmen's Village in Arlington for nearby Washington, where they planned to attend a meeting of the National Freedmen's Aid Society. It was held in the basement of Calvary Church, where donations of clothing to freedpeople were gathered, sorted, and distributed.

Staying at Calvary Church at this time was a British reporter who perhaps could find no other lodgings in crowded Washington. Having been out for a while, he returned to the church and saw the entrance "blocked by about 200 women" desperate to get some of the clothing. So great was the clamor that the Freedmen's Aid Society meeting could not proceed. The reporter saw an old Black woman, neatly dressed, wearing a pair of gold-rimmed spectacles. "Clear this passage and don't hinder the business," she ordered. "You have freedom; you must now have regulation, or you are undone." Her voice had the ring of authority. No wonder Captain Carse called her "Queen Sojourner."[58]

After Truth established some order, the British reporter met her and shook her hand. He asked her how old she was. She replied "that her natural age was nearly seventy, but when the war broke out the Lord added twenty years to her life, so that she was now not quite fifty." Then he asked Truth if she found the people hard to manage. "Lord bless you child, no," she replied. "They are as gentle as lambs, but they must be brought under rule and regulation. Ah! The poor things, they have all to learn."

The unnamed British correspondent was probably Fred Tomkins, who later wrote about Truth in a pamphlet called *Jewels in Ebony*. Tompkins said Truth was "full of intelligence and tenderness . . . full of faith in the Holy Ghost." She was "the most remarkable woman that I ever met." Tomkins observed that Truth could "speak in correct and beautiful English" when she chose. She could also speak in "negro dialect . . . uttering the most telling truths with the most biting sarcasm."[59] Truth knew—to use a modern phrase—how to code-switch, depending on her audience and the result she wanted.

That evening, a grand reception was held at the White House. It was open to the public—the *white* public, that is. "Many colored people were in Washington," Elizabeth Keckley wrote, "and large numbers had desired to attend the levee, but orders were issued not to admit them."[60] Keckley did not say who gave this order, but it was probably not Lincoln himself, since the arrangements for these receptions fell to the White House staff.

Tomkins went to the reception. He recalled that the best musicians in the city played the music of Beethoven, which filled the reception hall and drawing rooms. The women wore their finest evening gowns and the men their best silk suits. All the notable white people in Washington came.

Tomkins saw Sojourner Truth at the entrance, escorted by Captain Carse. Then "I saw Sojourner refused admission," Tomkins wrote. She was told—perhaps by a guard or doorman—that Black people were not allowed at the reception. Carse said, "If she is not good enough to enter, I am not." He turned away, offered Sojourner his arm, and led the "dignified and lady-like old Black woman away" from the White House. "I saw the good old woman bent with grief, and the captain in disgust, leave the hall," wrote Tomkins.

The following Monday evening Tomkins had "a long interview with President Lincoln." Tomkins said he regretted "that so good and faithful a subject of the Republic" was refused admission. Lincoln "expressed his sorrow, and said he had often seen her, that it should not occur again, and that she should see him at the first opportunity: a promise which he kept by sending for her a few days afterwards."[61] If Truth saw Lincoln again, no record of it has been found.

Truth returned to Freedmen's Village and was there when news of General Lee's surrender came. After months of trench warfare around Petersburg, Lee's shattered army retreated, leaving the nearby Confederate capital of Richmond defenseless. Confederate political leaders left their capital as Lee's army fled to the west, hoping to link up with Confederate general Johnston's forces. Meanwhile Confederate sympathizers set Richmond's warehouses and factories ablaze to keep supplies out of Yankee hands. On April 4, Lincoln and his son Tad visited the smoldering ruin of a city. Black people crowded around Lincoln in the streets, many falling to their knees, but Lincoln told them not to bow to him.

Lee's Army of Northern Virginia was starving. On April 9, 1865, after one last skirmish at the little village of Appomattox Court House, Lee surrendered.

As word reached the North, bells pealed and bands played. Flags flew and fireworks shot up into the sky. "Every city blazed with its tens of thousands of lights," Elizabeth Keckley recalled. "But scarcely had the fireworks ceased to play, and the lights been taken down from the windows, when the lightning flashed the most appalling news over the wires. 'The President has been murdered.'"[62]

Abraham Lincoln was assassinated on April 15, 1865—just days after Lee's surrender. Telegrams and newspapers spread the dreadful news. All across the North and as far west as California, disbelief gave way to shock, followed by deep grief and gloom. People draped their homes and public buildings with black crepe. The same church bells that pealed out Lee's surrender now tolled Lincoln's death. Everyone who could afford it wore black mourning clothes; others found scraps of black cloth to pin to their clothing or to hang from their doors. But not everyone mourned. As historian Martha Hodes shows from letters written at the time, Copperheads in the North rejoiced (in private, lest they face reprisals). Many white Southerners blamed Lincoln for the war and took grim satisfaction in the news of his death.

Black people across the nation were grief-stricken, having revered Lincoln as their deliverer, protector, and friend. In the North, African Americans wept to see "the hope of our people . . . again stricken down."[63] In the South, many whites taunted Blacks with threats of reenslavement now that Lincoln was gone.

Truth is said to have held a memorial service for Lincoln at Freedmen's Village.[64] She had always known that Lincoln was in danger, like Daniel in the lions' den. When she met him in the White House, she had said she rejoiced that God "spared him" thus far. Truth was a firm believer in Providence. If Truth, like many others at the time, felt that Lincoln had finished the work God set out for him to do, she may have found some consolation. Whatever her feelings were, she knew that her people passed through desolation on their way to freedom, and they must keep walking.

In the summer of 1865, Truth decided to leave Freedmen's Village. Her friend Captain Carse had been replaced by a new superintendent, who "forced residents to work by reducing their rations."[65] Sojourner wanted no part of such cruel measures.

Besides, she may have felt her own effectiveness waning. Some of the freedpeople rejected her message. In a letter to her friend Amy Post, she expressed frustration that some in the camp "desire nothing higher than the lowest and the vilest of habits." Truth judged her work to be "acceptably to the good," but she would not stay to see it slip lower. "For you know I must be a faithful Sojourner everywhere." She was grateful that "those in authority even to the President" usually treated her with "kindly attention." Yet she could not be satisfied until her people were truly free. Evoking the exodus story, in which God led the people through the wilderness with a pillar of cloud by day and a pillar of fire by night, she wrote to Post: "I see dark spots still in the great cloud that leads us by day, and occasionally angry flashes in the pillar of fire that guides us through this long dark night." Perhaps she referred to the trauma of Lincoln's assassination. "Yet my comfort in all this is in the thought that God rules."[66]

Despite their sorrow over Lincoln's death, Black people celebrated the Union victory as a great jubilee. "The end of the war [was] a time of unparalleled optimism . . . for the entire Black community,"[67] writes historian Henry Louis Gates Jr. Yet no one knew what the future held for the freedpeople. The exodus from slavery had been made, but now came the wilderness time, when the promised land was nowhere in sight. Sojourner Truth would stay a while longer in Washington among the freedpeople.

15

Reconstruction

In the summer or fall of 1865, Sojourner Truth left Freedmen's Village and returned to nearby Washington. There she lived with her friend Josephine Griffing, who was now the general agent for the National Freedmen's Relief Association of the District of Columbia. Griffing had rented a large house near the Capitol building, which she turned into "a relief depot" for distributing "food, clothing and fuel." Griffing kept her office there and had space for a few lodgers. The house was "usually surrounded by a ragged crowd of freed people" seeking assistance and "was for years a symbol of the unsolved issues of freedom," wrote historian Eric Melder. With the war over and the period of Reconstruction already under way, both Truth and Griffing were entering a new phase of their work.

Truth's work often overlapped with that of the Freedmen's Bureau. Officially called the Bureau of Refugees, Freedmen and Abandoned Lands, this government agency was launched in March 1865. Griffing was among the reformers who lobbied Congress to create the Bureau.[1] She had hoped the new agency would have a budget of its own and be run by abolitionists and humanitarians. Instead, it had no independent budget and was run by the War Department.

The Bureau sought to remake the South without slavery. This required sweeping changes in education, labor laws, and land reform. According to historian Eric Foner, the Freedmen's Bureau was based on the view "that the federal government must shoulder broad responsibility for the emancipated slaves, including offering them some kind of access to land."[2] But any form of Southern land redistribution was thwarted by President Andrew Johnson and by ex-Confederates as they regained power.[3] Both Griffing and Truth came to see land ownership—not in the South, but in the North or West—as the key to self-sufficiency for freedpeople.

Soon after returning to Washington, Truth began working at the Freedmen's Hospital on the northwest edge of town. An official at the Freedmen's Bureau wrote a recommendation for Truth on September 13, 1865: "Sojourner Truth has good ideas about the industry and virtue of the colored people. I commend her energetic and faithful efforts to Surgeon Gluman, in charge of Freedmen's Hospital, and shall be happy to have him give her all facilities and authority so far as she can aid him in promoting order, cleanliness, industry, and virtue among the patients."[4]

Truth also volunteered at the National Colored Home, an orphanage in nearby Georgetown. The orphanage was in an abandoned house whose owner, a Confederate sympathizer, left town at the start of the war.[5] Now it housed between sixty and seventy children plus several old women. Sanitation was poor, and many children died from disease.[6] Truth's friend Lucy Colman was appalled by the conditions there and may have asked Sojourner to help. Truth brought donations of food and clothing, and likely also visited with the children.

Thinking of her own family, Sojourner sent a letter to her friend Amy Post in Rochester. Truth asked Post to find out how her daughters were doing and to tell them to write to her in care of the Freedmen's Hospital.[7] Truth's grandson Sammy had left Washington, perhaps to see his cousin James (now discharged from the army).[8]

Truth missed Sammy, but she was always on the move between her lodgings, the Freedmen's Hospital, the Georgetown orphanage, and various meetings. Though strong for her age, she could not walk everywhere—especially when carrying supplies for the hospital or the orphanage. Friends might give her a ride in a buggy from time to time, but what she needed was public transportation.

In those days Washington had streetcars, called "horse cars" because horses pulled them along a rail track. These cars were for whites only, but Blacks could ride standing up at the front of the car near the horses. The drivers felt no obligation to stop for Blacks. Jim Crow cars were introduced, but these were so scarce that Blacks had to wait for long periods or walk.[9]

Congress had passed a law against excluding anyone from public transportation "on account of color" in Washington, DC. A company that refused to serve Blacks could lose its license to operate.[10] Lincoln had signed the law on March 3, 1865, several weeks before he died.

However, unwritten rules of segregation prevailed, and Washington's transportation remained largely segregated. Truth did not accept this state of affairs. As the prologue to this book shows, she fought to desegregate public transportation in Washington.

Truth joined a battle already in progress. In the spring of 1865, "a Black Union army sergeant boarded a streetcar" and was attacked by four white men. Police arrested two of the attackers. And "for the rest of the year, streetcars were at the heart of the local debate about equality," writes historian Kate Masur. Black people claimed their "right to ride," and many whites, including "streetcar conductors, reacted with hostility and sometimes violence."[11]

This conflict was part of Truth's work in Washington. Sojourner's *Book of Life* (a later addition to her *Narrative*) says she tried to catch one of the horse-drawn trollies as she was returning to the city from the orphans' home at Georgetown. The conductor pretended not to see her and kept ringing his bell to drown out her cries. She pursued the car to the next stop and climbed in. "It is a shame to make a lady run so," she told the conductor. He threatened that he would put her off the car if she said another word. She replied that if he tried to put her off, it would cost him more than his car and horses were worth. Just then a man "wearing a general's uniform, interfered in her behalf, and the conductor gave her no further trouble."

Truth's *Book of Life* relates that she was sent to Georgetown to get a nurse for the Freedmen's Hospital. On the return trip, Truth and the nurse (who was Black) "went to the station and took seats in an empty car." Then two white "ladies" came into the car. They sat across from Truth and the nurse, whispering to each other and casting "scornful glances" at the two Black women. The nurse Truth had brought "hung her poor old head nearly down to her lap," while Truth held her head high and "looked fearlessly about."

Then one of the white women, playing the role of helpless female, drawled "in a weak, faint voice, 'conductor, conductor, does n*****s ride in these cars?'" The conductor hemmed and hawed and finally admitted it was so. "'Tis a shame and a disgrace," said the white women, "they ought to have a n***** car on the track."

Truth spoke up: "Of course colored people ride in the cars," she said. "Street cars are designed for poor white, and colored, folks. Carriages are for ladies and gentlemen." Truth pointed out the window to some carriages "standing ready to take you three or four miles for sixpence!!!'" Outwitted, the white women arose to leave. "Ah!" said Sojourner, "now they are going to take a carriage. Good bye, ladies."[12]

Another time, Truth was going to take a car with Griffing. The car had been stopped, but the moment Griffing stepped aboard, the conductor started his horses in order to leave Truth behind. Truth reached out to hang on to the car's handrail, but the conductor kept going. Griffing was trying to make the conductor stop, but he dragged Truth several yards before allowing her to get on. Griffing "reported the conductor to the president of the City Railway, who dismissed him at once."[13] Almost a century after Sojourner Truth made her own freedom rides, Blacks and whites risked their lives riding together to desegregate busses. The civil rights Freedom Riders carried on the work of Reconstruction, so long delayed.

Truth told audiences about her experiences on the horse cars in Washington. "I tell you," she said, "there's nothing like standing up for your rights."[14] It took "years of struggle, both in the streets and in Congress," for Black people to secure their "right to ride on the capital's streetcars,"[15] writes Kate Masur. This was part of a much larger movement involving New York City, San Francisco, Cincinnati, Cleveland, and many other cities that desegregated their streetcars during the Civil War.[16] Unfortunately, many of these gains were reversed when Reconstruction was abandoned.

———

During the first four years of Reconstruction, the seventeenth president of the United States was one of the least competent men ever to hold the office. Andrew Johnson, a Democrat from Tennessee, served in Congress and remained loyal to the Union. He became Lincoln's running mate in 1864 and was elected vice president. After the assassination of Lincoln elevated Johnson to the presidency, he sought to restore Southern states to their full rights as soon as possible, with no regard for the future of the freedpeople.

Johnson's archfoes were the Radical Republicans. They wanted Reconstruction to rebuild the South on a whole new footing. To fulfill the promise of emancipation, said the Radicals, Black people must have equal rights *and* reparations in the form of land redistribution. Politically, Sojourner Truth stood with the Radicals. She was not alone in this, since "American Blacks emerged from slavery convinced that the federal government had committed itself to land distribution."[17] As Truth said, "We Black folks earned a right to some land. It's wet with our blood in some places. Ain't that earned it?"[18]

Between Johnson and the Radicals stood the "moderate Republicans," who saw Reconstruction as "a set of practical problems" to be solved before the Southern states could return to their "full rights and powers."[19] Truth also wanted to solve practical problems, but she saw that if the roots of slavery were left intact, something like slavery would grow back again.

Sojourner wanted to meet President Johnson in the White House, so Lucy Colman again arranged the visit and accompanied Truth. Colman's *Reminiscences* hints that the meeting was awkward but offers no account of the visit.[20] Truth later said she had "a poor opinion" of Johnson. He "reminded her of the fig tree that Jesus cursed—there was not much to him."[21] More is known about Johnson's meeting with a delegation of Black leaders (including Frederick Douglass) in 1866. Johnson told the delegation that promoting civil rights would "result in the extermination of one [race] or the other."[22]

Johnson wanted the freedpeople to be subject to white rule. He actively opposed ratification of the Fourteenth Amendment (which guaranteed citizenship to all people born in the United States and increased federal power to protect civil rights). But the Radical Republicans passed legislation requiring Southern states to ratify the Fourteenth Amendment as a condition for reentering the Union. One by one the former Confederate states transitioned out of military rule and returned to the Union, in a process called "Redemption." In 1870 Georgia was the last state to return. The planter aristocracy regained political power at the state and local level, and strove to force Blacks into peonage. As Truth often said, "Slavery is dead but the spirit of slavery lives on."

On December 6, 1865, the Thirteenth Amendment was ratified, completing what Lincoln's Emancipation Proclamation had begun. This was the first of several constitutional amendments in the Reconstruction era, intended to secure the rights of Black people. As the old year ended, Sojourner Truth continued her relief work, but she searched for ways to help her people move into the fullness of their freedom over the long term.

Truth's first public appearance in 1866 was not at a lecture podium but on a stage. On January 2 she joined in a tableaux exhibition to help raise money for wounded soldiers. Now a vanished art form, the tableau was very popular in the nineteenth century. It allowed women to participate in drama while avoiding the theater (which for many was morally suspect). Women in a tableau wore costumes and posed on a stage or other special setting to create "living works of art, or scenes of literature or history."[23] Tableaux were meant to inspire, instruct, or entertain.

Before the war, tableaux were used for fund-raising at antislavery fairs; Truth attended many of these. During the war, "Sanitary Fairs" raised a great deal of money to buy bandages and other supplies for the soldiers, and tableaux inspired people to give generously. After the war, tableaux were staged to raise money for freedpeople, wounded soldiers, and war widows.

As 1866 dawned, thousands of Civil War soldiers lay sick and wounded. The Ladies of the National Union Relief Association staged a tableaux exhibition to raise money for these men. A newspaper described the event as "patriotic." The brass band of the Eighth Regiment of Hancock's corps offered background music, and "ice cream, oysters, cake and coffee were served" at the intermission.

Truth was well known among the reformers of the city, so "the audience were agreeably surprised by the appearance of the 'Contraband Sibyl,' represented by Sojourner Truth," reported the *Daily National Republican*. She "appeared in an appropriate costume and sang words and music of her own composition, with good effect."[24] The newspaper did not describe Truth's costume, or what song she sang, but one imagines her clothed in rags and singing "I Am Pleading for My People."

Truth had a growing sense of urgency to get freedpeople to leave Washington, as did her friend Josephine Griffing. Washington was so packed with refugees that there was little hope of finding work or a decent place to live. Griffing used her contacts in the North to locate homes and jobs for freedpeople. Working closely with the Freedmen's Bureau, she is said to have moved between three thousand and five thousand people to new locations between 1865 and 1868.[25] Yet, even these efforts may have seemed like trying to empty the ocean with a teacup: "thousands of people did depart the capital . . . but thousands more continued to arrive."[26]

Truth joined Griffing's work to help resettle freedpeople in the North. She wanted them to go where they could gain control of their lives and start to build a future. As the twentieth-century author Toni Morrison wrote in *Beloved* (a novel set during slavery and Reconstruction), "Freeing yourself was one thing, ownership of that freed self was another."[27]

Truth's new cause was vast. It was also very personal. She too had left slavery with nothing. After years of struggle and setbacks, she became a homeowner and public speaker. Perhaps she thought that what was good for her was good for everybody else.

And yet, freedpeople had reasons to stay in Washington. Some were already creating communities and chose not to be uprooted one more time. The strongest motive for staying was family. The capital was a hub for reunions. Here many found—or were found by—long-lost relatives who had been cruelly sold apart under slavery. For many, freedom meant finding family and staying together.[28] Leaving Washington too soon might mean never seeing loved ones again. Many employers in the North wanted young single men, but if these left, who would care for their families?[29]

Truth herself intended to move back to Michigan to reunite with family. In the summer of 1866, she shipped some boxes to her friend Amy Post in Rochester, planning to pick them up on her way back to Michigan. The letter Sojourner sent along asked Amy to air out the blankets in those boxes, because Truth had few possessions and could not afford to replace them. Her letter told Post of the plan to find homes and jobs in the North for freedpeople. Truth reported that freedmen could earn up to thirty-six dollars a month, while freedwomen could make only a fraction of that doing domestic work or farm labor. It was easier for men to earn money than for women, though even the men would be underpaid. It was a challenge to find places where entire families could go.[30]

Truth would get her abolitionist friends to find homes and jobs for freedpeople in the North. She herself would travel with the freedpeople to make sure everybody got to the right place. Before the war, fugitive slaves headed north on the Underground Railroad. After the war, Truth conducted freedpeople on the aboveground railroad and became "an active agent in the making of Reconstruction."[31]

As Black people continued moving northward, it became clear that "the consequences of emancipation extended well beyond the slaveholding South," writes historian Leslie Schwalm. During the war, some white Northerners feared a migration of Blacks to the North, thinking that "any Black gains in the region would diminish their own status and citizenship." These Northerners resented having what they deemed a "Southern problem" foisted upon them. Thus "northern whites participated in a powerful national amnesia" about Northern slavery and its aftereffects. This "set the stage for a much longer battle of 'place' and citizenship," writes Schwalm, "a battle that would last well into the 20th century."[32] Despite such resistance, antislavery activists led the way in bringing Black people into the Upper Midwest and other parts of the North, finding jobs and homes for them.

Truth partnered with Griffing in this effort.[33] If Truth and Griffing could supply names and addresses of employers in the North who had jobs to offer, the Freedmen's Bureau would pay traveling expenses for freedpeople and also for Truth and Griffing. Truth's first group left Washington on a north-bound train pulling several cars of freedpeople. Some went to towns in Ohio, where activists found work and shelter for them. Twenty-eight more people went on to Battle Creek, where Frances Titus (a mutual friend of Truth and Griffing) helped with resettlement.[34]

Most stories of the people Truth conducted north have been lost. An exception is the story of Payton Grayson, who was seventy years old when the *Battle Creek Enquirer* interviewed him in 1929.[35] He was said to be the last living person Truth brought to Battle Creek.

Grayson was born into slavery in Virginia near the Potomac River, a few years before the Civil War broke out. As the Union army advanced, white masters fled and Payton's mother, Liza, remained on an abandoned plantation with her three children. Fearing that the master would return, Liza decided to take her children toward freedom. With young Payton in her arms, a second child clinging to her skirt, and the third walking alongside, she made her way to the river. Standing on the bank, she waved a white rag until a northbound boat stopped and took the family on board. After a while someone on the boat pointed to a high hill and said, "There sits the house of old General Lee."

Soon the Graysons were let off the boat and directed to Freedmen's Village. After some time passed, they met Sojourner Truth, who was recruiting people to go north. Truth said the place was too crowded; people should go where they could get work and do better. Payton's mother trusted Truth and did "whatever she said," Mr. Grayson later recalled.

In November 1866, Liza Grayson and her three children boarded a train with "four or five coaches" full of freedpeople heading north. The trip was paid for by the Freedmen's Bureau, with Truth and Griffing riding along to make sure people got off at the right places and met their local hosts.

When the travelers got to Battle Creek, Truth told Liza Grayson, "You better get off here. It is my home and I think you'll find it will make a good home for you." Mrs. Grayson no doubt told her children these details in years to come, so they would always remember their freedom story. "Sojourner wanted to help us help ourselves," Payton Grayson said. "That's the reason she had us come to Battle Creek and small towns, instead of to the big cities, so we could find work."

Mr. Grayson saw Truth from time to time in Battle Creek. She "was always busy, working for her people," giving lectures and preaching, he said. "She did a world's wonder of good for the colored people." She "took us out of the crowded freedmen's camp and brought us out here where we could find new homes and do something for ourselves."

———

Truth moved back to Michigan in 1867. Before the war she had bought a house in Harmonia (the spiritualist enclave on the outskirts of Battle Creek). That house was now occupied by Truth's daughter Sophia and her husband and children. Sojourner had friends in Battle Creek and wanted to be closer to them. But she had no money to buy property, having used what little she had to help the freedpeople. "I wish I had the money,"[36] she admitted. She may have mortgaged the house in Harmonia in order to buy property in Battle Creek.

The only place she could afford in Battle Creek was a lot with a barn but no house. "I am trying to get this barn fixed over into a house," Truth told Amy Post in a letter. "I mortgaged everything I have got" except "my body and a few rags." Sojourner wanted Amy to visit but asked her to bring food, she said, "for I am too poor to get anything to eat." Truth said she was digging out the cellar of the barn. The dirt was so heavy she could not shovel it and had to carry it out in her apron.[37] The result of her labors was a house with two rooms furnished with a cot, a table, and a few chairs.

While working on her house, Truth lived with Mrs. E. M. Rhoades in Battle Creek. In September 1867, Truth asked Rhoades to make an appeal for funds and have it printed in the *National Anti-Slavery Standard*. Truth "is indeed very poor," Rhoades wrote, because she devoted all her time and money to "taking care of the freed people" in Washington. Truth was helping others to find homes when she herself needed a home. Any contribution would help, because Truth "is very needy in the way of money and clothing." Mrs. Rhoades urged Truth's friends to "take hold of the matter at once" so that Truth could get her house ready before winter set in.[38]

Another friend who sought funds for Sojourner was Frances Titus, who would become Truth's closest friend and coworker in her old age. Truth first met Titus in 1856 at a Progressive Friends meeting in Battle Creek. And now Titus wrote to friends asking for money as well as warm clothing and blankets for Truth.

Frances Walling was born in 1816 to a Quaker family. She grew up in Cleveland and married Richard Titus, a prosperous miller. They moved to Battle Creek, where in 1867 Frances "started a school . . . to teach the fundamentals of reading, writing and arithmetic" to Black children. Richard Titus died in 1868, leaving Frances financially secure and free to devote herself to reform work. She was active in the woman's suffrage movement and became a founder of the Michigan Suffrage Association. After Truth moved to Battle Creek, she often visited Titus. In contrast to Sojourner's made-over barn, Frances lived in a colonial-style house, embellished with Victorian-style gables.[39] The friendship of these two women reached across race and class in a shared passion for human rights.

After Sojourner finished work on her house, she returned to public speaking. Titus did Truth's correspondence and helped arrange speaking engagements for her.[40] Truth either charged a small admission fee or received freewill offerings at the end of each speech. These funds, combined with the sales of her book and pictures, provided Truth some income.

Truth also began to gather her family. Her daughter Elizabeth and family moved in with her. Another daughter, Diana Corbin, lived with her husband and son nearby, according to the 1870 census.[41] Daughter Sophia and her family were already in Harmonia. Truth's adult children had few resources and could not support their mother. But for Sojourner, public speaking was more than an income stream; it was her divine vocation that started all those years ago with a vision of Jesus.

In the fall of 1868, Truth began a several-month tour of western and central New York. While she spoke for the freedpeople, she also campaigned for U. S. Grant. It was the first presidential election since the war—and the first in which Southern Black men could vote. Truth was counting on Grant to uphold Reconstruction in the South and, with it, Black citizenship. Ever since the war, Truth said, "rebels . . . have been murdering" Black people and any whites who try to help them. Truth told audiences that when she was with the freedpeople, she saws scars from slavery that made her heart bleed. "I said, 'oh God! Was there no mercy? Is there no justice?'" Truth warned against forgiving the rebels "before they repent."[42] She hoped that, as president, Grant would keep the rebels in check.

Truth's tour was a success. In the small hamlet of North Collins, she drew a crowd of six hundred to an outdoor meeting. Truth's speech could "melt away the prejudice of color and creed," an eyewitness said, because her preaching touched "the *Soul* of an audience." At another event, a throng packed the church where Truth was speaking—despite a heavy snowstorm. Her message there was "touching, and at times, extremely witty."[43] Another reporter described Truth as "witty, sarcastic, sensible and oftentimes profound."[44]

After Grant won the election, Truth could relax in the home of her friend Amy Post. In a letter to the *National Anti-Slavery Standard*, Post said that Truth suffered "lameness brought on by some long cold rides" during her speaking tour. Truth asked Post to send "gratitude for kind and helping hands, extended to her everywhere, from friends she never met before, as well as her old and well-tried friends." Truth would "continue in her public labors, not for her own good but for that of others both for this life and in the life to come."

Getting down to personal matters, Post said Truth had not smoked tobacco for three months.[45] A story about Truth and her smoking circulated for years. True or not, it was part of the lore about Sojourner. As the story goes, Truth on her travels once stayed in the home of a minister named Brother Goodrich, a strict temperance man and "a devoted hater of tobacco." One morning Goodrich saw Truth "puffing away with a long pipe in her mouth." Offended, her host asked Sojourner if she considered herself a Christian.

"Yes, brother," she replied. "I expect I am."

"Do you know the Scriptures say that nothing unclean shall enter the kingdom of heaven?"

"Yes Brother Goodrich, I have heard tell of it," Truth replied.

"Well," said Goodrich, "you smoke, and you cannot enter the kingdom of heaven, because there is nothing so unclean as the breath of a smoker. What do you say to that?"

"Why, Brother Goodrich," Sojourner replied. "When I go to heaven, I expect to leave my breath behind me."[46]

Truth knew that smoking was bad for her health. Friends encouraged her to quit, and she tried, but without success. In a letter to Post, Truth told of her prayer that God would make her "feel the necessity to give it up." She said that God answered her prayer: "I have had no taste or appetite to take it again." The part of her that longed for tobacco, God "filled . . . with his own love and spirit," Truth testified. It was now a "big prayer of her heart" for others to lose all desire for tobacco.[47]

———

Sojourner continued to worry about the freedpeople in Washington, convinced that her efforts to move them north were insufficient. Something more must be done. Early in 1870, Truth began to call for the government to set aside lands for freedpeople. Speaking in Providence, Rhode Island, she proclaimed that the North had a "duty" to grant lands in the West to "emancipated negroes."[48] The best way for freedpeople to become fully independent, Truth thought, was to grant them western lands. Unlike earlier colonization schemes that called for people to leave the country, Truth's plan was for freedpeople to stay within the United States, to go someplace where land was still available.

During the Civil War, some attempts to redistribute Southern lands to the freedpeople were made.[49] In January 1865, General Sherman ordered lands along the coastline of South Carolina, Georgia, and northern Florida to be given in forty-acre plots to former slaves who had worked those lands. Lincoln approved Sherman's order, but Johnson reversed it. Throughout the South, opposition from ex-Confederates made it hard for freedpeople to get or keep land.

To get land for freedpeople, it seemed necessary to look beyond the South. In 1869 President Grant tried to annex Santo Domingo (now the Dominican Republic) through a treaty. Grant wanted a naval base to strengthen US influence in the Caribbean. But he "also saw Santo Domingo as a kind of safety-valve solution for the biggest problem of Reconstruction—Ku Klux violence and the fate of millions of freedpeople in the South," writes Grant biographer David Blight. Grant was not for "large-scale colonization," but he saw Santo Domingo "as a Black country, a place where African Americans could choose to make a new home."[50] However, Grant's treaty failed to win Senate approval.

Truth went back to Washington in 1870 to get support for her idea. Celebrations were planned in the capital to mark the passing of the Fifteenth Amendment, which guaranteed that "the right of citizens of the United States to vote shall not be denied or abridged by the United States or by any state on account of race, color, or previous condition of servitude." In February, the required number of states ratified the amendment, with more soon to come. The amendment was set to pass into law on March 30.

On her return to the city, Truth was dismayed to find freedpeople still coming into the already-crowded refugee camps.[51] This strengthened her resolve to find a better place for them to settle. She spoke on this theme several times while she was in town.

She also took care of some personal business. Truth had received no pay from the government for her twenty-six months of work at Freedmen's Village and Hospital. And she had spent the small stipend she got from the New York agency that sponsored her Freedmen's Village work helping others. Now she met with General Howard, the head of the Freedmen's Bureau. He saw to it that Truth received back pay from the federal government: "three hundred and ninety dollars, being fifteen dollars per month for twenty-six months." While in Washington she "collected other funds to the amount of four hundred and fifty dollars." Truth could now pay off her mortgage in Battle Creek.

General Howard also helped Truth get an appointment to meet with President Grant. Truth was accompanied by Giles Stebbins, an antislavery activist who was part of Truth's network. They waited while other visitors met with the president. When Truth's turn came, Grant shook her hand. She said she was glad that Black men got the right to vote. She showed him her autograph book (which she called her "Book of Life"). Lincoln had signed it, and Grant signed it too. "I then handed him two of my photographs, which he took," Truth said. "He gave me a five-dollar bill, for which I thanked him."[52] Stebbins later described Grant as "reticent but kindly."[53] Truth agreed that Grant was "not such a talker as Lincoln, but he's a good man and thinks a great deal."[54]

While in Washington, Truth visited the Capitol building. She met and socialized with congressmen in the Marble Room, a "long narrow space just outside the Senate Chamber" that "served as a general meeting place." Its marble halls and "ornate mirrors" reflected the light of a huge chandelier and made for an impressive setting.[55] There Truth met several members of Congress and may have told them about her idea for western lands for freedpeople. Several congressmen signed her autograph book, including Senator Hiram Revels of Mississippi, who wrote "colored" after his name.[56]

The Marble Room, like other grand places in Washington, reminded Truth of slavery's role in building the Capitol. When she saw the majestic government buildings in Washington, she reflected that "*we helped* pay this cost. We [enslaved people] have been a source of wealth to this republic. . . . Our unpaid labor has been a stepping-stone to its financial success." Truth believed that the government owed something to the people who had toiled so long for no pay, and also that her people "would rather become independent" by their own labor than remain in the refugee camps.[57] Truth thought she knew what was best for others, but, as historian Nell Irvin Painter points out, Truth did not consult the freedpeople. "With the help of northern supporters, she would deliver freedpeople to a better place. She and her friends would *get* them out of Washington and *put* them in the West."[58]

On April 13, 1870, Sojourner Truth took part in a grand celebration of the ratification of the Fifteenth Amendment. According to the *Washington Evening Star*, a long parade of carriages, followed by hundreds marching on foot, wound its way out to Georgetown and back. Along the parade route, flags and bunting fluttered from homes and churches, stores and public buildings. Crowds gathered to watch the procession, and the day grew so hot that the carriages had to stop so the horses could rest and drink.

Late in the afternoon, the procession reached City Hall,[59] where the outdoor ceremony would take place. As a brass band played near the speakers' platform, the carriages unloaded their dignitaries and trundled off to make way for the crowd, which soon filled "the entire space in front of City Hall." Sojourner Truth was in the crowd, and one of the organizers spotted her and invited her to sit on the speakers' platform. After the opening prayer, several members of Congress spoke, with the band playing between speeches.

Every orator hailed the Fifteenth Amendment as the crowning glory of emancipation. One speaker said that all the races now lived "under a Constitution that acknowledges the rights of all." Another declared that "revolutions never go backward" and expressed his confidence that women would surely have the right to vote in less than five years.

Sojourner Truth sat on the platform awaiting her turn to speak. At the end of the program, her name was called, and she rose and went to the podium.

"Children," Truth said, "I came here today to join with you in this cele-bration . . . on this great day." Ever since she became free, she said, she strove to make the people see how wrong slavery was. Truth said she rejoiced in emancipation and the Fifteenth Amendment. But the fight for freedom wasn't over. "My children, much has been said to-day about men's rights, but I am a woman, and how could I be other than in favor of woman's rights? Now that the men have got their rights they must recognize the rights of the woman."

Truth also said she was proud of the name God gave her. "For the truth does not stay where there is any kind of slavery." She closed with good wishes: "may you always be as joyful as you are today." After the ceremony, people came forward to shake Truth's hand. That night the celebrations continued, with many homes and public buildings "brilliantly illuminated."[60]

———

Two years later when President Grant ran for reelection, Truth campaigned for him again. She could not vote, but she could speak, and she meant to get men—especially Black men—to vote for Grant. In the summer and fall of 1872, Truth stumped for Grant in Michigan. Grant's main opponent was New York newspaper editor Horace Greeley. Because Greeley said it was time to end Reconstruction, Truth said he was a traitor to all the North had fought for.

Truth told Blacks that their "safety . . . as a race depended on keeping the Government with those they knew to be their friends."[61] Grant was their proven friend because in his first term he suppressed the Ku Klux Klan (KKK) in South Carolina.

When Grant was first elected, violence against Blacks ran rampant in parts of the South. Black men risked their lives to vote or run for public office. Black teachers and farmers were threatened and murdered, as were white Northerners working with Blacks in the South. In South Carolina and Mississippi especially, the KKK did all in its power to keep Black men from voting.

President Grant at first used peaceful means to "strengthen federal over-sight of the voting process," writes historian Ron Chernow. But white suprem-acists responded with "the worst outbreak of domestic terrorism in American history." Grant finally had to send in federal troops to crush the KKK. US soldiers arrested thousands of Klan members and charged them with crimes, so that by 1872, "the Ku Klux Klan had been smashed in the South."[62]

Wherever Truth went, she found Black people strongly supporting Grant. They remembered Lincoln and emancipation and "believe[d] Grant and the Republican Party . . . to be their truest friends." The *New York Times* endorsed Truth's opinions, saying that "she knows whereof she speaks."[63] Truth's words came "as oracles to the colored people of America,"[64] said the *Brooklyn Union.* And the *National Republican* ventured that "Sojourner Truth is perhaps even better known" among Black people than "Frederick Douglass himself, and in her way wields a power among them second to none."[65]

Frederick Douglass also campaigned for Grant. He wrote editorials and pamphlets and delivered many speeches. Douglass hailed Grant's friendship with Lincoln, his victory over Lee, and his support for the Black vote. He told Northern audiences that the atrocities committed by the KKK "hardly seemed possible in a civilized land." But since President Grant cracked down on the Klan, "the scourging and slaughtering of our people have *so far* ceased."[66] How long this *so far* would last, nobody knew.

In recent years, the Equal Justice Initiative has documented two thousand lynchings in the South during Reconstruction—but the true number may be much higher. White supremacist violence was "carried out by vigilantes, terrorist groups like the Klan and the local authorities themselves." Nothing infuriated white supremacists like Black men voting and being elected to public office.[67] Sojourner Truth could not have known the extent of the violence in the South, but she knew it was rampant. When she called Grant's reelection a matter of life or death, she did not exaggerate.

The stakes were so high that Truth decided to vote on Election Day. She would follow the advice she gave to other women: "If you want your rights, take them." At the polling place in Battle Creek, Sojourner tried to convince election officials that she had a right to vote. They turned her away.[68]

16

Give Woman Her Rights

The Civil War was a hurricane that drew everything into its vortex, including the women's movement. Women's rights leaders became nurses, worked with the freedpeople, and raised money or gathered supplies for war-related causes. On the home front, women kept farms and businesses running and mourned their menfolk killed in the war. When the storm finally passed, more Northern women than ever before felt "entitled to the vote" because of the sacrifices they had made for their country.[1] "When such women come up now and ask for the right of suffrage," said Frances Gage, "who will deny their request?"[2] If slaves could be set free, women could get the vote too.

After the war, many reformers pushed for universal suffrage so that all women and all Blacks would get the vote together. After all, the women's movement was born out of the antislavery movement, and both were part of a larger quest for human rights. But politics forced painful choices, splitting the women's movement into two rival camps.

Truth was still in Washington in January 1866 when she received a letter from Susan B. Anthony. It concerned the proposed Fourteenth Amendment (to guarantee citizenship to everyone born in the United States, meaning that former slaves would be citizens). That was great good news—except that the proposed amendment described voters as "male inhabitants." Anthony's letter to Truth said that if the amendment got adopted with this language, it would shut "all women out from voting" for national offices forever. "It is a most atrocious proposition," she said, "and I know Sojourner Truth will say 'no' to it." Anthony asked Truth to make her mark on a petition, get others to sign, and perhaps speak to a congressman about it.[3] The letter was signed, "your friend, Susan B. Anthony." Truth's response to Anthony's letter is unknown.

Meanwhile, Truth's friend Josephine Griffing called for Black rights and women's rights to be joined. She too "fought to keep the word 'male' out of the Constitution, lest it preclude women's right to vote."[4]

Tensions within the women's movement "emerged everywhere in the wake of the 14th Amendment's inclusion of the word 'male.'"[5] It forced the issue of who would get their rights first: freedmen or women. The amendment was ratified in 1868 and included the word "male."

The Fifteenth Amendment would deal specifically with voting rights. Those who wanted women to get the vote first clashed with those who wanted Black men to get the vote first. Things became so polarized that many old allies became enemies. A strong advocate for Black men to vote first was the orator Wendell Phillips, known before the war as "abolition's golden trumpet." Truth knew Phillips well and often shared the podium with him at antislavery rallies before the war, when Phillips supported both abolition and women's rights. After the war, he said that the women's vote must wait until the Black man's vote was secure, lest the women's vote "harm Black men's chances."[6]

In eleven Northern states, Black men still could not vote, and none of the five border states allowed them the franchise. According to historian Leslie Schwalm, some Republicans wanted to restrict Black voting in the North but expand it in the South (to keep the Southern Democrats in check).[7] In the South, freedmen were voting under the protection of Union troops. Yet these new voters were often harassed, beaten, or murdered by ex-Confederates. The handwriting was on the wall: when Reconstruction ended, white Southern leaders would put a stop to Black voting. Black people would be excluded from politics and denied representative government. And if that happened, warned Phillips, all the blood and treasure the Union spent to win the Civil War would be for nothing.[8] Emancipation was not complete without the vote, and only a constitutional amendment could secure that. "This is the Negro's hour," Phillips famously declared. But if the amendment included the women's vote, Phillips warned, it would be soundly defeated. Better to take one issue at a time and win than overreach and lose all. Stanton and Anthony opposed Phillips, but Lucy Stone and other women's rights leaders were more receptive to Phillips's message.

In May 1866, women's rights and antislavery activists met in New York City to form a new organization: the American Equal Rights Association (AERA). Its goal was "to secure Equal Rights to all American citizens, especially the right of suffrage, irrespective of race, color or sex."[9] Frederick Douglass was one of the leaders. He saw Black men's voting rights as a matter of life or death. However, he said there was "no reason to discourage women suffragists from agitating for their cause as well."[10] Truth had many friends in the AERA but did not attend its first meeting because her work with the freedpeople took all her time.

The next year when the AERA met for the second time, Truth was there. During the convention, Truth gave three short speeches and led some singing. Loud cheers greeted Truth as she took the podium on the first day. "Friends," she began, "I am rejoiced that you are glad, but I don't know how you will feel when I get through." She knew her work among the freedpeople gave her a different perspective from that of many people in the audience. "I come from another field," she said, "the country of the slave." There slavery was partly destroyed but not entirely. "I want it root and branch destroyed. Then we will all be free indeed."[11]

Truth said she heard "a great stir" about Black men getting their rights but "not a word" about Black women. If Black men get the vote and Black women do not, "the colored men will be masters over the women, and it will be just as bad as it was before," Truth said. (Truth was not putting down Black men; she was saying that when only men can vote, women have no voice. And people with too much power can easily abuse it.) She was glad to see Black men getting their rights, but she wanted the same for Black women.

Many women came out of slavery with no skills, Truth said. And now that they had to work for pay, most can reach "no higher than a clothesline." Whatever pittance a freedwoman earns belongs to her husband (also true for whites). He can take her money and then "scold because there is no food." Black women needed their rights. Truth asked what freedom means if you have no rights.

Then Truth spoke of the legal system. "In the courts women have no right, no voice, nobody speaks for them." Some folks say women have no place in a courtroom, Truth said, because shysters and crafty lawyers will take advantage of the weaker sex. Truth rejected that argument. If the court is not fit for women, she said, it is not fit for men either. Let woman "have her rights there [in court] among the pettifoggers."

And what about money? Black or white, women got paid half of a man's wage. "What we want is a little money." Why do men complain when women ask them for money, Truth asked, and then prevent women from making their own money? If men want women to stop asking them for money, then women should get the same pay as men.

Change will be hard for men, Truth said. "You have been having our rights so long that you think, like a slaveholder, that you own us." Giving up long-held power "cuts like a knife," but the wound "will feel all the better when it closes up again."

Truth felt the women's vote was within reach, but another moment like this might not come for a long time. To preach the urgency of the moment, she told the gospel story of a paralyzed man waiting beside a healing pool. Only when the water stirred could this man be healed; but when the water stirred, nobody helped him get into the pool. To be healed of injustice you must get your rights. And to get your rights you need the help of those who already have their rights. And for that help to change things, it must come at an opportune time.

The Union victory opened the way for Black men to get the vote. Well and good, Truth said, but "I am for keeping [women's voting rights] going while things are stirring," she said. "If we wait till it is still, it will take a great while to get it going again." She wanted to wade in the water of change. "Now that there is a great stir about colored men getting their rights is the time for women to step in and have theirs," before it was too late.

Even without her full rights, Truth took full responsibility for her life. "I feel that I have to answer for the deeds done in my body just as much as a man. I have a right to have just as much as a man." Most women were taught to look to men for guidance, but Truth was guided by the Holy Spirit, who told her she was a child of God.

Sojourner was like a lone oak on a hilltop. "I suppose I am about the only colored woman that goes about to speak for the rights of colored women," she said. (There were other Black women speaking for their rights, but their paths seldom crossed with Truth's.)

Truth was about seventy years old when she spoke to the AERA, but she did not know her true age. She told the audience she was old enough to be the mother of everyone there. "I am above eighty years old; it is about time for me to be going. . . . I suppose I am kept here because something remains for me to do; I suppose I am yet to help break the chain." She closed by saying, "People in the North, I am going round to lecture on human rights. I will shake every place I go to."

As Truth spoke, Frances Gage listened closely. During part of the war, Gage had worked at a freedmen's camp in South Carolina. When her turn came to speak to the AERA convention, she said that she, like Truth, came "from the country of the slave." What she saw in the South convinced her that Black women must get the vote. She had met Black women who refused to marry, lest their husbands take their earnings. Freedwomen had told Gage that they did not want to go "under the heel of [their] husbands who are tyrants almost equal to [their] masters."[12] Gage said that since Black women had the greatest need, they should get the vote first.

Anthony and Stanton pushed back. They believed *white* women should get the vote first because they had more education than Black men. White women's vote would counteract the "incoming tide of ignorance, poverty and vice" heralded by Black male suffrage, said Anthony.[13]

George T. Downing, a successful Black restauranteur, challenged Stanton: Was she "willing to have the colored man enfranchised before the woman?" Stanton replied that it would be ideal if everyone could "go into the kingdom together." But she would not support Black men getting the vote *before* women because the freedmen might be even "more despotic" than white men. "The wisest order of enfranchisement was to take the educated classes first," Stanton said. Why ask "educated women . . . to stand aside while two million ignorant men are ushered into the halls of legislation?"[14]

Some of the white women disagreed with Stanton. Abby Kelley (who had traveled with Truth on the antislavery circuit) said that if Black men could not vote, they could be subjected to conditions just as bad as slavery. And Truth's friend Josephine Griffing said she rejoiced that two million Black men could now vote. "We must work by degrees, accepting every inch . . . gained toward the right." She believed that the Black man's vote was a step toward the women's vote.[15]

Truth made her second speech late in the afternoon—a tough time for any speaker. If the convention planners hoped Truth would wake up the audience, she did not disappoint. Truth used humor to debunk common notions of women's inferiority. And she used the Bible to argue for women's rights.

"Some folks say women aren't fit to vote," Truth said. Just look at Mary Magdalene: she had seven devils, so that must prove women are unfit to vote or to govern. But "seven devils were nothing compared to that man who had a legion in him." Laughter rippled through the audience.

Now as for the man who had a legion, Truth continued, "when Jesus cast out those devils, they didn't know where to go. So they asked that they might go into the swine, [thinking that] was as good a place to go as the man they came out from." Truth said that the devils wanted to go into the hogs, because hogs are such selfish animals. "And man is so selfish that he has got women's rights and his own too, and yet he won't give women their rights. He keeps them all to himself." By now the crowd rocked with laughter.

"Now about that woman" (whose seven devils were cast out), Truth pressed. "She loved Jesus [and] followed him." And that man (whose legion of devils went into the swine) "wanted to follow Jesus too, but Jesus told him to go home, and didn't seem to want to have him round." Truth told more Bible stories in which men went astray but women followed Jesus. "See what a spirit woman has! Just let women have their rights, and the truth will reign triumphant."

Near the very end of the convention, Truth gave her third speech. She said she was working for the day when "the colored people" would "own their soul and body." That day finally came, though she was sorry "it came with blood." And the women "are now trying for liberty that requires no blood." Women want the vote. "Men," she said, "give them what belongs to them; they ask it kindly too. I ask it kindly." And quickly. "It can be done in a few years. How good it would be."

She said she paid taxes every year on her house in Battle Creek, but she could not vote. Didn't paying taxes and voting go together? Truth declared she would not die until she could vote. "Now, if you want me to get out of the world, you had better get the women voting soon."[16] Truth closed out with a song.

The AERA kept working for both women's and Black male suffrage, seeking to make headway in state campaigns about voting. They lost in both Kansas and New York in 1867. The hawk and the buzzard—Truth's old metaphor for the Blacks and the women—had once been allies against the white man, but now they were rivals contending for the vote.

On February 26, 1869, Congress passed a draft of the Fifteenth Amendment. "The right of citizens of the United States to vote shall not be denied
or abridged by the United States or by any State on account of race, color,
or previous condition of servitude," it said. Women were left out. Stanton
and Anthony rejected the Fifteenth Amendment and at that point dropped
all pretense of supporting the vote for all.[17] Stanton wrote that she deserved
to "be enfranchised before Hans, Yung, Tung, Patrick and Sambo."[18] She
objected not only to Black men getting the vote before women, but also to
enfranchising German, Asian, and Irish males. "Should women stand aside
and see 'Sambo' walk into the Kingdom first?" Stanton demanded. Historian Faye Dudden writes that by 1869 Stanton and Anthony were using their
newspaper, the *Revolution*, "to oppose the Fifteenth Amendment," going so
far as to engage in fearmongering about Black men. Stanton claimed that the
Black men's vote "under the 15th Amendment would 'culminate in fearful
outrages on womanhood especially in the southern states.'"[19]

Meanwhile, Lucy Stone and other moderate feminists supported the Fifteenth Amendment—even though it meant that women would not get the
vote at this time. The American Equal Rights Association, torn apart by
these conflicts, disbanded on May 15, 1869.

Stanton and Anthony immediately founded the National Woman's
Suffrage Association (NWSA). They opposed ratification of the Fifteenth
Amendment and made no commitment to racial equality. Later that year,
Lucy Stone founded a rival group—the American Woman's Suffrage Associ-
ation (AWSA). They supported the Fifteenth Amendment as a necessity for
Black men but said the women's vote must come next. For twenty years, the
two rival groups pursued their own strategies, before finally coming together
to form the National American Woman's Suffrage Association.

Truth had friends on both sides of the women's movement schism. As
noted in the previous chapter, Truth was in Washington in 1870 to celebrate
the passage of the Fifteenth Amendment and used the opportunity to call for
women's rights. Not long after that, Truth went to New York, where she saw
Elizabeth Cady Stanton. "I hope, dear Sojourner," Stanton wrote in Truth's
Book of Life, "that you will be enfranchised before you leave us for the better
land. Your True Friend, Elizabeth Cady Stanton, New York, May 4, 1870."[20]

Ten days later, Truth attended the rival organization—the American
Woman Suffrage Association (which supported the amendment). The

AWSA met in Steinway Hall, a concert venue in lower Manhattan. Despite a driving rain, the place was filled to its capacity of two thousand. Speakers included Rev. Henry Ward Beecher and other "luminaries," whose presence signaled "respectability to friends and foes."[21]

Truth spoke briefly in the afternoon session. She said that women should not have to beg for the right to vote because it was already theirs. "Woman . . . ought to have *all* rights. If she doesn't have them how are her sons and daughters to know about their rights? I don't want children to be saying to their mothers, 'you're nothing but a woman!' They learn this from their fathers. What kind of men will they make, I'd like to know?" Truth predicted that within a few years, women would be elected to Congress. "We'll have women lawyers, and your old brandy-nosed pettifoggers will have to get out of the way."

Truth told the journalists at the AWSA convention to report her speech "in a grammatical and smooth way."[22] She was tired of having her speech rendered in a dialect that wasn't hers to begin with. Someone must have listened to her, for the *New York Tribune* said Truth spoke "in a clear, resonant voice" and even reported the content of her speech. However, Truth had reason to be wary. Many newspapers ignored her message. Instead, they repeated old tales about her, speculated about her age, or made fun of her person or speech. Some were openly, even gleefully, racist. When Truth spoke at a Presbyterian church in Springfield, New Jersey, a writer ridiculed her as "that lively old negro mummy . . . a crazy, ignorant, repelling negress," whose "guardians" should "restrict her entirely to private life."[23] This hateful letter was included in a later version of Truth's *Narrative* and *Book of Life*, to show what she had to contend with.

Sojourner never shrank from controversy, and sometimes she critiqued her friends in the women's movement. At a woman's rights conference in Providence in the fall of 1870, Truth lampooned women's fashions as confining, impractical, and downright silly. The latest fashions did not help women prove their equality but reinforced stereotypes of female frivolity and helplessness. Truth was quite willing to ruffle the feathers of her friends when they failed to live up to their own ideals. In Providence in 1870, she told an audience:

> I'm awful hard on dress, you know. Women, you forget that you are the
> mothers of creation; you forget your sons were cut off like grass by the

war, and the land was covered with their blood; you rig yourselves up in panniers and Grecian-bend backs and flummeries; yes, and mothers and gray-haired grandmothers wear high-heeled shoes and humps on their heads, and put them on their babies, and stuff them out so that they keel over when the wind blows. O mothers, I'm ashamed of ye! What will such lives as you live do for humanity? When I saw them women on the stage at the Woman's Suffrage Convention the other day, I thought, "what kind of reformers be you, with goose-wings on your heads, as if you were going to fly, and dressed in such ridiculous fashion, talking about reform and women's rights?" [It appears] to me, you had better reform yourselves first. But Sojourner is an old body, and will soon get out of this world into another, and wants to say when she gets there, Lord, I have done my duty, I have told the whole truth and kept nothing back.[24]

In the decades after the Civil War, African American women were more likely to identify "with the suffragists who had supported the Fifteenth Amendment than those who had opposed it."[25] Even so, both NWSA and the AWSA were primarily white, and they seldom encouraged or welcomed the Black women who attended their meetings.[26] Black women formed their own organizations, where they could have their own leaders and set their own priorities. In 1896, a merger of several Black women's organizations created the National Association of Colored Women (NACW), to work on civil rights issues, including the vote. Sojourner Truth did not live to see the founding of the NACW, but she was among its foremothers. All women who vote, regardless of their race, owe a debt of gratitude to Sojourner Truth.

17

"I Go in for Agitating"

On New Year's Day 1871, Sojourner Truth was in Boston to celebrate the eighth anniversary of the Emancipation Proclamation at Tremont Temple. The large Baptist church had a long history of antislavery activism and was packed to standing room only for this event.

The choir opened with an anthem, followed by Scripture reading and prayer. Truth was the last of several speakers. She told of her life as a slave and how God changed her hatred for white people into love. Since then, Truth said, "the love has continued and kept me among the white people." But her love for white people was that of an activist seeking change. "I go in for agitating," Truth said. And "there is work belongs with agitating."

Then she got down to cases. The freedpeople in Washington were living on the government, Truth said. It was costing a lot of money, and instead of helping the freedpeople, "it degrades them worse and worse." She would rather see them "go west where they can make something of themselves by their own labor."

So, who should make this happen? Truth asked. Not "the good people in the South." They might be willing to change, but "the rebels won't let them." Some say let the freed folks take care of themselves, Truth said. But "you've taken all that away from them. Ain't got nothin' left." You can't expect people to pull themselves up if they don't even have a bootstrap to pull on. Now if the Northerners got a place out west for the former slaves, "they would soon be able to be a people among you." Not a *de*pendent people, but an *in*dependent people. "That is my commission," said Truth: to get lands in the West.

The audience had work to do too. First, "agitate" for lands in the West. Then get the freedpeople to move there. And finally, teach the people to "read one part of the time and to work the other part of the time."

Just then a man got up and walked out, interrupting Truth and distracting her audience. "Hold on," Truth said. *Some folks like to leave before they get a chore to do.* Her quip made the audience laugh and showed that Truth was in charge. "I tell you these things," said Truth, "so that when a paper comes for you to sign you can sign it." (Truth referred to a petition she was preparing.) Then the pastor gave the benediction, and the meeting ended at 9:30 p.m. Truth stayed to answer questions, proving herself still "apt and keen at repartee."[1]

Truth was going to get up a petition asking Congress for lands in the West for freedpeople. She found a writer, probably Gilbert Haven, "a radical Methodist editor."[2] The petition addressed the Senate and House of Representatives:

> Whereas, through the faithful and earnest representations of Sojourner Truth (who has personally investigated the matter), we believe that the freed colored people in and about Washington, dependent upon Government for support, would be greatly benefitted and might become useful citizens by being placed in a position to support themselves:
>
> We, the undersigned, therefore earnestly request your honorable body to set apart for them a portion of the public land in the West, and erect buildings thereon for the aged and infirm, and otherwise so to legislate as to secure the desired results.[3]

Truth used her own money to print copies of the petition. She solicited signatures wherever she went; others helped gather signatures too. Some trusted friends agreed to collect the signed petitions from each state and send them to Washington.[4] Sometimes people gladly signed the petition. But if any balked, Truth spoke her mind: "How is it that with all your opportunities for reading and writing you don't take hold and do anything? My God, I wonder what you are in the world for!"[5]

Truth's petition asked for "public land in the West" but didn't say where. Then she received a letter from a Mr. Smith in Kansas, whom Truth had never met. Smith expressed admiration for her work and invited her to come to Topeka. He offered to pay her train fare and other expenses and welcomed her to stay at his home.[6] Truth took Smith's letter as a sign from God. She had it printed in the *National Standard* and mentioned it in many of her speeches.

Kansas was a symbol of freedom and struggle to many abolitionists. After years of guerilla warfare over slavery, it entered the Union as a free state in 1861. At that time, several hundred Black people were living in Kansas. After the Civil War, "free and cheap land provided by the Homestead Act and the railroads attracted many settlers," according to the Kansas Historical Society. "By 1870 just over 17,000 Blacks lived in Kansas . . . concentrated primarily in the eastern part of the state."[7] Truth was eager to see Kansas for herself, but first she wanted to gather more signatures.

Truth took her campaign to Northampton, Massachusetts, where she still had many friends. Early in 1871, she held several meetings in the area. Several of these were arranged by Samuel Hill, her old friend from the Northampton Association. Having already done so much speaking and traveling, Truth was exhausted by the time she reached Northampton. She had no time to rest before her first engagement. She told her audience, "Children, I have come here to-night like the rest of you to hear what I have got to say."[8] A wave of friendly laughter let Truth ease into her message on behalf of the freedpeople.

Truth believed Congress must do what the majority demanded, so she was out to "make majorities." And to do that, said the *National Standard*, she had to change minds. Her first appeal was to simple justice: the freedpeople, she said, built the nation and deserve recompense for their unpaid labor. Next, she appealed to thrift and common sense: it would be "cheaper and better for the government" to give lands in the West to the freedpeople than to keep them in poverty and idleness at government expense. "Giving lands in the west would pay a little of the great debt we owe this long-oppressed people," Truth summed up, "while at the same time leading them to support themselves, enrich the nation and become useful citizens." Therefore, the people should "petition Congress to do this work at once."[9]

Truth had a friend write down her words to send to the *National Standard*. "I have been making my appeal to the people," she said. "I have been hoping somebody would print a little of what I am doing, but the papers seem to be content simply in saying how old I am."[10]

In the spring and summer of 1871, Truth traveled widely. When she met whites who thought that they bore no responsibility for slavery, she challenged them and urged them to help the freedpeople. She said she was giving her audience "a chance to get in on" what the "spirit of prophecy told her."[11]

Around this time, Truth saw Frederick Douglass and collected his signature for her *Book of Life*. "I rejoice to find you strong in health, vigorous in mind, warm in heart and as usual, full of noble purposes,"[12] Douglass wrote. But if they talked about Truth's Kansas plan, Douglass may have voiced misgivings. He always saw "integration as the only path to Black progress," writes Margaret Washington; he opposed "any type of relocation" or colonization. Before the Civil War, Truth had also opposed colonization and "embraced racial integration." But now during Reconstruction, the suppression of Black rights in the South "pushed her toward separation."[13] These two strategies for Black empowerment—integration versus separation—were under debate already and remain so today.

Truth left for Kansas in September 1871, accompanied by her beloved grandson Sammy. Now about twenty years old, Sammy was a seasoned traveler and a great help to his grandmother. "Her grandson is with her and takes the very best care of her," wrote a friend who hosted them in Wisconsin. Truth held several meetings along the way and "collected enough to pay all of her traveling expenses."[14]

Once in Kansas, Truth and Sammy moved from place to place and lodged with friends. Sojourner addressed Black and white audiences in many eastern Kansas towns. Crossing the river into Missouri, she spoke at a Black Baptist church in Quindaro, on the outskirts of Kansas City. It had been an abolitionist settlement and a station on the Underground Railroad; after the war, a freedmen's university was located there. Quindaro was part of the larger story of Black migration that grew after the Civil War and continued through the 1880s.[15]

Truth said that the freedpeople must "begin to *realize* they are now citizens and own themselves forever more." After Truth's speech, Sammy read out the petition, and they left copies of it for people to sign. A reporter from the *Wyandotte Gazette* who attended this event said Truth "has a gift of thought and speech from on high, such as is seen but once in a life time."[16]

Truth's reception by the press was mixed. Several Kansas newspapers reported Truth's talks favorably and gave the substance of her message. The

Western Home Journal said Truth "is a very smart old woman, and says a great many very sensible things."[17] But other reporters belittled her, claiming that she was really a man and dismissing her as ignorant and old, a relic from times gone by.[18]

———

"Reservation" was a word Truth sometimes used for land for freedpeople. It was already a loaded word. "Old Sojourner Truth's idea that the Government ought to set apart a reservation for the freedmen seems to us in every respect a good one," reported the *Daily Kansas Tribune*. Since the government gave vast tracts of land to the railroads and set aside huge parcels for Indian reservations, it could also designate lands for freedpeople. But Truth may not have known that the reservations being formed in the West were places of defeat, poverty, and isolation. The reservation system gave white people control of the best lands, leaving native tribes to subsist on poor land.

In "A Reservation for the Freedmen," the *Daily Kansas Tribune* expressed typical attitudes about race. Whites sent "agricultural implements, agents, teachers, etc. to the Indians," who were "intractable and averse to lives of industry," said the *Tribune*. How much better to provide these things to freedpeople, "who are naturally teachable, and who have been workers all their lives."[19] The writer saw Native Americans as too wild to work, and Blacks as docile folk who were more likely to do the white folks' bidding.

Meanwhile, Kansas railroads already had Jim Crow and "whites only" cars. Truth saw this for herself when she rode from Kansas City to Leavenworth on the Missouri Pacific Railroad. As she started to board, a conductor and the brakeman told her she must ride in a car further back. Truth refused to budge. She "was finally, but very ungraciously, admitted" to the railcar of her choice, reported the *Wyandotte Gazette*. The *Gazette* lamented that Truth, an illustrious woman now getting up in years, had been so ill-treated.[20] But the *Gazette* stopped short of calling for equal treatment of all Black people on the trains. An exception was made for Truth, but the Jim Crow system remained in place.

All her adult life Truth spoke out for temperance: the movement to curb excessive drinking. But when Truth spoke to the Topeka Temperance Society in February 1872, she said that she believed in prohibition: the campaign to make the manufacture and sale of alcohol illegal. The prohibition movement was gaining strength, with the Woman's Christian Temperance Union to be founded the following year. Because women were often at the mercy of alcoholic husbands, Truth and many others linked women's rights with prohibition.[21]

Truth came to believe that alcohol should be banned. "I believe that it is at the bottom of a great many crimes," she said. Most likely "it is not the man that murders, but whisky." Truth had no confidence in the practice of "taking the pledge," that is, signing a document declaring that you would never drink again. Taking the pledge didn't stick, she said. If a man drank too much, he should "get to work, and carry food and clothing to his poor starving wife and children." And if the rest of us treated these "converts as human beings should be treated . . . fewer would backslide."[22]

When Sojourner was speaking at a temperance meeting in Kansas, she noticed tobacco juice all over the floor, and an expression of disgust came over her face. The Methodists used to "kneel in the house of God during prayers," she said, but "how could anyone kneel on *these* floors?" Truth was on a goodwill mission to Kansas, but she would not hide her principles. "If Jesus was here, he would scourge you from this place."[23] For Truth, cleanliness was next to godliness.

Sojourner and Sammy left Kansas in the spring of 1872. Truth returned to Battle Creek "with scrolls of signatures and trophies of success," wrote her friend Frances Titus, "over which she felt as jubilant as 'great Caesar bringing captives home to Rome.'"[24] Truth saw each signature she gathered as a vote for her Kansas plan. She meant to get even more signatures and then take the petitions to Washington, DC.

And yet, Truth did not identify a particular place in Kansas for Black settlement. Her trip did not persuade more freedpeople to leave Washington for points west. And she was no closer to getting government action.[25] She was like a soloist with no orchestra to back her up.

After campaigning for Grant's reelection (as noted in the previous chapter), Truth went back to work on her Kansas project. In 1873 she traveled around Michigan, speaking in Black and white churches and collecting signatures on her petition. When she stayed with friends in Detroit, one of her hosts described her appearance in a journal: Truth's clothes were simple, like Quaker garb. Sojourner wore a plain, dark dress and a red vest, topped by a long white apron. A white turban crowned her head. As she sat in a big straight-back chair, her elbows on her knees and her hard, knotty hands clasped, one could clearly see the stump where her right index finger had been lost in a farming accident long ago. Truth spoke with "unusual power" about the poor folk she had seen in Washington and wondered why "Congress was so reluctant" to do anything for them.[26]

Meanwhile, Sojourner herself lived in near poverty. Freewill offerings from her talks and the sales of her pictures and *Narrative* did not cover her basic needs. At summer's end in 1873, Amy Post received a letter from Truth. "I write to you to get a little money. I am hard up. I don't want to mortgage my house because I can't pay it again. Please send right off and I will pay you. S. T."[27] She may have sent similar letters to other friends. Perhaps she did get some help, for by October she was in Lafayette, Indiana, giving a lecture at the AME church entitled "The Condition of the Poor Colored People in the South."[28]

At last Truth was ready to go to Washington. She left Battle Creek in the early spring of 1874. Her grandson Sammy joined her en route, and they traveled on together. Truth had entrusted various people to send signed petitions to Washington, but she may also have brought some with her. Along the way they stopped in Baltimore (and probably other places) for Truth to give talks and get more signatures.[29]

When she got to Washington, Truth heard bad news: Senator Charles Sumner had died on March 11, 1874. It was a hard loss for her, since she had been counting on Sumner's support in the Senate for her Kansas project. "Mr. Sumner said he'd help me, but the Lord took him,"[30] Truth lamented.

Sojourner needed people with influence to promote her project in Congress. With Sumner gone, Truth turned to General Howard, whom she knew from the Freedmen's Bureau. "Howard advocated Black land ownership," wrote historian Carleton Mabee, but was reluctant to ask for "government aid to Blacks to help them secure it." However, Howard loaned Truth money and helped arrange a speaking engagement for her at Washington's First Congregational Church. Howard also wrote to Massachusetts congressman and former Union general Benjamin Butler, asking him "to help the freedmen by trying 'an experiment in the direction that Truth indicates.'"[31] Butler's response (if any) is unknown; but Truth later claimed that both Howard and Butler "approved of my general recommendation."[32]

Butler did nothing to bring Truth's plan to Congress. He was in charge of getting the Civil Rights Bill through the House, and would take on nothing else. This bill, drafted by the late senator Sumner and coauthored by Butler, would ban discrimination in public accommodations and transportation and guarantee the right of Black men to serve on juries. The Civil Rights Bill—also known as the Enforcement Act or the Force Act—passed in March 1875. It was the last major legislation of Reconstruction, and was later ruled unconstitutional by the Supreme Court.

Truth's Kansas project lacked political support. There is no surviving record that she ever presented her petitions to congressmen. Even if she did, the politicians knew that many voters in the North "believed that government had already done enough for the victims of slavery."[33] Northern whites were getting weary of Reconstruction, but Southern white resistance to Reconstruction held firm.

Truth blamed the failure of her Kansas project on the Civil Rights Bill. "After the slaves were freed I traveled four years getting signers to a petition asking Congress to give public lands to the ex-slaves," Truth later said. "The Civil Rights bill was up and crowded mine out." Truth thought that the Civil Rights Bill "did the Black man no good." Perhaps she meant that it made life harder for Black people because it provoked a white backlash. Besides, she believed that if rights were only on paper, it was better to own land.[34]

Four years had passed since Truth had been in Washington, and she was eager to see for herself how the freedpeople were doing. She sat up in the gallery of the House of Representatives and listened to Black people testify about slavery.[35] Before the Civil War, it was almost unheard of for African Americans to observe Congress in action. But "as Reconstruction dawned, Black men and women of various classes and social positions demanded a place in the public life of the capitol."[36]

Truth also paid a visit to the police court. What she saw that day, she later told audiences, was Black "people being thrown into jails, and their children growing up in vice and ignorance."[37] Indeed, Blacks were often harassed "by local whites, and they could not expect fair treatment by police and other law enforcement officials," writes historian Kate Masur. The most common charges against the freedpeople were vagrancy, theft, and prostitution.[38]

A reporter from the National Republican spotted Truth at the police court, and described her as an "old colored woman" sitting quietly in the back, watching the workings of the court "with absorbing interest."[39] The reporter interviewed Truth. They discussed her age, and she reminisced about her visit to President Lincoln ten years earlier. But Truth was not stuck in the past. She said it pleased her greatly that Hiram Revels, a Black man, had become a United States senator and held "the very seat Jeff Davis disgraced." Truth was full of hope that things could change. "I tell you, child, the world moves, and all things in it."

This same reporter came to hear Truth speak at a Congregational church. She described her visit to the police court, where freedpeople accused of crimes waited to see the judge. Life was so bad on the streets, Truth said, that some people might feel safer in jail. They would be much better off in Kansas, she declared.

Just the other day, Truth told her audience, she saw a Black woman begging in the street. This woman had a little music box about the size of a coffee mill. She cranked the music box and begged for pennies to buy food, while her children, crouched beside her, looked like heaps of rags. "It is an outrage," Truth declared. She would rather see the "beggars put to work and their children doused with water and scrubbed." Truth told her audience that slavery was to blame for the condition of the freedpeople after the war. "God will hold you responsible for these crying wrongs . . . which require the daily routine of the Police Court." The suffering she saw on the streets must not be passed down to the next generation, she said. The freedpeople needed a place to make a life for themselves.

Truth spoke of her own enslavement. "I have been robbed of every God-given right—children, husband, education and everything," she said. Yet God directed her life, she declared. The same God who had permitted her to be the subject of a great wrong could enable her to do a great work. Therefore, said Truth, "I want to do something for my race while I live, so that when I quit my work here, I shall go to the sweet rest of Heaven."

Truth said she had tried moving freedpeople herself, but it was too big a job for even the most dedicated volunteers. The government needed to take action. "I wish I was a Congressman; indeed I do," Truth said. Then *she* would make things happen. Apparently, a titter of laughter ran through the audience, as though they thought Truth was joking. "You laugh," she said, "but you don't know how far a toad can jump."

When she finished speaking, her petition was read "by a male attendant," probably her grandson Sammy. Signatures were gathered and a collection taken up for Sojourner's benefit, "during which she entertained the audience with songs from her slave life."[40]

Truth was invited to a May Day benefit concert for the Lincoln Mission Sabbath School. Located near Howard University, the school served about six hundred Black children. The concert program included several songs performed by the children and the teachers.[41] A newspaper reported that Sojourner Truth sang two antislavery songs and gave a short speech. "Great respect was shown to her"—but not by everyone. When she was speaking, a few Black youth "snickered." She ignored their rudeness until she had finished her speech. And then she pointed at them and gave them "such a 'talking to' as they will not probably forget for many a day." She reprimanded them for making fun of a woman who came there to do them good and who was old enough to be their grandmother. The offenders were silent, but the audience gave Truth "thunders of applause." Truth could "paddle her own canoe," a reporter wrote, despite "her weight of years."[42]

Sojourner Truth made news by worshiping at Methodist Metropolitan Church, where President Grant often attended. There she "partook of the communion . . . being the first colored person" ever to do so, according to the *Los Angeles Evening Express*.[43]

———

That fall, Truth left Washington abruptly. Her grandson Sammy suffered from a swelling in his neck, and she decided to take him back to Michigan. When they arrived in Battle Creek, Sammy had a large and painful growth, thought to be goiter.

Truth herself was in pain from a gangrenous sore on her leg. For many weeks she could not walk. Truth sought help from several doctors and finally turned to a veterinarian. "I got a horse doctor who took the swelling out. . . . It seems I am a horse," she said. Truth's horse joke must have amused her, for she told it often. Truth "says she is more like a horse than any animal" and thinks the veterinarian is "the proper one to employ," Frances Titus told a friend.[44]

Truth's jest about her own health could not hide her dismay as Sammy's health worsened. He was diagnosed with a subclavian aneurism (a weakness or bulging in the wall of the subclavian artery, located below the collarbone). Sojourner got the best medical care she could for Sammy, borrowing money to pay for it. A complicated surgery was done on Sammy in December 1874 in an attempt to save his life.

Sammy struggled on as Sojourner prayed and kept vigil. On February 24, 1875, Sammy Banks died. He was twenty-three years old. Sammy had been to Truth like the son she had lost so long ago. She had helped to raise Sammy, and he may have been the only family member who took an active part in her work. Truth was brought low by the loss of her beloved grandson, traveling companion, and friend. "Would to God I had died for thee,"[45] Truth lamented. He was the future she would not live to see, but now he was cut short, and with him, many of Truth's hopes.

Samuel Banks was buried at Oak Hill Cemetery in Battle Creek. To pay for his doctor bills and burial, Truth remortgaged her little house.[46] Once more she sought financial help from friends. Among the respondents were William Lloyd Garrison and Wendell Phillips.[47]

Another great abolitionist, Parker Pillsbury, visited Truth around this time. He described her dwelling as a "miserable little house" of only two rooms, in which were a cot, a cookstove, and a couple of chairs. Truth became so poor that she could not afford to subscribe to a Battle Creek newspaper, and asked the editor if he could "continue sending her the paper" in hopes that she would be able to pay later.

During Truth's grief and slow recovery from her own illness, her friend Frances Titus took action on Sojourner's behalf. Titus added new material to Truth's *Narrative* and had it published. Truth was grateful that the expanded version of her book "was got up to pay my debts and help me in my old age." Since Truth was in debt, Titus advanced $350 to the publisher,[48] trusting Sojourner to repay her later on. Titus "seldom mentioned her own name" in the book, and like Olive Gilbert before her, "kept her name off the title page."[49] She hoped that book sales would generate income for Truth, keep Sojourner's story before the public, and describe Truth's life and labors in the twenty-five years since the *Narrative of Sojourner Truth* first came out. Titus reprinted the original *Narrative* and added material from Truth's *Book of Life*, resulting in a book nearly twice as long as the original.

The *Book of Life* consisted of three scrapbooks in which Truth kept newspaper clippings, letters, and autographs.[50] Truth's "trusted scribe," Frances Titus, selected the items to be printed in the book.[51] The clippings reported on Truth's speeches and travels, her work with the freedpeople, and her meeting with Lincoln.

The autographs were from personal friends and from famous people, including Presidents Lincoln and Grant, Frederick Douglass, Elizabeth Cady Stanton, and Susan B. Anthony. These autographs often included a brief message. When Truth wanted a signature from someone, she would ask, "Don't you want to write your name in the Book of Life?" The New Testament uses the phrase "Book of Life" several times, suggesting that God knows those who love and serve him and is preparing their eternal reward; so when Truth asked people to write their names in the Book of Life, she was giving them a holy invitation.

Like Olive Gilbert (who collaborated with Sojourner on the 1850 *Narrative*), Frances Titus made mistakes. Titus's foreword to the new version added ten years to Truth's enslavement and twenty years to her age. Titus also left gaps in Truth's story. Little is said about Truth's family or her friendships with Black people. One is left wondering if all of Truth's close friends were white, and if so, why.

Titus portrayed Truth's religion as "exceedingly practical," all about doing good to others. "'How can you expect to do good to God,' Truth asked, 'unless you first learn to do good to each other?'" And Titus made Truth's view of the afterlife sound like spiritualism, quoting Truth as comparing death to "stepping out of one room into another, stepping out into the light."[52] Truth may have said this, but her view of the afterlife also included judgment and justice at the mercy seat of God.

Truth said she could remember seeing pictures of hell, perhaps used to promote revivals. She recalled one picture that showed a narrow stair leading to heaven on one side and a "terrible abyss" on the other side, with smoke rolling up from it, and "numberless human beings swimming around in flames." The evil one had a "long snout and tail" and was stirring the people around with a pitchfork. When she first saw this frightful image, she said to herself, "My God, that is hell, sure enough." But as she got older, she found out there was no such thing as hell, "and the narrow stairs only showed the narrowness of the mind that conceived the picture." She said she had found out that "God's brightness and goodness and glory is hot enough to scorch all the sinners in the world."[53]

Truth's faith was distinctly Christian and deeply African American. Sojourner believed that God created all people equal. She loved Jesus and prayed in the power of the Spirit. She worshiped a God of mercy and justice. "I talk to God and God talks to me," she often said. She believed that God answers prayer, and she did not rule out miracles. Truth's own experience proved to her the power of divine guidance and providence. As a perfectionist, she pursued holiness both for herself and for society. She put body and soul into worship—especially singing. Her early vision of Jesus guided her life, and she may well have had other luminous experiences that she kept between herself and God.

Though a Christian, Truth did not find a resting place with any one church or denomination. Like Noah's dove, she circled the flood waters, looking for a place to call home. In 1879 Truth told a reporter that "she had been a Methodist till that church outgrew her; it had changed but not she."[54] Modern Pentecostalism had not yet emerged as a movement in Truth's time, but its seeds were already growing in Holiness churches (offshoots of Methodism) and in many African American churches. Its marks were ecstatic worship, faith in supernatural powers, charismatic leadership, and openness to new revelations from the Holy Spirit. These qualities are not emphasized in the *Narrative of Sojourner Truth* because, as historian Nell Irvin Painter wrote, Truth's story was told by "politically minded reformers."[55]

These reformers were not attuned to the transcendent dimension of Truth's religious experience. They did glimpse Truth's charismatic gifts: her singing, her preaching, and the power she had to change people's hearts and minds. In Truth's lifetime, many observers commented on Truth's powers of speech and song. But, as scholar Judith Castleberry has observed, "When African American women's religious work is viewed through the lens of civic and political work the nuances of spiritual labor and spiritual authority can be obscured."[56] Truth's faith often gets "obscured" when her life is seen only through the lens of social reform. And yet it was Sojourner Truth's quest for holiness that propelled her work for human rights.

18

"My Name Was Up"

"There is no language between heaven and earth that can express how much I wish to see you since Sammy died," Truth told a friend. She was still too lame to get around, yet she hoped to get better in time to go to Philadelphia for the Centennial Exposition, a world's fair commemorating one hundred years since the signing of the Declaration of Independence. The centennial would run for several months in 1876. Truth at first planned to go in May and then delayed her trip until fall, hoping that she would be stronger by then. "If the Lord will spare me until that great time in Philadelphia I will see you all."[1] She told another friend that she was "very anxious" to get to the centennial, where, she continued, "I think I can sell my books fast and then I can pay my debts."[2]

That fall Truth began her journey, but in Chicago a health crisis (probably a stroke) forced her to return to Battle Creek. The right side of her body was temporarily paralyzed, and her eyesight, poor for years, now seemed to be failing entirely.

Sojourner recovered . . . reluctantly. "I really thought to myself the Lord wanted me to die while my name was up," Sojourner later told a reporter. When she started getting better, "I felt quite sad, almost . . . but the Lord has been good; he has given me business to do and has moved me to do it." Truth regained the use of her limbs, and her vision improved, prompting her to give thanks that "The Lord put new glasses in the windows of my soul."[3]

Ulysses S. Grant declined to run in 1876 for a third term as president, so the Republicans nominated the former Civil War general Rutherford B. Hayes.

The Democrats chose Samuel Tilden, the governor of New York. For the first time since the Civil War, it seemed possible for a Democrat to win the White House. In the North, the political will to uphold Reconstruction was crumbling. And in the South, the old planter class regained control of state governments one by one. By the fall of 1876, only Florida, South Carolina, and Louisiana continued with Reconstruction under Republican control.

Samuel Tilden barely won the popular vote. But electoral votes in South Carolina, Florida, and Louisiana were disputed. A commission, created to decide the results of the election, reached a compromise on March 4, 1877. By that time, a great many Union troops had already left the South. Republican Rutherford Hayes was declared the winner of the presidency—on condition that the remaining federal troops be removed. The "Compromise of 1877" came to be known as the end of Reconstruction because "the fall of the South's last Republican governments and the removal of federal troops from . . . regional politics marked a definitive turning point in American History," writes historian Eric Foner.[4] Sojourner Truth had worked hard during Reconstruction, first among the freedpeople in Washington and then in her attempts to relocate them. And now her own strength was fading as Reconstruction was ending.

Sojourner needed support in her old age, and so Frances Titus brought forth another edition of the *Narrative*. It was called *The Life of Sojourner Truth, the Libyan Sibyl, the Oldest Lecturer in the World! A Graphic Volume about the Colored Centenarian.* Truth was approaching eighty years of age, but apparently both Truth and Titus believed that she was one hundred years old. "People ask me . . . how I came to live so long and keep my mind," Truth said. It was "because I think of the great things of God, not little things. I don't fritter my mind away in caring for trifles."[5]

It seemed that everyone asked Truth about her age. She had a good stock of answers at the ready. "Bless you, child," Truth told a reporter. "I don't tell my age! I'm looking out for a good chance to marry."[6] To another she said, "I don't know my age exactly. I was a slave in the State of New York and was sold a good many times. When too old I was made younger, and when too young I was made older. I am between eighty and ninety."[7] Sometimes Truth joked that she charged $5 to tell how old she was. A few people handed over the $5 (worth more than $120 today).

Truth was getting too frail to travel alone, and Frances Titus became her traveling companion. To test the waters, Titus took Truth on a speaking tour of western Michigan.[8] Sojourner stood the trip well, and so the two women set out on a ten-month tour of New York State in 1878.

They attended a woman's rights event marking the thirtieth anniversary of the Seneca Falls Convention. Truth made some brief remarks there and at several events in the area. She scolded women for dressing up like dolls. Women "should be something better than mere toys," Sojourner said, but "vanity and pride" were their downfall. "If women would live as they ought to, they would get their rights as they went along."[9]

Truth saw the latest fashions as a form of bondage, little better than alcohol and tobacco. Chewing tobacco was especially obnoxious because chewers had to spit out their tobacco juice. The habit was so common that spittoons were placed in hotels, train cars, and even courtrooms. As one who revered cleanliness, Truth could not abide this form of tobacco consumption, and she was not shy about telling her audiences.

On reaching New York City, Sojourner and Frances stayed with friends. While there, Truth spoke at the Cooper Institute, the grand Italianate brownstone in Manhattan's Lower East Side. Truth spoke in the "small hall" to a modest audience. A reporter noted that Truth got off to a slow start as she fumbled to untie her old bonnet. She began with a prayer and then, speaking "as loud as a man," she warned that "Christ is coming soon!" and believers must "keep their lamps trimmed and burning."

The *Times Union* reported that "the old lady has become somewhat of a Second Adventist." Well, why not, the reporter condescended, if it consoles her in her old age? But others "have not the excuse of senility and ignorance." Educated people surely understand that "the promised reign of Christ is a spiritual and not a material reign." God's throne is "in the universal heart of man," not a literal place on earth. If Sojourner Truth believed the "hobgoblin" and "delusion" of the second coming, she was entitled to do so, said the reporter; but more enlightened souls do better to love God and serve their fellow man.[10]

This reporter misunderstood Truth. She *had* spent her life serving others. In her old age, Truth "still believed in the second coming of Christ" but not "in a literal sense," wrote historian Carleton Mabee. In New York in 1878, she said that Jesus was coming. Not "flying in the air, the way those Second Advent folks say, but he's coming in the spirit, bless the Lord!" Truth told people to take action and not sit passively waiting for the second coming. "Don't wait for the Lord to come to clean up this wicked world. But take hold and clean it up for yourselves." In Lansing in 1881, she told her listeners not to wait "for God to come. He is with you now, all the time, and what more can you want?"[11]

Truth and Titus returned to Battle Creek in 1879. Local newspapers reported that Truth was renovating her house, spending time with her family, chatting with friends and neighbors. People noticed that her speech and memory were clear and sharp.[12] Sojourner was excited by news of a fresh wave of Black migration to the West. She knew she must return to Kansas and see this great movement of people for herself.

The freedpeople now heading west called themselves the "Exodusters." The name suggested a biblical-type exodus heading to the dusty western plains. By the tens of thousands, freedpeople were leaving the South and going to Kansas, Colorado, and Oklahoma. Truth hailed the migration as "the greatest movement of all time."[13]

She now admitted that her first trip to Kansas (in 1872) was "for the time being a failure" because Congress did not set aside western lands for freedpeople. But now, Truth said, God is "finally taking my people there in such numbers" as to bring "regeneration, temporally and spiritually, of the American Colored Race."[14] She believed God would compensate them for all their suffering. Truth felt personally "responsible for the negro exodus," said the *Chicago Tribune*, "having prayed earnestly for it during the past five years."[15]

Historically, the Exoduster movement was a response of Southern Blacks to the end of Reconstruction. Without Northern troops in the South, there was no protection against white violence. And so, under the leadership of people like Benjamin "Pap" Singleton (a former slave from Tennessee), many freedpeople were voting with their feet. "The movement generated immense excitement among ordinary Blacks." And yet Frederick Douglass, among others, "opposed the Kansas migration" because it seemed to abandon "the struggle for citizenship rights in the South."[16]

The migration peaked in 1879, when twenty-six thousand Exodusters arrived in the West. The relationship between Blacks and whites in eastern Kansas appears to have been relatively friendly until that point, according to the Kansas Historical Society. But many whites perceived the rapidly growing Black population as a threat. Racial tensions rose, "with at least two lynchings and with institutionalized discrimination becoming the norm."[17]

In 1921, in Topeka, whites murdered up to three hundred Black people and destroyed their homes and businesses, but the story was hushed up for almost a century.

In the summer of 1879, Truth and Titus left for Kansas, stopping off in Chicago for a few days en route. Sojourner spoke at the Langley Avenue Methodist Church. The old woman "hobbled" to the front of the church, leaning on her cane, reported one Chicago paper. She wore "a plain dark dress, a small shawl across her shoulders, and a white lace cap drawn tight over her head." She climbed into the pulpit and spoke to a full church for almost an hour.

"The spirit of God has followed me all my days," Truth began. She gave her testimony of how she became a follower of Jesus. She described herself as "ignorant" in her youth, but she kept on learning. Now in her old age, she "believed no mind was big enough to appreciate the glories of God." God made all good things come to pass. But there was still evil in the world, Truth warned. If we have "Jesus for a guide . . . we shall conquer the devil" and enjoy "all that is good upon our side here and hereafter." In words that now seem to anticipate Martin Luther King Jr., Truth said that although Black people in the South "are subjected to terrorism . . . God can make a way when there is no way."[18]

Leaving Chicago by train, Truth and Titus arrived in Topeka in September. The freedpeople from the South were coming in a constant stream. Most were destitute, owning nothing but the clothes on their backs. Sojourner later told the *Chicago Inter Ocean*, "I have not language to tell you what rags and wretchedness and hunger and poverty I saw among them." She wanted them to get land as soon as possible and cultivate the soil so they could become self-supporting.[19]

As before, Truth spoke to racially segregated audiences in Kansas. "The white people will have a chance to hear Sojourner tomorrow, Tuesday evening at the first Baptist church, corner of Ninth and Jackson," said the *Topeka Daily Capital*; the paper also reported that "Sojourner Truth spoke to a good audience, principally of colored people, at the A. M. E. church, Saturday evening. Her remarks were good and well received."[20] The *Topeka Colored Citizen* revealed Truth's rage at Southern whites. The *Citizen* quoted her as saying that God wants "Black people [to be] in full possession of their rights, even if the entire [Southern] white population has to be annihilated in the accomplishment of His purpose."[21] This strikes a discordant note with Truth's higher vision of love and forgiveness, but it shows her as a human being who sometimes felt rage against those who made her people suffer, just as she felt gratitude toward any, Black or white, who tried to ameliorate that suffering.

Temporary relief societies sprang up to help the Exodusters, but they could not keep pace with the demand.[22] The *Topeka Daily Capital* reported that Black Kansans supported the Exodusters. After a rousing worship service at the Second Baptist Church, the Kansas Freedmen's Relief Association held a business session. They passed a resolution to honor the relief work done on behalf of "about 5,000 of our people" who were "driven from the savage districts of the south by murder, fraud and intimidation." The resolution invoked patriotism and equal rights. The Southern Black people, it said, came to Kansas to "enjoy all the rights guaranteed to them by the 13th, 14th and 15th amendments to the Constitution of the United States." Attendees pledged their spiritual, political, and practical support for the new arrivals.

Another motion was passed to honor Truth and Titus as "Christian women" who were helping refugees from the South to find "the protection of their life, liberty and happiness." Truth was affirmed for "her motherly-like counsel," and the congregation pledged to pray without ceasing for Sojourner, an ambassador "presenting the grievances of our people" to the rest of the country.[23]

White people also paid tribute to Sojourner Truth. The *Smith County Pioneer* hailed her as a "great humanitarian" who has done more for her people than anyone else.[24] And Richard Cordley, a white minister in Emporia, remembered how hard Truth had worked to bring freedpeople from the South to Kansas. But when, despite all her efforts, the government did nothing, Truth "laid the matter before the Lord." Cordley saw the new migration as proof that "the Lord is doing just what she asked him to do."

Cordley also hailed Truth as a spiritual inspiration to others. Although Truth often spoke of her vision of Jesus, she knew that God worked with individuals in different ways. Sometimes people said to her, "I wish I had your faith, Sojourner," and she would reply, "Well, child, you can have it, without money and without price—not mine, but just as good." Cordley said he had often heard her sing "I Am Pleading for My People" as "a memento of the old struggle with slavery in which her soul still lives."[25]

Not everyone appreciated what Sojourner Truth stood for. She spoke at a white Baptist church in Topeka, to an audience that—in the eyes of the reporter, at least—came "more through curiosity to see the old lady than to hear her talk."[26]

As these public comments were being made, so was private correspondence between friends. Truth is "in very good health and spirits," Frances Titus wrote to Mary Gale, a friend back east. However, Truth had her limits, and had stayed behind while Titus went to bring supplies to some remote Exoduster settlements. Led by the Kansas Freedmen's Relief Association, the group traveled seventy-five miles "in an open wagon across the prairies, following the old Mormon trail for a guide." They "distributed clothing and bedding to over 300 people," Titus wrote. Truth no longer had the stamina to make such a trip.

The letter went on to say that Truth wanted Titus to take her on a trip to collect money and supplies for the Exodusters. However, winter was closing in, and Sojourner was "very sensitive to the cold," Titus wrote. Titus was torn between Truth's needs and her own desire to do more relief work in Kansas. In the end, she decided to take Truth back to Michigan in December.

"I have taken upon myself the whole responsibility of [Truth's] support, else she would have been a public charge for the last five years," Titus wrote. She wished more people would give money for Truth's support. If only they could get funds to open an account in the Battle Creek bank, so Truth "could draw three or four dollars per week." Titus hoped that maybe "the way will open when least expected."[27]

After returning to Michigan, Titus collected food and supplies for the Exodusters. She wanted to go back to Kansas, but she stayed in Battle Creek to "manage Truth's correspondence and to care for Truth's physical needs."[28] Sojourner stayed home that winter, hoping to get out again when the seasons turned.

19

"We Will All Be as One"

Despite her wealth of experience, Sojourner Truth spent her last years in near poverty. She shared her little house with her daughter Elizabeth (now a widow in her midfifties) and with Elizabeth's son William. Elizabeth did domestic work for neighbors but didn't make enough to support herself. "The City Poormaster is frequently called upon to assist the family through the cold winters," said the *Chicago Tribune*.[1] The poormaster was a county official who visited needy families and issued vouchers for them to get food in local stores. How sad that one who gave so freely of her own great strength needed public assistance in her final years. As an enslaved person, Isabella worked for no pay. In freedom, she was underpaid and gave away much of what she earned. She had provided for her family as much as she could, but now her daughters were not in a position to support her.

Friends sent her small cash contributions or gifts of food. When someone in England sent her a new silk dress, she said she must live longer so she could wear it. "I want to live now more than ever. There is no better world than this."[2]

Truth kept up on the news from Kansas and remained an avid supporter of the Exodusters. She was glad when she found out that Kansas, in 1881, prohibited "the manufacture and sale of intoxicating liquors."[3] Truth credited the Black voters with helping "make Kansas a prohibition State." This was just "one of the blessings these people will bring to the home of their adoption," Truth said in a public letter to the *Chicago Daily Inter Ocean*.

In the same letter, Truth thanked the editor for publishing her message and encouraged many old friends who had lost touch with her to write letters and to request her books and pictures. "I have said for many years that the newspaper is the last gospel, which carries good tidings to all the world," Truth said. An example was the paper's coverage of the Exodusters, whom Truth called "the refugees from Southern cruelty." Like the good Samaritan in Jesus's parable, "You have picked up this mutilated human brother . . . dressed his wounds, set him on your own beast, have taken him to the wayside inn . . . till he can care for himself." Truth thanked *Inter Ocean* for carrying "this gospel of humanity" far and wide, inspiring people to send aid to the destitute refugees. Sojourner said she hoped "to live another hundred years to witness the prosperity of my people."[4]

Truth cared deeply about her adopted home state of Michigan, and was therefore dismayed to learn that capital punishment might be reinstituted there. The so-called Wyckoff Hanging Bill was introduced to the Michigan state legislature on February 3, 1881. Truth spoke out against the bill, and later on the *Owasso Times* credited her speeches with defeating it.[5]

Truth went to Lansing and spoke to the Michigan state legislature on a June evening in 1881. It was her last public speech.

"I have come here to-night, to see about a thing that fairly shocked me," Truth said. "I've heard that you are going to have hanging again in this state. Before God only think of it!" For many years, Truth thought Michigan was the most blessed state in the Union. And now she could not bear to think that Michigan would hang people by the neck until dead. Who could sanction such a thing? she asked. And where did this "stupid spirit" come from that would make murderers of the people of Michigan?

"The religion of Jesus is forgiveness," Truth declared. How could she pray, "Father, forgive me as I forgive those who trespass against me," and then turn around and condone hanging? Even to punish a killer, hanging was murder in cold blood, Truth said. When a man is in jail awaiting hanging, the ministers go to convert him. They pray that God will forgive him, and when he is converted, "they put a rope around his neck and swing him off, but that is not Jesus' law."

Truth said she had heard people say "we must abide by the public laws." But she could not agree with any law that upholds murder. "I am against it! I am against it!" Jesus taught us better than "an eye for an eye and a tooth for a tooth," Truth said. He "commanded us to love one another." We give God no glory by killing other people with "the awful system of hanging." Those who sanction "such a barbarous thing have murder in their hearts," and they must one day answer to God, she told the Michigan state legislature.

As Truth neared the end of her speech, someone informed her that the Wyckoff Hanging Bill was *already* defeated. (It was voted down on May 19, 1881, a few weeks before Truth went to Lansing to speak against it.) Without skipping a beat, Truth "shouted for joy" and proclaimed Michigan the best state in the Union. "I believe that God has spared me to do good to this white population, which has done so much good to the Black race. How wonderful God turns things."[6] Truth's words about race relations may seem naïve even for her day. One historian says that "Truth's last speech casts too positive a light on Black-white relations in post-Reconstruction America," even if Truth's motive was to improve race relations.[7]

Truth also praised new inventions that could make life better, including the telegraph, the locomotive, and the telephone. She said that "spiritual doctrines should keep pace with all the wonderful inventions for the benefit of mankind." If only someone would "write a bible" discarding "Mosaic laws which teach 'an eye for an eye and a tooth for a tooth.'" She exhorted her audience to "acts of kindness" rather than revenge.[8]

It seems that Truth's friend, Eliza Leggett, either heard or read Truth's speech against capital punishment. In June 1881, she wrote to the poet Walt Whitman and told him that Truth saw God at work in modern inventions. Sojourner thought there should be "scriptures telling of railroads, and telephones and the Atlantic cable." Leggett told how Truth "sees God in a steam engine and electricity."[9]

After Truth spoke in Lansing, she went to Detroit. There she sat for a photographic portrait session at the studio of Corydon Randall. This was the first of three portrait sessions Truth had before she died, writes photographic historian Darcy Grimaldo Grigsby. Truth ordered quantities of these pictures both as an income source and as a statement of her identity. Again she used her famous caption: "I sell the shadow to support the substance," with her name printed below. In these final portraits, her clothing was very plain; white cap, white shawl, dark dress. She didn't wear glasses or hold her knitting. "Among her very last photographic portraits are two cartes de visite prominently featuring her face. . . . The frontal view is intimate and soft; we see a woman who looks older and more fragile, but also tender."[10] The photographs did not show that Truth had by now lost so many teeth;

she had a set of false teeth made. "They are the only thing false about me," Truth told a reporter.[11]

Truth's health and strength were now in steep decline. Her daughters Elizabeth, Diana, and Sophia "faithfully attended" her, reported the *Battle Creek Nightly Moon*, and "kindly neighbors" did all they could to ease her last days. Many people came to visit Truth, often leaving gifts for her.[12]

Truth's friend Frances Titus wrote that "the last three months of her life was a period of intense suffering."[13] The ulcers on Truth's leg were gangrenous and very painful. Truth was attended regularly by physicians from the Seventh-day Adventist Sanitarium; Dr. John Harvey Kellogg is said to have used his own skin to attempt a skin graft for Truth.[14] "She has known for some weeks that she must die," reported the *Nightly Moon*, "and often remarked that God knew best and she was prepared to meet him."[15]

As Truth lay dying, the racial equality she had long fought for was pushed further away. On October 15, 1883, the Supreme Court overturned the Civil Rights Act of 1875 that prohibited segregation in public places. The Court ruled the act did not apply to privately owned businesses such as restaurants and hotels. The Supreme Court legitimated "Jim Crow" segregation and rolled back many of the gains made by Reconstruction. It would take generations of hard work before the civil rights movement forced a national reckoning with the unfinished business of Reconstruction. More recently, Black Lives Matter arose to take up the still-unfinished business of racial justice and equity. Both of these movements can proudly claim Sojourner Truth as a forerunner.

During Truth's last illness, a few newspaper reporters came seeking one last story about her. A Grand Rapids journalist wrote that Truth's eyes were keen and her mind sharp, although she was very thin. She told him that the movement of Black people to Kansas must continue. She sang a favorite hymn and told the reporter and his readers to be followers of Jesus.[16]

One morning when Frances Titus came to visit, she saw that Sojourner had "suffered all night long." Through her pain Truth sang a hymn she wrote many years earlier: "It was early in the morning, just at the break of day, when he rose . . . and went to heaven on a cloud."

The next time Frances came, she saw her friend lying down with her eyes closed. "Sojourner, can you look at me?" Frances asked. Sojourner "slowly opened those wondrous orbs which seemed filled with spiritual and prophetic light," as if to say, "Let not your heart be troubled." Then Sojourner "slowly closed her eyes . . . [and] sank into a comatose state, from which she never rallied." She was about eighty-six years old when she died on November 26, 1883.

As the body of Sojourner Truth was prepared for burial, a service she so often provided for others was done for her. Frances Titus recalled that loving hands robed Truth in black, "with white muslin cap and folded kerchief." Flowers were arranged in "emblems . . . a cross, a sheaf of ripened grain, a sickle, and a crown," and laid on her casket. In her right hand, long ago maimed by an injury during her enslavement, someone placed a bouquet of white flowers.[17] In the following weeks, newspapers around the country claimed she had reached the age of 104, 106, even 110. Yet it hardly matters, since Truth did so much with the years she had.

Two days after Truth's death, friends and family gathered at her house. They formed a funeral procession to the Congregational/Presbyterian church on Main Street. The pallbearers placed the casket in the vestibule, removing the lid so that mourners could take a last look as they filed by. The church quickly filled with nearly a thousand people "composed of all classes and creeds," reported the *Battle Creek Daily Journal*. Many floral tributes were brought to Truth's funeral, including "a basket of ferns and delicate cream, pink and white flowers by the Band of Hope," a temperance group in Battle Creek.[18]

Rev. Reed Stuart preached the sermon, and Giles Stebbins, Truth's old friend from Northampton days, gave a eulogy on Truth's character and contributions. The service probably included singing, prayer, and Scripture readings that Sojourner loved in life.

Then came the procession to Oak Hill Cemetery, where an open grave awaited. "The short November day, now drawing to its close, was the perfect day of the season," wrote Frances Titus. "The long line of carriages, the hearse with its black plumes, the people—all so motionless—the cloudless sky, the great round, red sun lying low in the horizon, all made up a whole of solemn but exquisite beauty." Her sojourn at an end, Truth was buried beside her beloved grandson Samuel Banks. The casket was lowered into the grave, and the benediction was spoken as the sun went down.[19]

For the next several weeks, obituaries and tributes appeared in newspapers all around the country. Truth was "distinguished for insight into human nature," wrote Frederick Douglass, "remarkable for independence and courageous self-assertion, devoted to the welfare of her race . . . an object of respect and admiration to social reformers everywhere."

But let Sojourner Truth have the last word, from her 1881 New Year's greeting in the *Chicago Daily Inter Ocean*.[20]

Dear Friends:

. . . We talk often of a beginning, but there is no beginning but the beginning of a wrong. All else is from God, and is from everlasting to everlasting. All that has a beginning will have an ending. God is without end, and all that is good is without end. We shall never see God only as we seen Him in one another. He is a great ocean of love, and we live and move in Him as the fishes in the sea, filled with His love and spirit, and His throne is in the hearts of His people. Jesus, the Son of God, will be as we are, if we are pure, and we will be like Him. There will be no distinction. He will be like the sun and shine upon us, and we will be like the sun and shine upon Him; all filled with glory. We are all the children of one Father, and He is God; and Jesus will be One among us. God is no respecter of persons, and we will all be as one . . .

                                                        Sojourner Truth

SOJOURNER TRUTH.

A Picture taken in the days of her Physical Strength.

Sojourner Truth, a picture taken in the days of her physical strength (Lincoln Financial Foundation Collection, Indiana State Museum, Allen County Public Library)

Ulster County Courthouse in Kingston, NY, where Isabella won custody of her son Peter in 1828 (County Atlas of Ulster, New York, by F. W. Beers, published by Walker & Jewett, 1875, courtesy of the Ulster County Clerk's Office, Kingston, NY)

Prophet Matthias (Print collection, New York Public Library)

Frederick Douglass (Library of
Congress Prints and Photographs
Division)

William Lloyd Garrison
(H. W. Smith, engraver)

Sketch by Charles C. Burleigh Jr. thought to represent Sojourner Truth working in the laundry at the Northampton Association (Historic Northampton, Northampton, Massachusetts)

Anti-slavery image from March 17, 1832, Liberator. Similar pictures were used in the anti-slavery movement on both sides of the Atlantic. (Granger Historical Picture Archive)

The Libyan Sibyl, *William Wetmore Story, 1861 (Metropolitan Museum of Art, gift of the Erving Wolf Foundation in memory of Diane R. Wolf, 1979)*

Freedpeople in the Washington, DC, area during the Civil War (Library of Congress Prints and Photographs Division)

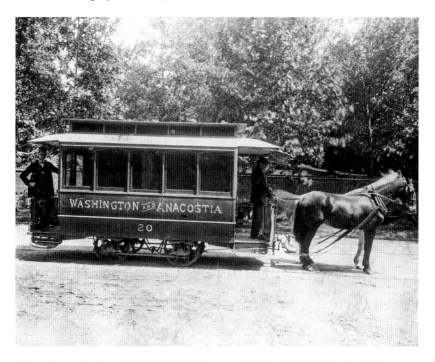

Horse-drawn streetcar similar to what Sojourner Truth rode in Washington, DC (Kiplinger Research Library, Washington, DC, CHS 06298, DC History Center)

Harriet Tubman, "The Moses of Her People" (Library of Congress, Emily Howland Photograph Album)

Sojourner Truth, "I Sell the Shadow to Support the Substance," 1864 (Library of Congress)

Sojourner Truth in patriotic costume, probably from Indiana, 1861 (Chicago History Museum)

APPENDIX

Three Versions of Truth's Most Famous Speech, "Ain't I a Woman?"

Version 1: Women's Rights Convention, Akron, Ohio, *Anti-Slavery Bugle*, May 28, 1851

One of the most unique and interesting speeches of the convention was made by Sojourner Truth, an emancipated slave. It is impossible to transfer it to paper, or convey any adequate idea of the effect it produced upon the audience. Those only can appreciate it who saw her powerful form, her whole-souled, earnest gesture, and listened to her strong and truthful tones. She came forward to the platform and addressing the President said with great simplicity: "May I say a few words?" Receiving an affirmative answer, she proceeded:

I want to say a few words about this matter. I am a woman's rights. I have as much muscle as any man, and can do as much work as any man. I have plowed and reaped and husked and chopped and mowed, and can any man do more than that? I have heard much about the sexes being equal. I can carry as much as any man, and can eat as much too, if I can get it. I am as strong as any man that is now.

As for intellect, all I can say is, if a woman have a pint, and a man a quart—why can't she have her little pint full? You need not be afraid to give us our rights for fear we will take too much,—for we can't take more than our pint'll hold. The poor men seem to be all in confusion, and don't know what to do. Why children, if you have woman's rights, give it to her and you will feel better. You will have your own rights, and they won't be so much trouble.

I can't read, but I can hear. I have heard the bible and have learned that Eve caused man to sin. Well, if woman upset the world, do give her a chance to set it right side up again. The Lady has spoken about Jesus, how he never spurned woman from him, and she was right. When Lazarus died, Mary and Martha came to him with faith and love and besought him to raise their brother. And Jesus wept and Lazarus came forth. And how came Jesus into the world? Through God who created him and the woman who bore him. Man, where was your part? But the women are coming up blessed be God and a few of the men are coming up with them. But man is in a tight place, the poor slave is on him, woman is coming on him, he is surely between a hawk and a buzzard.[1]

Version 2: Mrs. F. D. Gage, "Sojourner Truth"
National Anti-Slavery Standard, May 2, 1863

The story of *Sojourner Truth*, by Mrs. H. B. Stowe, in the April number of *The Atlantic*, will be read by thousands in the East and West with intense interest; and as those who know this remarkable woman will lay down this periodical, there will be heard in home-circles throughout Ohio, Michigan, Wisconsin and Illinois many an anecdote of the weird, wonderful creature, who was at once a marvel and a mystery.

"Well, chillen, whar dar's so much racket dar must be som'ting out o' kilter. I tink dat, 'twixt de n*****s of de South and de women at de Norf, all a-talking 'bout rights, de white men will be in a fix pretty soon. But what's all this here talking 'bout? Dat man ober dar say dat woman needs to be helped into carriages, and lifted over ditches, and to have de best place eberywhar. Nobody eber helps me into carriages, or ober mud-puddles, or gives me any best place"; and, raising herself to her full height, and her voice to a pitch like rolling thunder, she asked, "And ar'n't I a woman? Look at me. Look at my arm," and she bared her right arm to the shoulder, showing its tremendous muscular power. "I have plowed and planted and gathered into barns, and no man could head me—and ar'n't I a woman? I could work as much and eat as much as a man (when I could get it), and bear de lash as well—and ar'n't I a woman? I have borne thirteen chillen, and seen 'em mos' all sold off into slavery, and when I cried out with a mother's grief, none but Jesus heard—and ar'n't I a woman? Den dey talks 'bout dis ting in de head. What dis dey call it?" "Intellect," whispered some one near. "Dat's it, honey. What's dat got to do with woman's rights or n*****s' rights? If my cup won't hold but a pint and yourn holds a quart, wouldn't ye be mean not to let me have my little half-measure full?" and she pointed her significant finger and sent a keen glance at the minister who had made the argument. The cheering was long and loud. "Den dat little man in black dar, he say woman can't have as much right as man 'cause Christ wa'n'nt a woman. *Whar did your Christ come from?*"

Rolling thunder could not have stilled that crowd as did those deep, wonderful tones, as she stood there with outstretched arms and eye of fire. Raising her voice still louder, she repeated—"Whar did your Christ come from? From God and a woman. Man had not'ing to do with him." Oh! what a rebuke she gave the little man. Turning again to another objector, she took up the defence of Mother Eve. I cannot follow her through it all. It was pointed and witty and solemn, eliciting at almost every sentence deafening applause; and she ended by asserting "that if de fust woman God ever made was strong enough to turn de world upside down all her one lone, all dese togeder," and she glanced her eye over us, "ought to be able to turn it back and git it right side up again, and now dey is asking to, de men better let 'em" (long continued cheering). "Bleeged to ye for hearin' on me, and now ole Sojourner ha'n't got nothin' more to say."

Amid roars of applause she turned to her corner, leaving more than one of us with streaming eyes and hearts beating with gratitude. She had taken us up in her great, strong arms and carried us safely over the slough of difficulty, turning the whole tide in our favor.

I have given but a faint sketch of her speech. I have never in my life seen anything like the magical influence that subdued the mobbish spirit of the day, and turned the jibes and sneers of an excited crowd into notes of respect and admiration. Hundreds rushed up to shake hands and congratulate the glorious old mother, and bid her "God speed" on her mission of "testifying agin concernin' the wickedness of this here people."[2]

Version 3: "Ain't I a Woman?" 1972

Well, children, where there is so much racket there must be something out of kilter. I think that 'twixt the negroes of the South and the women at the

North, all talking about rights, the white men will be in a fix pretty soon. But what's all this here talking about?

That man over there says that women need to be helped into carriages, and lifted over ditches, and to have the best place everywhere. Nobody ever helps me into carriages, or over mud-puddles, or gives me any best place! And ain't I a woman? Look at me! Look at my arm! I have ploughed and planted, and gathered into barns, and no man could head me! And ain't I a woman? I could work as much and eat as much as a man—when I could get it—and bear the lash as well! And ain't I a woman? I have borne thirteen children, and seen most all sold off to slavery, and when I cried out with my mother's grief, none but Jesus heard me! And ain't I a woman?

Then they talk about this thing in the head; what's this they call it? [member of audience whispers, "intellect"] That's it, honey. What's that got to do with women's rights or negroes' rights? If my cup won't hold but a pint, and yours holds a quart, wouldn't you be mean not to let me have my little half measure full?

Then that little man in black there, he says women can't have as much rights as men, 'cause Christ wasn't a woman! Where did your Christ come from? Where did your Christ come from? From God and a woman! Man had nothing to do with Him.

If the first woman God ever made was strong enough to turn the world upside down all alone, these women together ought to be able to turn it back, and get it right side up again! And now they is asking to do it, the men better let them.

Obliged to you for hearing me, and now old Sojourner ain't got nothing more to say.[3]

A Note on the Sources

Everyone who writes about Sojourner Truth has to grapple with the fact that she herself did not read or write. Source materials tend to come in smaller bits and have to be pieced together, like a mosaic. And everything comes mediated through those who wrote her words down.

Yet Truth did get her life story into print. The *Narrative of Sojourner Truth*, first published in 1850, is practically the only source for Truth's early years. To get the story down on paper, Truth worked with Olive Gilbert, whose voice offers opinions and interpretations together with Truth's story. A great help for navigating this double-stranded work is the journal article by Jean M. Humez, "Reading the *Narrative of Sojourner Truth* as a Collaborative Text," in *Frontiers: A Journal of Women's Studies* 16, no. 1 (1996): 29–52.

Selections from Truth's scrapbooks were added to Truth's *Narrative* in 1875, and published by her friend Frances Titus. This addition, called the *Book of Life*, contains newspaper clippings, autographs, and letters that Truth received. (Since the *Book of Life* became part of the *Narrative*, in the notes it is cited simply as *Narrative*.)

Truth also collaborated on an earlier book that documents Isabella's sojourn in the Kingdom of Matthias. Interviews with Isabella Van Wagenen (before she changed her name to Sojourner Truth) were the foundation of Gilbert Vale's *Fanaticism: Its Source and Influence; Illustrated by the Simple Narrative of Isabella* . . . (London: Dalton House, 2015; original 1835).

Sojourner Truth also sent letters, which she dictated to friends and then sent to other friends or to newspapers, such as the *Chicago Inter Ocean* or the *National Anti-Slavery Standard*, for publication. Sometimes letters she sent to friends also made their way into newspapers. Some of Truth's correspondence is available in online databases, for example, the Post Family Papers Project, University of Rochester, River Campus Libraries, https://rbscp.lib .rochester.edu/exhibits/show/post-family-papers/post-project.

This biography weaves together many newspaper articles about Sojourner Truth. These articles report on her speeches, her travels, and the effect she had on her audiences. Often, they comment on her appearance. Newspaper reports reveal Truth's power as a public speaker, yet many reporters used what they thought was Black southern dialect to report Truth's words (discussed in the book). Others used standard English. Many of these newspaper articles express the racism so prevalent in nineteenth-century America, but many others also bear witness to Truth's wit, courage, and dignity. Of course, Truth got the most coverage in the antislavery press, including the *Liberator*, *National Anti-Slavery Standard*, *Anti-Slavery Bugle*, and others. Now available online are many historical newspapers, which one can access on services like Newspapers.com or Accessible Archives. Yet there remain many newspapers that can only be accessed by visiting archives or, if need be, quoting from secondary sources.

The voices of Truth's contemporaries have entered into this book through their memoirs and ongoing legacy. Examples include *The Narrative of the Life of Frederick Douglass, an American Slave, Written by Himself* (New Haven: Yale University Press, 2001; original 1845) and Elizabeth Keckley, *Behind the Scenes* (Columbia, SC: Loki's Publishing, 2019; original 1868).

Several books and articles from the late nineteenth century have material about Sojourner Truth. For example, Charles A. Sheffeld, ed., *The History of Florence, Massachusetts, Including a Complete Account of the Northampton Association of Education and Industry* (Florence, MA: Sheffeld, 1895), is a key source for my chapter "The Moral Reform Depot." And Fred Tomkins, *Jewels in Ebony* (London: British and Foreign Freedmen's Aid Society, 1870), has a chapter on Sojourner Truth in Washington.

Modern biographies of people who shaped Truth's world have contributed to this work. These include David W. Blight, *Frederick Douglass, Prophet of Freedom* (New York: Simon & Schuster, 2018); Ron Chernow, *Grant* (New York: Penguin, 2017); Catherine Clinton, *Harriet Tubman: The Road to Freedom* (New York: Little, Brown, 2004); Graham Russell Gao Hodges, *David Ruggles: A Radical Black Abolitionist and the Underground Railroad in New York*

City (Chapel Hill: University of North Carolina Press, 2010); Andrea Moore Kerr, *Lucy Stone: Speaking Out for Equality* (New Brunswick, NJ: Rutgers University Press, 1992); and Henry Mayer, *All on Fire: William Lloyd Garrison and the Abolition of Slavery* (New York: St. Martin's Griffin, 1998).

One of the joys of writing a biography is learning about places as they were in the past. Edwin Burrows and Mike Wallace, *Gotham: A History of New York City to 1898* (New York: Oxford University Press, 1999), helped me to write about New York City during the years Isabella lived there. Kate Masur, *An Example for All the Land: Emancipation and the Struggle for Equality in Washington, D.C.* (Chapel Hill: University of North Carolina Press, 2010), helped me locate Sojourner Truth's work among the freedpeople in the context of wartime and Reconstruction Washington.

Three biographies of Sojourner Truth, by historians Carleton Mabee, Nell Irvin Painter, and Margaret Washington, were so foundational to my project that they are noted in the acknowledgments. I also quoted Isabelle Kinnard Richman, *Sojourner Truth: Prophet of Social Justice* (London: Routledge, 2016). Darcy Grimaldo Grigsby, *Enduring Truths: Sojourner's Shadows and Substance* (Chicago: University of Chicago Press, 2015), probes the historical context and meaning of Truth's photographs.

Several biographies of Sojourner Truth have been written, so why another one? Each author has a unique perspective and writes within her own historical context, and may reach a different audience. Until everyone has their rights, there should never be a last biography of Sojourner Truth.

Abbreviations

CM, *Sojourner Truth*
Carleton Mabee, with Susan Mabee Newhouse. *Sojourner Truth: Slave, Prophet, Legend.* New York: New York University Press, 1993.

IR, *Sojourner Truth*
Isabelle Kinnard Richman. *Sojourner Truth: Prophet of Social Justice.* London: Routledge, 2016.

MW, *Truth's America*
Margaret Washington. *Sojourner Truth's America.* Urbana: University of Illinois Press, 2009.

NIP, *Sojourner Truth*
Nell Irvin Painter. *Sojourner Truth: A Life, a Symbol.* New York: Norton, 1996.

ST, *Narrative*
Sojourner Truth. *Narrative of Sojourner Truth.* Edited by Nell Irvin Painter. London: Penguin Books, 1998.

Notes

Prologue

1. ST, *Narrative*, 124.

2. An Act to Amend an Act Entitled "An Act to incorporate the Metropolitan Railroad Company in the District of Columbia," 38th Cong., 2nd sess. [March 3, 1865]; U.S. Congress, U.S. Statutes at Large, Volume 13-1865, 38th Congress, United States, 1865, 1864, periodical, https://www.loc.gov/item/llsl-v13/.

3. ST, *Narrative*, 125.

4. ST, *Narrative*, 126.

5. Truth to Amy Kirby Post, Washington, October 1, 1865, Post Family Papers Project, University of Rochester, Rare Books and Special Collections (rochester .edu), accessed August 21, 2018.

Chapter 1

1. Eric Foner, *Gateway to Freedom* (New York: Norton, 2016), 28, 42.

2. Firth Haring Fabend, *Zion on the Hudson: Dutch New York and New Jersey in the Age of Revivals* (New Brunswick, NJ: Rutgers University Press, 2000), 181.

3. Shane White, *Somewhat More Independent: The End of Slavery in New York City, 1770–1810* (Athens: University of Georgia Press, 1991), 16–20.

4. "When Did Slavery End in New York State?" New-York Historical Society Museum and Library, accessed March 14, 2022, http://www.nyhistory.org/community/slavery-end-new-york-state.

5. Deborah Gray White, *Ar'n't I a Woman? Female Slaves in the Plantation South* (New York: Norton, 1999), 15.

6. Nell Irvin Painter, introduction to ST, *Narrative*, xiii.

7. "Sojourner Truth," *New York Daily Herald*, December 16, 1878, 2.

8. William Still, "Sojourner Truth: Her Strange Career, Some Very Interesting Reminiscences," *Philadelphia Evening Bulletin*, July 19, 1876; reprinted in *Friends' Review: A Religious, Literary and Miscellaneous Journal* 29 (1876): 829.

9. Jean M. Humez, "Reading the *Narrative of Sojourner Truth* as a Collaborative Text," *Frontiers: A Journal of Women's Studies* 16, no. 1 (1996): 37.

10. ST, *Narrative*, 56.

11. MW, *Truth's America*, 10.

12. MW, *Truth's America*, 9–10.

13. ST, *Narrative*, 10.

14. MW, *Truth's America*, 15.

15. ST, *Narrative*, 9, 11.

16. ST, *Narrative*, 10, 12. See also Eugene D. Genovese, *Roll, Jordan, Roll: The World the Slaves Made* (New York: Vintage Books, 1976), 247.

17. MW, *Truth's America*, 32.

18. ST, *Narrative*, 18, 14.

19. ST, *Narrative*, 15.

20. ST, *Narrative*, 18.

21. ST, *Narrative*, 19.

22. MW, *Truth's America*, 34.

23. ST, *Narrative*, 19.

24. ST, *Narrative*, 248n33.

25. Comment from Anne Gordon, county historian for Ulster County, while giving a tour of Ulster County, July 7, 2014.

26. CM, *Sojourner Truth*, 5.

27. ST, *Narrative*, 22.

28. ST, *Narrative*, 20.

29. ST, *Narrative*, 55, 56.

30. ST, *Narrative*, 248–49n34.

31. ST, *Narrative*, 22, 20.

32. ST, *Narrative*, 22, 23.

33. ST, *Narrative*, 16.

34. Spelled "Catlin" in ST, *Narrative*, but "Catton" in other sources.

35. MW, *Truth's America*, 52.

36. ST, *Narrative*, 24.

37. Deborah Gray White, *Ar'n't I a Woman?*, 98.

38. CM, *Sojourner Truth*, 7, 9.

39. ST, *Narrative*, 25.

40. Deborah Gray White, *Ar'n't I a Woman?*, 101.

41. "Proceedings of the Annual Meeting of the Friends of Human Progress in Michigan," *Anti-Slavery Bugle*, November 8, 1856, in *Sojourner Truth as Orator: Wit, Story, and Song*, ed. Suzanne Fitch and Roseann Mandziuk (Westport CT: Greenwood, 1997), 117–18.

42. ST, *Narrative*, 26.

43. ST, *Narrative*, 25.

44. Fabend, *Zion on the Hudson*, 184.

45. MW, *Truth's America*, 54, 55.

46. ST, *Narrative*, 40.

47. ST, *Narrative*, 41.

48. MW, *Truth's America*, 28.

49. Shane White, *Somewhat More Independent*, 103, 98.

50. Genovese, *Roll, Jordan, Roll*, 212.

51. MW, *Truth's America*, 44, 45.

52. Shane White, *Somewhat More Independent*, 105, 99.

53. *Narrative of the Life of Frederick Douglass, an American Slave, Written by Himself*, ed. John W. Blassingame, John R. McKivigan, and Peter P. Hinks (New Haven: Yale University Press, 2001), 56.

Chapter 2

1. CM, *Sojourner Truth*, 13–14.

2. MW, *Truth's America*, 38.

3. ST, *Narrative*, 27, 28, 29.

4. MW, *Truth's America*, 58.

5. ST, *Narrative*, 29.

6. MW, *Truth's America*, 76.

7. ST, *Narrative*, 45, 42.

8. MW, *Truth's America*, 29.

9. ST, *Narrative*, 44.

10. ST, *Narrative*, 45.

11. ST, *Narrative*, 108.

12. ST, *Narrative*, 46, 47.

13. *New York Daily Tribune*, September 7, 1853.

14. Catherine A. Brekus, *Strangers & Pilgrims: Female Preaching in America, 1740–1845* (Chapel Hill: University of North Carolina Press, 1998), 183.

15. Kyle T. Bulthuis, *Four Steeples over the City Streets: Religion and Society in New York's Early Republic Congregations* (New York: New York University Press, 2014), 58.

16. CM, *Sojourner Truth*, 22, 23.

17. NIP, *Sojourner Truth*, 32, 33.

18. ST, *Narrative*, 47, 30.

19. ST, *Narrative*, 32.

20. MW, *Truth's America*, 63.

21. ST, *Narrative*, 48.

22. MW, *Truth's America*, 64.

23. ST, *Narrative*, 32, 33.

24. CM, *Sojourner Truth*, 18.

25. Giselle Rhoden, "New Documents Reveal Abolitionist's Court Case to Free Her Child from Slavery," CNN, February 27, 2022, https://www.cnn.com /2022/02/27/us/sojourner-truth-court-battle-ny-archives/index.html.

26. ST, *Narrative*, 33.

27. ST, *Narrative*, 34, identifies this lawyer as Demain; however, CM, *Sojourner Truth*, 18, identifies him as Romeyn.

28. MW, *Truth's America*, 67.

29. ST, *Narrative*, 36.

30. People v. Gedney, March 18, 1828, New York State Archives, Supreme Court of Judicature (Utica), Writs of Habeas Corpus, 1807–1832, J0029-82, Box 3, Digital Collections: Text: People v. Solomon Gedney [NYSA_J0029-82 _1828_People_v_Gedney] (nysed.gov).

31. "Render unto them double" was a curse used in several biblical passages (see Ps. 28:4; Zech. 9:12; Rev. 18:6) asking God to repay evil deeds. NIP, *Sojourner Truth*, 35, interprets "render them double" as "everyday witchcraft." In any case, it was a plea for vengeance.

32. ST, *Narrative*, 37.

33. Rhoden, "New Documents Reveal Abolitionist's Court Case to Free Her

Child from Slavery," quoting Dr. James D. Folts, head of Researcher Services at the New York State Archives.

34. ST, *Narrative*, 39.

35. ST, *Narrative*, 56.

36. ST, *Narrative*, 49.

37. NIP, *Sojourner Truth*, 36.

38. ST, *Narrative*, 50.

39. Bulthuis, *Four Steeples*, 58.

40. Nell Irvin Painter, "Difference, Slavery and Memory: Sojourner Truth in Feminist Abolitionism," in *The Abolitionist Sisterhood: Women's Political Culture in Antebellum America*, ed. Jean Fagan Yellin and John C. Van Horne (Ithaca, NY: Cornell University Press, 1994), 143.

41. CM, *Sojourner Truth*, 22, 23.

Chapter 3

1. CM, *Sojourner Truth*, 24.

2. Edwin G. Burrows and Mike Wallace, *Gotham: A History of New York City to 1895* (New York: Oxford University Press, 1999), 547.

3. Jonathan Daniel Wells, *The Kidnapping Club: Wall Street, Slavery, and Resistance on the Eve of the Civil War* (New York: Bold Type Books, 2020), 7.

4. Wells, *The Kidnapping Club*, 39.

5. Kyle T. Bulthuis, *Four Steeples over the City Streets: Religion and Society in New York's Early Republic Congregations* (New York: New York University Press, 2014), 199.

6. Graham Russel Gao Hodges, *David Ruggles: A Radical Black Abolitionist and the Underground Railroad in New York City* (Chapel Hill: University of North Carolina Press, 2010), 90.

7. IR, *Sojourner Truth*, 86.

8. Wells, *The Kidnapping Club*, 68.

9. Hodges, *David Ruggles*, 145.

10. "Address by a Slave Mother," *New York Daily Tribune*, September 7, 1853, 5.

11. ST, *Narrative*, 54.

12. MW, *Truth's America*, 141.

13. ST, *Narrative*, 51.

14. Burrows and Wallace, *Gotham*, 547.

15. MW, *Truth's America*, 142.

16. Margaret Washington, "Going 'Where They Dare Not Follow': Race, Religion, and Sojourner Truth's Early Interracial Reform," *Journal of African American History* 98, no. 1 (Winter 2013): 51.

17. MW, *Truth's America*, 83.

18. Bulthuis, *Four Steeples*, 159.

19. Bulthuis, *Four Steeples*, 155, 179.

20. MW, *Truth's America*, 89.

21. Washington, "Going 'Where They Dare Not Follow,'" 53.

22. ST, *Narrative*, 55; see also MW, *Truth's America*, 89.

23. "Address by a Slave Mother," 5.

24. Bulthuis, *Four Steeples*, 185.

25. Nell Irvin Painter, "Sojourner Truth in Feminist Abolitionism," in *The Abolitionist Sisterhood: Women's Political Culture in Antebellum America*, ed. Jean Fagan Yellin and C. Van Horne (Philadelphia: Library Company of Philadelphia, 1994), 144.

26. Gilbert Vale, *Fanaticism: Its Source and Influence, Illustrated by the Simple Narrative of Isabella, in the Case of Matthias . . .* , 2 vols. in 1 (London: Forgotten Books, 2015; original 1835), 2:21.

27. Burrows and Wallace, *Gotham*, 483–84, 547.

28. ST, *Narrative*, 59.

29. MW, *Truth's America*, 91.

30. ST, *Narrative*, 59.

31. Washington, "Going 'Where They Dare Not Follow,'" 56.

32. ST, *Narrative*, 60.

33. Wendy E. Chmielewski, "Sojourner Truth: Utopian Vision and Search for Community, 1797–1883," in *Women in Spiritual and Communitarian Societies in the United States*, ed. Wendy Chmielewski, Louis J. Kern, and Marilyn Klee-Hartzell (Syracuse, NY: Syracuse University Press, 1993), 25.

34. MW, *Truth's America*, 95.

35. ST, *Narrative*, 60.

36. Paul E. Johnson and Sean Wilentz, *The Kingdom of Matthias: A Story of Sex and Salvation in 19th Century America* (Oxford: Oxford University Press, 1994), 28.

37. CM, *Sojourner Truth*, 27, 28.

38. Johnson and Wilentz, *The Kingdom of Matthias*, 43.

39. Washington, "Going 'Where They Dare Not Follow,'" 57.

40. MW, *Truth's America*, 99.

41. ST, *Narrative*, 62.

42. MW, *Truth's America*, 96.

43. ST, *Narrative*, 66.

44. Washington, "Going 'Where They Dare Not Follow,'" 58.

Chapter 4

1. ST, *Narrative*, 62.

2. Paul E. Johnson and Sean Wilentz, *The Kingdom of Matthias: A Story of Sex and Salvation in 19th Century America* (Oxford: Oxford University Press, 1994), 61.

3. Johnson and Wilentz, *The Kingdom of Matthias*, 63, 64.

4. Gilbert Vale, *Fanaticism: Its Source and Influence, Illustrated by the Simple Narrative of Isabella, in the Case of Matthias . . .* , 2 vols. in 1 (London: Forgotten Books, 2015; original 1835), 1:38; Johnson and Wilentz, *The Kingdom of Matthias*, 71.

5. Johnson and Wilentz, *The Kingdom of Matthias*, 88, 89.

6. ST, *Narrative*, 63.

7. Vale, *Fanaticism*, 1:18, 43.

8. MW, *Truth's America*, 98, 102.

9. Johnson and Wilentz, *The Kingdom of Matthias*, 99.

10. MW, *Truth's America*, 103.

11. Vale, *Fanaticism*, 1:50.

12. MW, *Truth's America*, 104.

13. Vale, *Fanaticism*, 1:111.

14. Johnson and Wilentz, *The Kingdom of Matthias*, 99, 103, 104.

15. Vale, *Fanaticism*, 1:25.

16. Kyle T. Bulthuis, *Four Steeples over the City Streets: Religion and Society in New York's Early Republic Congregations* (New York: New York University Press, 2014), 198.

17. Nell Irvin Painter, "Difference, Slavery and Memory: Sojourner Truth in Feminist Abolitionism," in *The Abolitionist Sisterhood: Women's Political Culture in Antebellum America*, ed. Jean Fagan Yellin and John C. Van Horne (Ithaca, NY: Cornell University Press, 1994), 145.

18. CM, *Sojourner Truth*, 33.

19. W. E. Drake, *The False Prophet! The Very Interesting and Remarkable Trial of Matthias, the False Prophet* (New York: J. W. Mitchell, 1835), 8.

20. NIP, *Sojourner Truth*, 54.

21. CM, *Sojourner Truth*, 33.

22. Johnson and Wilentz, *The Kingdom of Matthias*, 125.

23. Vale, *Fanaticism*, 2:54–57.

24. Vale, *Fanaticism*, 2:60–61.

25. Johnson and Wilentz, *The Kingdom of Matthias*, 137.

26. CM, *Sojourner Truth*, 36.

27. CM, *Sojourner Truth*, 37. See also Vale, *Fanaticism*, 1:14 and 2:109, for Vale's defense of Isabella's character.

28. "New York Anti-abolitionist Riots," *New York Times*, August 8, 1834, 2, under "Anti-Slavery Riots," https://en.wikipedia.org/wiki/New_York_anti-abolitionist_riots_(1834).

29. "Another Riot in Centre Street—a Church and Four Houses Injured," *New York Evening Post*, July 12, 1834.

30. Bulthuis, *Four Steeples*, 172, 173.

31. Vale, *Fanaticism*, 1:11–1.2

32. Johnson and Wilentz, *The Kingdom of Matthias*, 154.

33. Vale, *Fanaticism*, 2:116.

34. Drake, *The False Prophet!*, 3.

35. Vale, *Fanaticism*, 2:118.

36. Vale, *Fanaticism*, 1:18.

37. Vale, *Fanaticism*, 2:116, 126.

38. CM, *Sojourner Truth*, 253n39, quoting diary of Joseph Smith.

Chapter 5

1. Gilbert Vale, *Fanaticism: Its Source and Influence, Illustrated by the Simple Narrative of Isabella, in the Case of Matthias . . .* , 2 vols. in 1 (London: Forgotten Books, 2015; original 1835), 2:122.

2. Maria Stewart, "Why Sit Ye Here and Die?" (speech given to the New England Anti-Slavery Society, Boston, 1832, BlackPast, accessed October 30, 2019, https://www.blackpast.org/african-american-history/speeches-african-american-history/1832-maria-w-stewart-why-sit-ye-here-and-die/).

3. MW, *Truth's America*, 142.

4. ST, *Narrative*, 51.

5. Edwin G. Burrows and Mike Wallace, *Gotham: A History of New York City to 1895* (New York: Oxford University Press, 1999), 549.

6. Jonathan Daniel Wells, *The Kidnapping Club: Wall Street, Slavery, and Resistance on the Eve of the Civil War* (New York: Bold Type Books, 2020), 101.

7. ST, *Narrative*, 51.

8. NIP, *Sojourner Truth*, 67.

9. ST, *Narrative*, 52.

10. Sidney E. Kaplan, "Sojourner Truth's Son Peter," *Negro History Bulletin* 19 (November 1955): 34.

11. ST, *Narrative*, 52.

12. Catherine A. Brekus, *Strangers & Pilgrims: Female Preaching in America, 1740–1845* (Chapel Hill: University of North Carolina Press, 1998), 134.

13. ST, *Narrative*, 75.

14. "Sojourner Truth," *New York Daily Herald*, December 16, 1878, 2.

15. IR, *Sojourner Truth*, 79.

16. MW, *Truth's America*, 147.

17. ST, *Narrative*, 67.

18. ST, *Narrative*, 67.

19. Nell Irvin Painter, "Difference, Slavery and Memory: Sojourner Truth in Feminist Abolitionism," in *The Abolitionist Sisterhood: Women's Political Culture in Antebellum America*, ed. Jean Fagan Yellin and John C. Van Horne (Ithaca, NY: Cornell University Press, 1994), 145.

20. Stewart, "Why Sit Ye Here and Die?"

21. ST, *Narrative*, 68.

22. "Sojourner Truth," *Detroit Press and Tribune*, November 28, 1883, reprinted in the *Akron (OH) Summit County Beacon*, December 12, 1883, 3.

23. Harriet Beecher Stowe, "Sojourner Truth, the Libyan Sybil," *Atlantic Monthly*, April 1863, quoted in ST, *Narrative*, 111.

24. "Personal Reminiscences," *Chicago Inter Ocean*, August 13, 1879, 3.

25. "Emancipation and the Fifteenth Amendment: The Celebration Yesterday," *Washington Evening Star*, April 14, 1870.

Chapter 6

1. ST, *Narrative*, 68.

2. Nell Irvin Painter, "Difference, Slavery and Memory: Sojourner Truth in

Feminist Abolitionism," in *The Abolitionist Sisterhood: Women's Political Culture in Antebellum America*, ed. Jean Fagan Yellin and John C. Van Horne (Ithaca, NY: Cornell University Press, 1994), 145.

3. MW, *Truth's America*, 150.

4. Painter, "Difference, Slavery and Memory," 146.

5. ST, *Narrative*, 69.

6. "Cold Spring–Anniversary of the Fourth of July," NYS Historic Newspapers, *Long Islander*, June 30, 1843, http://nyshistoricnewspapers.org/lccn/sn 83031119/.

7. ST, *Narrative*, 71.

8. Painter, "Difference, Slavery and Memory," 153.

9. ST, *Narrative*, 72.

10. ST, *Narrative*, 74.

11. ST, *Narrative*, 76–78.

12. Rachel Stearns to Maria Chapman, 184[3], photocopy from David Ruggles Center, Florence, MA.

13. Christopher Clark, *The Communitarian Moment: The Radical Challenge of the Northampton Association* (Amherst: University of Massachusetts Press, 2003), 13, 43, 46, 57.

14. ST, *Narrative*, 77, 78.

15. CM, *Sojourner Truth*, 50.

16. Christopher Clark, introduction to *Letters from an American Utopia: The Stetson Family and the Northampton Association, 1843–1847* (Amherst: University of Massachusetts Press, 2004), 15, 9.

17. David Rhinelander, "Silk: An Important Thread in State's Fabric," *Hartford Courant*, May 21, 1999, https://www.courant.com/news/connecticut/hc -xpm-1999-05-21-9905210388-story.html.

18. IR, *Sojourner Truth*, 83.

Chapter 7

1. MW, *Truth's America*, 158.

2. Charles A. Sheffeld, ed., *The History of Florence, Massachusetts* (London: Forgotten Books, 2015; original 1895), 76.

3. Sheffeld, *History of Florence*, 77.

4. Kathryn Grover, "Nomination of the Hill/Ross Farm at 123 Meadow

Street, Florence, Massachusetts to the National Register of Historic Places-Underground Railroad Context" (unpublished paper, David Ruggles Center, Florence, MA, n.d.), 3.

5. ST, *Narrative*, 82.

6. "Northampton Association of Education and Industry," Historic Northampton, accessed November 29, 2020, http://www.historic-northampton .org/highlights/educationindustry.html.

7. Christopher Clark, *The Communitarian Moment: The Radical Challenge of the Northampton Association* (Amherst: University of Massachusetts Press, 2003), 87–88, 94.

8. Arthur Hill, "Florence, the Sanctuary of the Colored Race" (unpublished manuscript, David Ruggles Center, Florence, MA, 1912).

9. Sheffeld, *History of Florence*, 71.

10. ST, *Narrative*, 89.

11. MW, *Truth's America*, 165.

12. ST, *Narrative*, 78–82.

13. CM, *Sojourner Truth*, 221.

14. ST, *Narrative*, 81–82.

15. Graham Russel Gao Hodges, *David Ruggles: A Radical Black Abolitionist and the Underground Railroad in New York City* (Chapel Hill: University of North Carolina Press, 2010), 183.

16. Clark, *The Communitarian Moment*, 89.

17. Sheffeld, *History of Florence*, 130–33; Clark, *The Communitarian Moment*, 89.

18. Rebecca Edwards, *36 Antislavery Songs* (Poughkeepsie, NY: Vassar College, 2011), 41, 42.

19. Frederick Douglass, "What I Found at the Northampton Association," in Sheffeld, *History of Florence*, 131–32.

20. Hodges, *David Ruggles*, 178–79.

21. Grover, "Nomination of the Hill/Ross Farm," 3.

22. MW, *Truth's America*, 158.

23. Dolly W. Stetson to James Stetson, May 4, 1845, in *Letters from an American Utopia: The Stetson Family and the Northampton Association, 1843–1847*, ed. Christopher Clark (Amherst: University of Massachusetts Press, 2004), 106.

24. Clark, *The Communitarian Moment*, 93.

25. ST, *Narrative*, 74.

26. Arthur G. Hill, "Anti-Slavery Days in Florence" (unpublished manuscript, David Ruggles Center, 1912), 3.

27. ST, *Narrative*, 239, 240.

28. Hill, "Anti-Slavery Days," 1.

29. Sheffeld, *History of Florence*, 74.

30. Clark, *The Communitarian Moment*, 95, 92.

31. Clark, introduction to *Letters from an American Utopia*, 13.

32. Sheffeld, *History of Florence*, 102.

33. MW, *Truth's America*, 163.

34. Dolly Stetson to James Stetson, October 6, 1844, "Emerging Equality," accessed October 20, 2021, http://radicalequality.emergingamerica.org/sources/letter-dolly-w-stetson-to-james-a-stetson-1844-10-06/.

35.Dolly Stetson to James Stetson, September 1, 1844, "Emerging Equality," accessed October 20, 2021, http://radicalequality.emergingamerica.org/sources/letter-dolly-w-stetson-to-james-a-stetson-1844-09-01/.

36. Nell Irvin Painter, introduction to ST, *Narrative*, xviii. Painter writes that Truth's daughter Diana's servitude expired in 1840, Elizabeth's in 1850, and Sophia's in 1851. Dumont's role, if any, in the daughters' visit to the NAEI is unclear.

37. Dolly Stetson to James Stetson, July 26 [1844], in *Letters from an American Utopia*, 47.

38. MW, *Truth's America*, 163.

39. Almira Stetson to James Stetson, [June 9, 1844], in *Letters from an American Utopia*, 47.

40. MW, *Truth's America*, 43, 164.

41. Dolly Stetson to James Stetson, [March 18, 1845], "Emerging America," accessed November 7, 2021, http://radicalequality.emergingamerica.org/sources/letter-dolly-w-stetson-to-james-a-stetson-1845-03-18/.

42. Henry Mayer, *All on Fire: William Lloyd Garrison and the Abolition of Slavery* (New York: St. Martin's Griffin, 1998), 323.

43. William Lloyd Garrison, "Song of the Abolitionist," in Edwards, *36 Antislavery Songs*, 26.

44. IR, *Sojourner Truth*, 85.

45. Sheffeld, *History of Florence*, 103.

46. Clark, *The Communitarian Moment*, 212.

47. Clark, *The Communitarian Moment*, 94.

48. ST, *Narrative*, 239.

Chapter 8

1. CM, *Sojourner Truth*, 53.

2. CM, *Sojourner Truth*, 93, 62, 63.

3. Elizabeth Cady Stanton, Matilda Joslyn Gage, Susan B. Anthony, eds., *History of Woman Suffrage* (1862), Project Gutenberg, accessed October 21, 2021, https://www.gutenberg.org/ebooks/28039, 2009, 2:926–27.

4. Jean M. Humez, "Reading the *Narrative of Sojourner Truth* as a Collaborative Text," *Frontiers: A Journal of Women's Studies* 16, no. 1 (1996): 31.

5. Eugene D. Genovese, *Roll, Jordan, Roll: The World the Slaves Made* (New York: Vintage Books, 1976), 242.

6. Sojourner Truth, "Letter to the Editor of the Inter Ocean," *Chicago Daily Inter Ocean*, April 16, 1881, 9.

7. MW, *Truth's America*, 182.

8. Humez, "Reading the *Narrative of Sojourner Truth*," 45, 30, 33, 36.

9. Sojourner Truth, *Book of Life*, in *Narrative*, 187. The *Book of Life* was first added to Truth's *Narrative* in 1875.

10. NIP, *Sojourner Truth*, 111–12. George Brown Yerrinton (also spelled Yerrington) was the first printer of the *Narrative of Sojourner Truth*.

11. NIP, *Sojourner Truth*, 107. The author of the unattributed quote is the poet Martin Farquhar Tupper.

12. Humez, "Reading the *Narrative of Sojourner Truth*," 42, 37, 31.

13. ST, *Narrative*, 91–92.

14. NIP, *Sojourner Truth*, 263.

15. *National Era*, April 25, 1850, 4.

16. *Anti-Slavery Bugle*, June 15, 1850, 158.

17. "N. E. Anti-Slavery Society," *New York Daily Tribune*, June 3, 1850.

18. Roseann Mandziuk, "'Grotesque and Ludicrous, but Yet Inspiring': Depictions of Sojourner Truth and Rhetoric of Domination," *Quarterly Journal of Speech* 100, no. 4 (2014): 468.

19. "Editorial Correspondence," *Richmond Enquirer*, June 7, 1850, 1.

20. Andrea Moore Kerr, *Lucy Stone: Speaking Out for Equality* (New Brunswick, NJ: Rutgers University Press, 1992), 58.

21. Kerr, *Lucy Stone*, 59.

22. MW, *Truth's America*, 195–97.

23. [Frances Titus], "A Memorial Chapter," in ST, *Narrative*, 240.

24. MW, *Truth's America*, 268.

25. IR, *Sojourner Truth*, 95.

26. Rebecca Edwards, *36 Antislavery Songs* (Poughkeepsie, NY: Vassar College, 2011), 24.

27. "Celebration at Abington," *Liberator*, July 12, 1850. Italics indicate slight adaptations in quotations, to make them work as a dialogue.

28. *Rhode Island Anti-Slavery Standard*, November 28, 1850.

29. *Massachusetts Spy*, October 30, 1850, quoted in http://www.worcester history.org.

30. "Affairs in New York; Political and Legal," *Washington (DC) Southern Press*, October 29, 1850, Chronicling America, Library of Congress, http://chron iclingamerica.loc.gov/lccn/sn82014764/1850-10-29/ed-1/seq-3/.

31. MW, *Truth's America*, 203, quoting *New York Herald*, October 25, 1850.

32. "Woman's Rights Convention," *Lancaster (WI) Grant County Herald*, November 14, 1850, 4.

33. "The Woman's Convention," *Athens (TN) Post*, November 22, 1850, Chronicling America, Library of Congress, http://chroniclingamerica.loc.gov /lccn/sn84024443/1850-11-22/ed-1/seq-1/.

34. "Awful Combination of Socialism, Abolitionism, and Infidelity," *New York Herald*, October 25, 1850, Chronicling America, Library of Congress, http:// chroniclingamerica.loc.gov/lccn/sn83030313/1850-10-25/ed-1/seq-1/.

35. "Rediscovered Voices, Jane Swisshelm," Worcester Women's History Project, accessed October 21, 2021, http://www1.assumption.edu/WWHP/Re discovered.html. Swisshelm did not attend the 1850 National Women's Rights Convention, but she objected to combining the issues of antislavery and women's rights. "We are pretty nearly out of patience with the dogged perseverance with which so many of our Reformers persist in their attempt to do everything at once," Swisshelm wrote. "In a Woman's Rights Convention, the question of color had no right to a hearing."

36. "Pillsbury Letter," Worcester Women's History Project, accessed October 21, 2021, http://www.wwhp.org/Resources/WomansRights/pillsbury_letter.html.

37. J. G. Forman, "Woman's Rights Convention," *New York Daily Tribune*, October 26, 1850, 6.

Chapter 9

1. "Refuge of Oppression," *Liberator*, December 6, 1850.

2. "Enthusiastic Reception of George Thompson, by the Colored Citizens," *Liberator*, November 22, 1850.

3. See MW, *Truth's America*, 207–14, for details of Truth's trip with Thompson, and CM, *Sojourner Truth*, 57.

4. Dorothy Sterling, *Ahead of Her Time: Abby Kelley and the Politics of Anti-Slavery* (New York: Norton, 1994), 270.

5. "Domestic Correspondence, Geo. Thompson in New York State," *National Anti-Slavery Standard*, March 6, 1851, 8.

6. George Thompson, "Anti-Slavery Convention at Rochester, March 15, 1851," *Liberator*, April 4, 1851, 1.

7. "George Thompson in Union Village," *Liberator*, February 28, 1851, 8.

8. George Thompson, "Anti-Slavery Convention at Rochester, March 15, 1851."

9. Truth to Garrison, April 11, 1864, Boston Public Library, Anti-Slavery Collection of Distinction, accessed October 22, 2021, https://www.digitalcommon wealth.org/search/commonwealth:6w9254678.

10. CM, *Sojourner Truth*, 57–58.

11. Truth to Isaac Post and Amy Post, n.d., University of Rochester, Isaac and Amy Post Family Papers, accessed January 4, 2019, https://rbscpexhibits .lib.rochester.edu/viewer/2630.

12. "The Rights of Woman: Ohio Woman's Rights Convention," *New York Daily Tribune*, June 6, 1851, 7.

13. "The Proceedings of the Woman's Rights Convention, Held at Akron, Ohio, May 28 and 29, 1851," Woman's Rights Convention, Lucy Stone, National American Woman Suffrage Association Collection, and Susan B. Anthony Collection, Library of Congress, accessed September 10, 2018, https://www.loc.gov /resource/rbnawsa.n8317/?sp=9&st=text.

14. "The Rights of Woman."

15. Michael Phillips-Anderson, "Sojourner Truth, 'Address at the Woman's Rights Convention in Akron, Ohio' (29 May 1851)," *Voices of Democracy* 7 (2012): 24.

16. Lucy Colman, *Reminiscences* (London: Forgotten Books, 2018; original 1891), 24.

17. Truth to Garrison, August 28, [1851], Boston Public Library, Anti-Slavery Collection of Distinction, accessed August 6, 2018, https://www.digitalcommon

wealth.org/search?f%5Bcollection_name_ssim%5D%5B%5D=Anti-Slavery
+%28Collection+of+Distinction%29&f%5Binstitution_name_ssim%5D%5B
%5D=Boston+Public+Library&page=1&per_page=20&q=Sojourner+Truth&utf8
=%E2%9C%93.

18. Russell B. Nye, "Marius Robinson, a Forgotten Abolitionist Leader," *Ohio Archaeological and Historical Quarterly* 55 (April-June 1946): 151.

19. Eric Foner, *Reconstruction: America's Unfinished Revolution, 1863–1877* (New York: Harper Perennial, 2014), 85.

20. "Woman's Convention, Akron May 28," *Liberator*, June 13, 1851, 4; "Woman's Rights Convention," *New York Daily Tribune*, June 6, 1851, 7.

21. "Woman's Rights Convention," *Lancaster (WI) Grant County Herald*, November 14, 1850, 4.

22. Phillips-Anderson, "Sojourner Truth, 'Address,'" 33.

23. [Marius Robinson], "Women's Rights Convention: Sojourner Truth," *Anti-Slavery Bugle*, June 21, 1851, 4.

24. Phillips-Anderson, "Sojourner Truth, 'Address,'" 33.

25. Truth to Amy Post, n.d., University of Rochester, Isaac and Amy Post Family Papers, accessed January 4, 2019, https://rbscpexhibits.lib.rochester.edu/viewer/2630.

26. ST, *Narrative*, 93.

27. Colman, *Reminiscences*, 65.

28. Sallie Holley and John White Chadwick, *A Life for Liberty: Anti-Slavery and Other Letters of Sallie Holley* (New York: G. P. Putnam's Sons, 1899), 104.

29. "Convention in Salem," *Anti-Slavery Bugle*, October 25, 1852.

30. David Blight, *Frederick Douglass* (New York: Simon & Schuster, 2018), 185.

31. *National Anti-Slavery Standard*, July 4, 1863. Quotations are slightly updated. The story of the weasel in the wheat was retold by Phoebe Stickney, a white friend of Truth's who presented it as a reminiscence from before the Civil War.

32. *Narrative of the Life of Frederick Douglass, an American Slave, Written by Himself*, ed. John W. Blassingame, John R. McKivigan, and Peter P. Hinks (New Haven: Yale University Press, 2001), 54.

33. Blight, *Frederick Douglass*, 241.

34. Blight, *Frederick Douglass*, 268.

35. Douglass formed an alliance with Gerrit Smith, who ran for president on

the Liberty Party ticket in 1848, and was later elected to the US House of Representatives. Smith was also a philanthropist who supported antislavery efforts, including Douglass's paper, the *North Star*.

36. Sterling, *Ahead of Her Time*, 273.

37. Blight, *Frederick Douglass*, 216.

38. Kyle T. Bulthuis, *Four Steeples over the City Streets: Religion and Society in New York's Early Republic Congregations* (New York: New York University Press, 2014), 185.

39. [Oliver Johnson], "Anniversary of the Western Anti-Slavery Society," *Pennsylvania Freeman*, September 4, 1852.

40. "Western Anti-Slavery," *Frederick Douglass' Paper*, September 3, 1852.

41. Lillie Wyman, *American Chivalry* (Boston: W. B. Clarke, 1913), 104, 105.

42. William Still, "Sojourner Truth: Her Strange Career, Some Very Interesting Reminiscences," *Philadelphia Evening Bulletin*, July 19, 1876, reprinted in *Friends' Review: A Religious, Literary and Miscellaneous Journal*, 1876, 29, 829.

43. CM, *Sojourner Truth*, 85.

44. IR, *Sojourner Truth*, 97.

45. [Frederick Douglass], "Mrs. Sojourner Truth," *New Era*, April 21, 1870.

Chapter 10

1. Truth to Mrs. Gale, April 14, 1853, Collections of the Manuscript Division, Library of Congress.

2. CM, *Sojourner Truth*, 94.

3. "Anti-Slavery Meetings in New York City," *Liberator*, September 9, 1853.

4. "New York City Anti-Slavery Society," *New York Daily Tribune*, September 4, 1853.

5. "Exciting Week in New York," *Liberator*, September 16, 1853.

6. "Row at an Anti-Slavery Meeting in New York," *Pittsburgh Daily Post*, September 8, 1853.

7. Sojourner Truth, "Address by a Slave Mother," *New York Daily Tribune*, September 7, 1853, 5.

8. Edwin G. Burrows and Mike Wallace, *Gotham: A History of New York City to 1895* (New York: Oxford University Press, 1999), 530.

9. Margaret Hope Bacon, "By Moral Force Alone: Antislavery Women and Nonresistance," in *The Abolitionist Sisterhood: Women's Political Culture in Ante-*

bellum America, ed. Jean Fagan Yellin and John C. Van Horne (Ithaca, NY: Cornell University Press, 1994), 294.

10. "Mob Convention," in *History of Woman's Suffrage* (1882), 1:567–68, 111. See also NIP, *Sojourner Truth*, 135, 136.

11. "Woman's Rights Convention," *New York Daily Tribune*, September 8, 1853, 5.

12. "Mob Convention," 1:567–68, 111.

13. Bacon, "By Moral Force Alone," 294.

14. Harriet Beecher Stowe, "Sojourner Truth, the Libyan Sibyl," in ST, *Narrative*, 103.

15. Deborah Gray White, *Ar'n't I a Woman? Female Slaves in the Plantation South* (New York: Norton, 1999), 162.

16. "Lecture by Sojourner Truth," *National Anti-Slavery Standard*, December 10, 1853.

17. "Fugitive Slave Anthony Burns Arrested," Mass. Moments, accessed March 18, 2019, https://www.massmoments.org/moment-details/fugitive-slave-anthony-burns-arrested.html.

18. *Liberator*, July 7, 1854.

19. MW, *Truth's America*, 264, quoting the *Liberator*, July 14, 1854.

20. Ed Shanahan, "$27 Million for Reparations over Slave Ties Pledged by Seminary," *New York Times*, October 21, 2019, https://www.nytimes.com/2019/10/21/nyregion/princeton-seminary-slavery-reparations.html. See also Megan Flynn, "Slaves Helped Build Virginia Theological Seminary. The School will Spend 1.7 Million Dollars in Reparations," *Washington Post*, September 9, 2019, https://www.washingtonpost.com/nation/2019/09/10/virginia-theological-seminary-reparations-slavery/.

21. "Proceedings at the Anti-Slavery Celebration, Framingham, Massachusetts," July 4, 1854, *Liberator*, July 14, 1854, 2.

22. "Our Correspondence," *Frederick Douglass' Paper*, June 15, 1855, accessed March 5, 2019, https://www.accessible.com/accessible/print?AADocList=1&AADocStyle=&AAStyleFile=&AABeanName=toc1&AANextPage=/printFullDocFromXML.jsp&AACheck=1.1.1.2.1 (emphasis added).

23. Parker Pillsbury, quoted in Lillie Buffum Chase Wyman, *American Chivalry* (Boston: W. B. Clarke, 1913), 105–6. See also "Report by James A. Dugdale," *National Anti-Slavery Standard*, July 4,1863. Sojourner Truth, *Book of Life*, in

Narrative, 93, sets the story in Michigan and has Truth confronting a "young Methodist" during a violent thunderstorm.

Chapter 11

1. Brian C. Wilson, "The Battle for Battle Creek: Sectarian Competition in the Yankee West," *Quaker Theology*, accessed March 17, 2022, https://quakertheo logy.org/the-battle-for-battle-creek/.

2. CM, *Sojourner Truth*, 95–97.

3. Sojourner Truth, "Personal Reminiscences," *Chicago Inter Ocean*, August 13, 1879, 3.

4. Wilson, "The Battle for Battle Creek."

5. Patricia L. Humphrey, "Pioneer of Freedom," *Columbia (MD) Union Visitor*, February 15, 1989, 4–5.

6. CM, *Sojourner Truth*, 243.

7. Martin Ashley and Mary Butler, "Milestones in the Life of Truth," *Heritage Battle Creek: A Journal of Local History* 8 (1997): 8, 27.

8. Nell Irvin Painter, "Difference, Slavery and Memory: Sojourner Truth in Feminist Abolitionism," in *The Abolitionist Sisterhood: Women's Political Culture in Antebellum America*, ed. Jean Fagan Yellin and John C. Van Horne (Ithaca, NY: Cornell University Press, 1994), 149.

9. Frances Thornton, "Harmonia: Memories of a Lost Village," *Heritage Battle Creek*, accessed April 4, 2019, http://www.heritagebattlecreek.org/index.php ?option=com_content&view=article&id=137&Itemid=73. See also MW, *Truth's America*, 279.

10. Ann Braude, *Radical Spirits: Spiritualism and Women's Rights in Nineteenth-Century America*, 2nd. ed. (Bloomington: Indiana University Press, 2001), 12, 34, 29.

11. Eugene D. Genovese, *Roll, Jordan, Roll: The World the Slaves Made* (New York: Vintage Books, 1976), 217.

12. Nick Buckley, "The Rise and Fall of Harmonia, a Spiritualist Utopia and Home to Sojourner Truth," *Battle Creek Enquirer*, January 16, 2019, https://www .battlecreekenquirer.com/story/life/2019/01/16/rise-and-fall-harmonia-battle -creeks-spiritualist-utopia/2214809002/.

13. Braude, *Radical Spirits*, 68–69.

14. E. A. [Lukens], "Rochester Knockings," *Anti-Slavery Bugle*, May 3, 1851, 131.

15. NIP, *Sojourner Truth*, 146; CM, *Sojourner Truth*, 98, 99.

16. IR, *Sojourner Truth*, 93.

17. CM, *Sojourner Truth*, 102.

18. Lucy Colman, *Reminiscences* (London: Forgotten Books, 2018; original 1891), 25, 30.

19. Parker Pillsbury, "Progress of Disunionism at the West," *Liberator*, October 23, 1857.

20. *Anti-Slavery Bugle*, November 7, 1857, 3.

21. "Sojourner Truth and the Spiritualists," *Madison Wisconsin State Journal*, July 10, 1869, 2. A similar story appeared in the *Blue Rapids (KS) Times*, July 18, 1878, 2.

22. "Michigan Spiritualism, Semi-Annual Meeting of the State Association," *Detroit Free Press*, June 13, 1871.

23. "The Dred Scott Decision: Opinion of Chief Justice Taney," Library of Congress, accessed March 18, 2022, https://www.loc.gov/item/17001543/.

24. David Blight, *Frederick Douglass* (New York: Simon & Schuster, 2018), 227.

25. "Black Laws of 1807," Ohio History Central, accessed March 18, 2022, https://ohiohistorycentral.org/w/Black_Laws_of_1807.

26. ST, *Narrative*, 215, 94.

27. "Being Black in Indiana," Indiana Historical Bureau, accessed March 18, 2022, https://www.in.gov/history/2548.htm.

28. "Confrontation and Violence," Indiana Historical Bureau, accessed March 18, 2022, https://www.in.gov/history/3115.htm.

29. MW, *Truth's America*, 285, says Truth's invitations to speak in Indiana came from "Universalists, Progressive Friends, utopians, some traditional denominations and Blacks."

30. William Hayward, "Pro-Slavery in Indiana," *Liberator*, October 15, 1858, 1.

31. William Hayward, letter to the editor of *Warsaw Northern Indianan*, October 8, 1858, courtesy of Indiana State Library. See also ST, *Narrative*, 94–95, which derives from Hayward's report.

32. NIP, *Sojourner Truth*, 139.

33. Hayward, letter to the editor of the *Warsaw Northern Indianan*.

34. NIP, *Sojourner Truth*, 140.

35. *Warsaw Northern Indianan*, vol. 3, October 8, 1858.

36. NIP, *Sojourner Truth*, 141.

37. Nancy Koester, *Introduction to the History of Christianity in the United States*, 2nd ed. (Minneapolis: Fortress, 2015), 118, 120.

38. Harriet Beecher Stowe, "The President's Message," *New York Independent*, December 20, 1860, 1.

Chapter 12

1. Abraham Lincoln, "First Inaugural Address," in *Abraham Lincoln, Speeches and Writings, 1859–1865*, ed. Don E. Fehrenbacher (New York: Library of America, 1989), 224.

2. Alexander H. Stephens, "'Cornerstone' Speech," Learning for Justice, accessed March 18, 2022, https://www.learningforjustice.org/classroom -resources/texts/hard-history/cornerstone-speech?gclid=CjoKCQjwiNSLBhCP ARIsAKNS4_fqiYsk5VDWAK3i-jl2sSXv_k9XF3LhA4H2hiKLetqnoXfSqrdPWR waAlc_EALw_wcB.

3. Josephine Griffing, "Letter from Michigan," *Anti-Slavery Bugle*, March 16, 1861, 3.

4. ST, *Narrative*, 118, says the conflict at the courthouse in Angola occurred in the fall of 1863. But several other sources have it in May 1861. Truth was gathering supplies for the Michigan Colored Regiment in the fall of 1863.

5. Patrick Furlong, "Sojourner Truth Visits Indiana in 1861," Indiana Historical Bureau, accessed April 30, 2019, https://www.in.gov/history/4085.htm. Furlong notes that article 13 was unenforceable during and after the Civil War. It was repealed in 1881.

6. Keith E. Melder, "Angel of Mercy in Washington: Josephine Griffing and the Freedmen, 1864–1872," *Records of the Columbia Historical Society, Washington, D.C.*, vol. 63/65 (1963), 248.

7. Josephine Griffing, "Treason in Disguise," *Liberator*, June 21, 1861.

8. Josephine Griffing, "Shameful Persecution," *Liberator*, June 28, 1861.

9. Furlong, "Sojourner Truth Visits Indiana in 1861."

10. ST, *Narrative*, 96.

11. Furlong, "Sojourner Truth Visits Indiana in 1861."

12. Darcy Grimaldo Grigsby, *Enduring Truths: Sojourner's Shadows and Substance* (Chicago: University of Chicago Press, 2015), 33.

13. Griffing," "Treason in Disguise."

14. Griffing, "Shameful Persecution."

15. "Angola," *Steuben (IN) Republican*, May 18, 1861.

16. "Old Time Papers," *Steuben (IN) Republican*, November 28, 1900.

17. ST, *Narrative*, 96.

18. Griffing, "Treason in Disguise."

19. Two letters exchanged between "Many Citizens" and Mr. G. W. Phenicle, captain of the Home Guards, May 1861, reprinted in "Old Time Papers," 1.

20. Griffing, "Treason in Disguise."

21. ST, *Narrative*, 96, 97.

22. "Old Time Papers," 1.

23. ST, *Narrative*, 97.

24. Griffing, "Treason in Disguise."

25. "Old Time Papers," 1.

26. Patrick J. Furlong, "The 'Symbolic Rape,' Arrest and Defense of Sojourner Truth in Indiana," *Indiana History Blog*, June 5, 2018, https://blog.history.in.gov /tag/steuben-county-courthouse/.

27. ST, *Narrative*, 97, 98.

28. The Second Confiscation Act, July 17, 1862, Freedmen and Southern Society Project, accessed March 18, 2022, http://www.freedmen.umd.edu/conact2 .htm.

29. Doris Kearns Goodwin, *Team of Rivals: The Political Genius of Abraham Lincoln* (New York: Simon & Schuster, 2005), 688.

30. MW, *Truth's America*, 298, 299.

31. CM, *Sojourner Truth*, 243 (the pastor's name was Samuel J. Rogers).

32. Phebe Stickney, "Sojourner Truth," *National Anti-Slavery Standard*, April 25, 1863.

33. Phebe Stickney, "Sojourner Truth," *National Anti-Slavery Standard*, April 4, 1863.

34. MW, *Truth's America*, 303.

35. Stickney, "Sojourner Truth," April 25, 1863.

36. *National Anti-Slavery Standard*, July 11, 1863, 4.

37. David Blight, *Frederick Douglass* (New York: Simon & Schuster, 2018), 395.

38. Michael O. Smith, "Raising a Black Regiment in Michigan: Adversity in Triumph," in *A Question of Manhood: A Reader in U.S. Black Men's History and*

Masculinity, vol. 1, ed. Darlene Clark Hine and Ernestine Jenkins (Bloomington: Indiana University Press, 1999–2001), 509.

39. Catherine Clinton, *Harriet Tubman: The Road to Freedom* (New York: Little, Brown, 2004), 184.

40. MW, *Truth's America*, 305.

41. Stickney, "Sojourner Truth," April 25, 1863.

42. Truth to Mary Gale, Detroit, February 25, 1864, at "Sojourner Truth Ministers to the Colored Troops," African American Odyssey: The Quest for Full Citizenship, Library of Congress, accessed March 18, 2022, https://www.loc.gov/exhibits/african-american-odyssey/civil-war.html#obj17.

43. Tim Talbott, "Sojourner Truth's Grandson, 54th Massachusetts POW," *Random Thoughts on History*, December 17, 2017, http://randomthoughtsonhistory.blogspot.com/2017/12/sojourner-truths-grandson-54th.html.

44. *National Anti-Slavery Standard*, September 12, 1863.

45. "Says the *Commonwealth*," Truth letter to Mr. Redpath, *National Anti-Slavery Standard*, April 27, 1863.

46. Truth to Eliza Leggett, quoted in MW, *Truth's America*, 307.

47. Stacy Newman, "First Michigan Colored Regiment," *Encyclopedia of Detroit*, Detroit Historical Society, accessed March 18, 2022, https://detroithistorical.org/learn/encyclopedia-of-detroit/first-michigan-colored-regiment.

48. Smith, "Raising a Black Regiment," 509.

49. *Detroit Free Press*, November 22, 1863.

50. "Sojourner Truth," *National Anti-Slavery Standard*, January 2, 1864, quoting the *Detroit Advertiser and Tribune*.

51. Smith, "Raising a Black Regiment," 503.

52. ST, *Narrative*, 86.

53. Truth to Oliver Johnson, in *National Anti-Slavery Standard*, February 13, 1864.

54. Truth to Gale, Detroit, February 25, 1864, at "Sojourner Truth Ministers to the Colored Troops."

Chapter 13

1. Margaret Malamud, *African Americans and the Classics: Antiquity, Abolition, and Activism* (London and New York: I. B. Taurus, 2016), 4.

2. L. M. C., "A Chat with the Editor of the Standard," *Liberator*, January 20, 1865.

3. Malamud, *African Americans*, 173, 3.

4. "Libyan Sybil," High Museum of Art, accessed March 18, 2022, https://www.high.org/collections/libyan-sibyl/.

5. Harriet Beecher Stowe, "The Libyan Sibyl," in ST, *Narrative*, 106, 107, 109, 110.

6. Stowe, "The Libyan Sibyl," 104; MW, *Truth's America*, 302, for Truth "in blackface."

7. ST, *Narrative*, 188.

8. *Detroit Advertiser and Tribune*, January 11, 1869, quoted in ST, *Narrative*, 118.

9. Truth to editor, *Boston Commonwealth*, July 3, 1863; Darcy Grimaldo Grigsby, *Enduring Truths: Sojourner's Shadows and Substance* (Chicago: University of Chicago Press, 2015), 42. See also "Letter from Miss Holley: Sojourner Truth," *National Anti-Slavery Standard*, September 17, 1864.

10. *National Anti-Slavery Standard*, March 28, 1863.

11. Stowe, "Libyan Sibyl," in ST, *Narrative*, 108.

12. Nell Irvin Painter, "Difference, Slavery and Memory: Sojourner Truth in Feminist Abolitionism," in *The Abolitionist Sisterhood: Women's Political Culture in Antebellum America*, ed. Jean Fagan Yellin and John C. Van Horne (Ithaca, NY: Cornell University Press, 1994), 151.

13. Gage's article also appeared in the *National Anti-Slavery Standard*, May 2, 1863.

14. Elizabeth Cady Stanton, Matilda Joslyn Gage, and Susan B. Anthony, eds., *History of Woman Suffrage* (1862), Project Gutenberg, accessed October 21, 2021, https://www.gutenberg.org/ebooks/28039, 2009, 1:115–17.

15. Sojourner Truth, "Ain't I a Woman?" in *Feminism: The Essential Historical Writings*, ed. Miriam Schneir (New York: Vintage Books, 1994), 93–95.

16. Mrs. F. D. Gage, "Sojourner Truth," *National Anti-Slavery Standard*, May 2, 1863.

17. "The Proceedings of the Woman's Rights Convention, Held at Akron, Ohio, May 28 and 29, 1851," National American Woman Suffrage Association Collection, and Susan B. Anthony Collection, Library of Congress, accessed March 18, 2022, https://www.loc.gov/resource/rbnawsa.n8317/?sp=9&st=text.

18. See notes for chap. 9.

19. Gage, "Sojourner Truth."

20. Painter, "Difference, Slavery and Memory," 140.

21. Grigsby, *Enduring Truths*, 44.

22. NIP, *Sojourner Truth*, 186; see also Grigsby, *Enduring Truths*, 2.

23. Grigsby, *Enduring Truths*, 45, 47.

24. NIP, *Sojourner Truth*, 198.

25. Grigsby, *Enduring Truths*, 17.

26. David Blight, *Frederick Douglass* (New York: Simon & Schuster, 2018), 599.

27. Sojourner Truth, letter to *National Anti-Slavery Standard*, April 16, 1864.

Chapter 14

1. "Sojourner Truth," *Buffalo Weekly Express*, August 16, 1864.

2. "Sojourner Truth. Letter from Miss Holley," *National Anti-Slavery Standard*, September 17, 1864.

3. CM, *Sojourner Truth*, 188. See also Rosa Belle Holt, "A Heroine in Ebony," *Chautauquan* 23 (1896): 462, accessed July 16, 2019, https://books.google.com/books?id=mGkXAQAAIAAJ&printsec=frontcover&source=gbs_ge_summary_r&cad=0#v=onepage&q=%22Sojourner%20Truth%22&f=false, and Sandra A. Johnson, "Truth and Tubman: Women Who Fought against Slavery," *Austin (IL) Weekly News*, July 13, 2005, https://www.austinweeklynews.com/2005/07/13/truth-and-tubman-women-who-fought-against-slavery/.

4. ST, *Narrative*, 118.

5. CM, *Sojourner Truth*, 118.

6. *National Anti-Slavery Standard*, August 6, 1864.

7. Tom Lewis, *Washington: A History of Our National City* (Philadelphia: Basic Books, 2015), 162.

8. Kate Masur, *An Example for All the Land: Emancipation and the Struggle over Equality in Washington, D.C.* (Chapel Hill: University of North Carolina Press, 2010), 55.

9. Lewis, *Washington*, 173–75.

10. A. C. Richards to the Department of Metropolitan Police, in ST, *Narrative*, 127–29.

11. Lewis, *Washington*, 176.

12. Allen C. Guelzo, "Public Sentiment Is Everything: Abraham Lincoln and the Power of Public Opinion," *The Cupola: Scholarship at Gettysburg College: Civil War Era Studies Faculty Publications*, 2014, 171.

13. "Downstairs at the White House: The Blue Room," Mr. Lincoln's White House, accessed March 21, 2022, http://www.mrlincolnswhitehouse.org/the

-white-house/downstairs-at-the-white-house/downstairs-white-house-blue
-room/.

14. DeNeen L. Brown, "Frederick Douglass Needed to See Lincoln: Would the President Meet with a Former Slave?" *Washington Post*, February 14, 2018, https://www.washingtonpost.com/news/retropolis/wp/2018/02/14/frederick -douglass-needed-to-see-lincoln-would-the-president-meet-with-a-former -slave/?noredirect=on&utm_term=.b914c091a9c8.

15. [Lucy Colman], *National Anti-Slavery Standard*, November 26, 1864.

16. Lucy Colman, *Reminiscences* (London: Forgotten Books, 2018; original 1891), 66.

17. Elizabeth Keckley, *Behind the Scenes . . . Thirty Years a Slave, and Four Years in the White House* (Columbia, SC: Loki's Publishing, 2019; original 1868), 43.

18. [Fred Tomkins], "Reception at Washington," *Liverpool (UK) Mercury*, March 22, 1865, 3.

19. "Downstairs at the White House."

20. Colman, *Reminiscences*, 66–67.

21. Lewis, *Washington*, 177.

22. "Letter from Sojourner Truth: The Story of Her Interview with the President," *National Anti-Slavery Standard*, December 17, 1864. This article is the basis for my account of Truth's meeting with Lincoln, except where otherwise indicated.

23. *Anti-Slavery Reporter*, March 1, 1865, with thanks to Gilletta McGraw.

24. "Presentation of a Bible to the President," *New York Times*, Sept. 11, 1864, https://timesmachine.nytimes.com/timesmachine/1864/09/11/issue.html?ac tion=click&contentCollection=Archives&module=LedeAsset&region=Archive Body&pgtype=article.

25. ST, *Narrative*, 122.

26. Colman, *Reminiscences*, 68–69.

27. "Letter from Sojourner Truth," December 17, 1864.

28. [Lucy Colman], *National Anti-Slavery Standard*, November 26, 1864. Much later in her life, she included in her memoir a very negative interpretation of the visit with Lincoln. See Colman, *Reminiscences*, 66–67.

29. "Letter from Sojourner Truth," December 17, 1864.

30. CM, *Sojourner Truth*, 73; MW, *Truth's America*, 223; NIP, *Sojourner Truth*, 123.

31. "Letter from Sojourner Truth," December 17, 1864; CM, *Sojourner Truth*, 119.

32. Truth to [Amy Post], Mason's Island, VA, November 3, 1864, Historical Society of Battle Creek Archive, typed transcript.

33. Anthony Gaughan, *The Last Battle of the Civil War: United States versus Lee, 1861–1883* (Baton Rouge: Louisiana State University Press, 2011), 30.

34. Map of Freedmen's Village, National Museum of African American History and Culture, Transitions in Freedom, Records from the Freedmen's Bureau, accessed March 21, 2022, https://janelevinedesign.com/nmaahc/.

35. "The Small Pox," *Liberator*, April 14, 1865, 3.

36. NIP, *Sojourner Truth*, 214.

37. Allan Johnston, *Surviving Freedom: The Black Community of Washington, D.C., 1860–1880* (New York: Garland, 1993), 122.

38. "The Freedmen," *Washington Evening Star*, May 8, 1856, 1.

39. CM, *Sojourner Truth*, 159.

40. G. B. Carse, "Sojourner Truth among the Freedmen," *National Anti-Slavery Standard*, December 17, 1864.

41. Wendy E. Chmielewski, "Sojourner Truth: Utopian Vision and Search for Community, 1797–1883," in *Women in Spiritual and Communitarian Societies in the United States*, ed. Wendy E. Chmielewski, Louis J. Kern, and Marilyn Klee-Hartzell (Syracuse, NY: Syracuse University Press, 1993), 35.

42. "Letter from Sojourner Truth," December 17, 1864.

43. Eric Foner, *Reconstruction: America's Unfinished Revolution, 1863–1877* (New York: Harper Perennial, 2014), 146.

44. Masur, *An Example*, 61, 68.

45. Carse, "Sojourner Truth among the Freedmen."

46. CM, *Sojourner Truth*, 142.

47. ST, *Narrative*, 122, 123.

48. Truth and Mrs. E. M. Rhoades, in *National Anti-Slavery Standard*, October 19, 1876.

49. CM, *Sojourner Truth*, 145.

50. Truth to "Dear Friend," in *National Anti-Slavery Standard*, December 17, 1864. CM, *Sojourner Truth*, 120, 121, identifies this friend as Rowland Johnson, "a New Jersey Quaker and supporter of Lincoln whom Truth had visited on her way to Washington." Truth gave Johnson "permission to publish as much of the letter as he thought suitable."

51. Thavolia Glymph, *The Women's Fight: The Civil War's Battles for Home, Freedom, and Nation* (Chapel Hill: University of North Carolina Press, 2020), 180.

52. Gaughan, *Last Battle*, 31; see also Glymph, *The Women's Fight*, 181.

53. Masur, *An Example*, 75.

54. MW, *Truth's America*, 320.

55. ST, *Narrative*, 123–24.

56. "Sojourner Truth," *Cleveland Daily Leader*, February 16, 1865, 1.

57. MW, *Truth's America*, 323, 317.

58. [Tomkins], "Reception at Washington," 3.

59. Fred Tomkins, *Jewels in Ebony* (London: British and Foreign Freedmen's Aid Society, 1870), 1–6.

60. Keckley, *Behind the Scenes*, 53.

61. Tomkins, *Jewels in Ebony*, 1, 2.

62. Keckley, *Behind the Scenes*, 53.

63. Martha Hodes, *Mourning Lincoln* (New Haven: Yale University Press, 2015), 65–66, 80.

64. MW, *Truth's America*, 322.

65. NIP, *Sojourner Truth*, 216. Carse's replacement, Captain Alfred W. Lomas, arrived in June 1865.

66. Truth to Post, October 1, 1865, Historical Society of Battle Creek Archive, typed transcript.

67. Henry Louis Gates Jr., *Stony the Road: Reconstruction, White Supremacy, and the Rise of Jim Crow* (New York: Penguin Press, 2019), 20.

Chapter 15

1. Keith E. Melder, "Angel of Mercy in Washington: Josephine Griffing and the Freedmen, 1864–1872," *Records of the Columbia Historical Society, Washington, D.C.*, vol. 63/65 (1963), 251–55.

2. Eric Foner, *Reconstruction: America's Unfinished Revolution, 1863–1877* (New York: Harper Perennial, 2014), 28, 68–69.

3. Eric Foner and John A. Garraty, eds., "Freedmen's Bureau," in *Reader's Companion to American History* (Boston: Houghton Mifflin, 1991), 420.

4. ST, *Narrative*, 124.

5. Carlton Fletcher, "The Colored Home," Glover Park History, accessed March 21, 2022, https://gloverparkhistory.com/estates-and-farms/burleith/the-colored-home/.

6. Lucy Colman, *Reminiscences* (London: Forgotten Books, 2018; original 1891), 61–63.

7. Truth to Post, October 1, 1865, Historical Society of Battle Creek Archive (hereafter HSBCA), typed transcript.

8. MW, *Truth's America*, 323.

9. Kate Masur, *An Example for All the Land: Emancipation and the Struggle over Equality in Washington, D.C.* (Chapel Hill: University of North Carolina Press, 2010), 101, 102.

10. MC, *Sojourner Truth*, 130; *Statutes at Large*, US Congressional Documents and Debates, 1774–1875, 13:536–37, Library of Congress, accessed July 17, 2018, https://memory.loc.gov/cgi bin/ampage?collId=llsl&fileName=013/llsl013.db&recNum =566&itemLink=r%3Fammem%2Fhlaw%3A%40field%28DOCID%2B%40lit%28slo131%29%29%230130809&linkText=1.

11. Masur, *An Example*, 107.

12. ST, *Narrative*, 126.

13. Truth to Post, October 1, 1865.

14. "Sojourner Truth and Her Talks," *Syracuse (NY) Standard*, HSBCA, April 12, 1871.

15. Masur, *An Example*, 109.

16. Foner, *Reconstruction*, 28.

17. Foner, *Reconstruction*, 104.

18. "Sojourner Truth," *Fall River (MA) Daily News*, December 17, 1874, 1.

19. Eric Foner, *Forever Free: The Story of Emancipation and Reconstruction* (New York: Vintage Books, 2006), 113.

20. Colman, *Reminiscences*, 68.

21. MW, *Truth's America*, 324.

22. Ron Chernow, *Grant* (New York: Penguin Press, 2017), 568–69.

23. Beverly Gordon, *Bazaars and Fair Ladies: The History of the American Fundraising Fair* (Knoxville: University of Tennessee Press, 1998), 73, 56.

24. "The Tableaux Exhibition," *Daily National Republican*, January 3, 1866, 2.

25. Melder, "Angel of Mercy," 259.

26. Masur, *An Example*, 60, 69.

27. Toni Morrison, *Beloved* (New York: Knopf, 1998), 112.

28. Foner, *Reconstruction*, 84.

29. Allan Johnston, *Surviving Freedom: The Black Community of Washington, D.C., 1860–1880* (New York: Garland, 1993), 187–89.

30. Truth to Post, July 3, 1866, HSBCA, typed transcript.

31. Foner, *Reconstruction*, xxii.

32. Leslie Schwalm, *Emancipation's Diaspora: Race and Reconstruction in the Upper Midwest* (Chapel Hill: University of North Carolina Press, 2009), 81–84, 106.

33. ST, *Narrative*, 186.

34. CM, *Sojourner Truth*, 144–45.

35. "Brought Here by Sojourner Truth, Local Man Recalls Famous Worker," *Battle Creek Enquirer*, May 29, 1929, 7.

36. Truth to Post, August 25, 1867, HSBCA, typed transcript.

37. Truth to Post, November 4, 1867, HSBCA, typed transcript.

38. "Letter from Sojourner Truth," *National Anti-Slavery Standard*, October 19, 1866.

39. Martin Ashley, "Frances Titus: Sojourner's 'Trusted Scribe,'" *Heritage Battle Creek, a Journal of Local History* 38 (Fall 1997): 38, 36.

40. CM, *Sojourner Truth*, 201, 202.

41. Martin L. Ashley and Mary G. Butler, "Milestones in a Life of Truth," *Heritage Battle Creek, a Journal of Local History* 38 (Fall 1997): 27.

42. Truth, letter to *National Anti-Slavery Standard*, April 27, 1867.

43. George W. Taylor, *National Anti-Slavery Standard*, September 26, 1868.

44. "Sojourner Truth," *St. Albans (VT) Weekly*, October 15, 1869, 2.

45. Amy Post, *National Anti-Slavery Standard*, December 18, 1868.

46. "Sojourner Truth," *Daily Columbus Ohio State*, April 6, 1868, 1.

47. Truth to Post, January 18 and February 8, 1869, HSBCA, typed transcript.

48. ST, *Narrative*, 132–35.

49. Foner, *Reconstruction*, 28.

50. David Blight, *Frederick Douglass* (New York: Simon & Schuster, 2018), 537.

51. CM, *Sojourner Truth*, 156.

52. ST, *Narrative*, 197, 184, 186.

53. Giles Stebbins memorial of Sojourner Truth, *Detroit Tribune*, November 3, 1885, quoted in NIP, *Sojourner Truth*, 208.

54. ST, *Narrative*, 185.

55. "The Marble Room," United States Senate, accessed March 21, 2022, https://www.senate.gov/artandhistory/history/minute/The_Marble_Room.htm.

56. ST, *Narrative*, 206.

57. ST, *Narrative*, 132, 133.

58. NIP, *Sojourner Truth*, 236.

59. Today this building is known as "Old City Hall" or "District of Columbia City Hall"; it stands on D Street between Fourth and Fifth Streets NW.

60. "Emancipation and the Fifteenth Amendment: The Celebration Yesterday," *Washington Evening Star*, April 14, 1870, 4.

61. *Chicago Inter Ocean*, August 27, 1872, 4.

62. Chernow, *Grant*, xxii–xxiii, 704, 707–9.

63. "A Word from Sojourner Truth as to How the Colored People Feel in the Present Canvass," *New York Times*, August 22, 1872, 8.

64. "Truth," *Brooklyn Union*, August 22, 1872, 2.

65. "Sojourner Truth Rebukes Mr. Sumner," *National Republican*, August 27, 1872, 2.

66. Frederick Douglass, "U. S. Grant and the Colored People," Daniel Murray Pamphlet Collection, Library of Congress, accessed March 21, 2022, https://www.loc.gov/resource/lcrbmrp.t2407/?sp=1, 6 (emphasis mine). See also Chernow, *Grant*, xxii.

67. Campbell Robertson, "Over 2,000 Black People Were Lynched from 1865 to 1877, Study Finds," *New York Times*, June 16, 2020, updated June 29, 2020, https://www.nytimes.com/2020/06/16/us/reconstruction-violence.html.

68. ST, *Narrative*, 155.

Chapter 16

1. Eric Foner, *Reconstruction: America's Unfinished Revolution, 1863–1877* (New York: Harper Perennial, 2014), 25.

2. "Address of Frances D. Gage," *Proceedings of the First Anniversary of the American Equal Rights Association, Held at the Church of the Puritans, New York, May 9 and 10, 1867, Phonographic Report by H. M. Parkhurst* (hereafter *Proceedings*), General Collections, Library of Congress, accessed March 21, 2022, http://www.loc.gov/resource/rbnawsa.n3542.

3. ST, *Narrative*, 191.

4. Keith E. Melder, "Angel of Mercy in Washington: Josephine Griffing and the Freedmen, 1864–1872," *Records of the Columbia Historical Society, Washington, D.C.*, vol. 63/65 (1963), 268.

5. David Blight, *Frederick Douglass* (New York: Simon & Schuster, 2018), 488.

6. Faye E. Dudden, *Fighting Chance: The Struggle over Woman Suffrage and Black Suffrage in Reconstruction America* (New York: Oxford University Press, 2011), 8.

7. Leslie Schwalm, *Emancipation's Diaspora: Race and Reconstruction in the Upper Midwest* (Chapel Hill: University of North Carolina Press, 2009), 176, 177.

8. "Mr. Wendell Phillips' Speech: A Corrected Version," *New York Times*, June 10, 1865, 2.

9. "American Equal Rights Association," American History USA, accessed March 21, 2022, https://www.americanhistoryusa.com/topic/american-equal -rights-association/.

10. Dudden, *Fighting Chance*, 62.

11. Sojourner Truth, *Proceedings*. All quotations from Truth's speeches at the May 9 and 10, 1867, meeting of the AERA are from this source.

12. Frances Gage, *Proceedings*.

13. Teresa Zackodnik, *Press, Platform, Pulpit: Black Feminist Publics in the Era of Reform* (Knoxville: University of Tennessee Press, 2011), 68.

14. George Downing and Elizabeth Cady Stanton, *Proceedings*.

15. Josephine Griffing, *Proceedings*.

16. Truth, *Proceedings*.

17. Dudden, *Fighting Chance*, 8, 10.

18. Letter from Stanton to Edward M. Davis, April 10, 1869, Massachusetts History, Collections Online, accessed March 21, 2022, http://www.masshist.org /database/3314?mode=transcript.

19. Dudden, *Fighting Chance*, 71, 11, 169 (quoting the newspaper of Stanton and Anthony, *Revolution*, February 4, 1869).

20. ST, *Narrative*, 204.

21. Andrea Moore Kerr, *Lucy Stone: Speaking Out for Equality* (New Brunswick, NJ: Rutgers University Press, 1992), 153.

22. "[Sojourner Truth Speech at] American Woman Suffrage Association, Steinway Hall, New York City May 11, 1870," in *Sojourner Truth as Orator: Wit, Story, and Song*, ed. Suzanne Pullon Fitch and Roseann M. Mandziuk (Westport, CT: Greenwood, 1997), 175.

23. ST, *Narrative*, 137.

24. "*Providence Daily Journal* Nov. 1 1870," in Fitch and Mandziuk, *Sojourner Truth as Orator*, 177–78.

25. Rosalyn Terborg-Penn, "African American Women and the Vote: An Overview," in *African American Women and the Vote, 1837–1965*, ed. Ann Gordon (Amherst: University of Massachusetts Press, 1997), 15, 16.

26. Dudden, *Fighting Chance*, 182.

Chapter 17

1. ST, *Narrative*, 144, 145. This story was told in heavy dialect, which I edited.

2. CM, *Sojourner Truth*, 158.

3. "Letter from Sojourner Truth," *National Standard*, formerly *National Anti-Slavery Standard*, March 4, 1871.

4. ST, *Narrative*, 159.

5. "*Providence Daily Journal* Nov. 1 1870," in *Sojourner Truth as Orator: Wit, Story, and Song*, ed. Suzanne Pullon Fitch and Roseann M. Mandziuk (Westport, CT: Greenwood, 1997), 177.

6. "Letter from Sojourner Truth," *National Standard*, March 4, 1871.

7. "Settlement in Kansas"; Kansapedia, accessed March 21, 2022, https://www.kshs.org/kansapedia/settlement-in-kansas/14546; "African Americans in Kansas," Kansapedia, accessed March 21, 2022, https://www.kshs.org/kansapedia/african-americans-in-kansas/17878.

8. ST, *Narrative*, 198, 215.

9. Seth Hunt, letter to *National Standard*, March 4, 1871.

10. Sojourner Truth, "Land for the Freed-People," *National Standard*, March 4, 1871.

11. "Sojourner Truth and Her Talks," *Battle Creek (MI) Journal*, April 12, 1871, Historical Society of Battle Creek Archive.

12. ST, *Narrative*, 178.

13. MW, *Truth's America*, 361, 362.

14. D. H. Morgan (Frances Titus's brother) to Mary K. Gale, September 27, 1871, Sojourner Truth Papers, Library of Congress.

15. "Settlement in Kansas."

16. "Sojourner Truth in Quindaro," *Wyandotte (KS) Gazette*, January 4, 1872, 3.

17. "Sojourner Truth," *Western Home Journal*, October 12, 1871, 3.

18. ST, *Narrative*, 164.

19. "A Reservation for the Freedmen," *Daily Kansas Tribune*, October 6, 1871, 3.

20. "Sojourner Truth," *Wyandotte (KS) Gazette*, February 1, 1872, 3.

21. ST, *Narrative*, 165.

22. "Sojourner Truth: Extracts from Her Lecture on Capital Punishment, Lansing, Michigan June 3, 1881," in Fitch and Mandziuk, *Sojourner Truth as Orator*, 135–36.

23. ST, *Narrative*, 215.

24. ST, *Narrative*, 165.

25. CM, *Sojourner Truth*, 160; NIP, *Sojourner Truth*, 241; IR, *Sojourner Truth*, 114.

26. MW, *Truth's America*, 366–67, 453n27.

27. ST to Post, August 26, 1873, Historical Society of Battle Creek Archive.

28. "Sojourner Truth," *South Bend (IN) Tribune*, October 6, 1873, 1.

29. "Friends Meeting House," *Baltimore Sun*, March 5, 1874, 2.

30. "Miscellany, Sojourner Truth," *Fall River (MA) Daily News*, December 17, 1874, 1.

31. CM, *Sojourner Truth*, 163; ST, *Narrative*, 167.

32. Sojourner Truth, "Personal Reminiscences," *Chicago Inter Ocean*, August 13, 1879.

33. CM, *Sojourner Truth*, 163, 164; NIP, *Sojourner Truth*, 242.

34. Sojourner Truth, letter to *Chicago Daily Inter Ocean*, April 16, 1881, 9, in Fitch and Mandziuk, *Sojourner Truth as Orator*, 203–4.

35. MW, *Truth's America*, 368.

36. Kate Masur, *An Example for All the Land: Emancipation and the Struggle over Equality in Washington, D.C.* (Chapel Hill: University of North Carolina Press, 2010), 94.

37. ST, *Narrative*, 168.

38. Masur, *An Example*, 112.

39. "A Remarkable Old Lady: An Interesting Interview with Sojourner Truth," *National Republican*, April 21, 1874, 8.

40. "A Remarkable Old Lady," 8.

41. "May Day Concert," *National Republican*, May 2, 1874, 8.

42. "Sojourner Truth," *Watertown (WI) News*, May 20, 1874, 6.

43. "Sojourner Truth," *Los Angeles Evening Express*, June 11, 1874, 3.

44. F. Titus to Miss Mary K. Gale, Battle Creek, MI, March 31, 1876, Sojourner Truth Papers, Library of Congress.

45. MW, *Truth's America*, 368, 369.

46. NIP, *Sojourner Truth*, 242; CM, *Sojourner Truth*, 215, 202.

47. ST, *Narrative*, 192.

48. Martin Ashley, "Frances Titus: Sojourner's 'Trusted Scribe,'" *Heritage Battle Creek, a Journal of Local History* 38 (Fall 1997): 40.

49. CM, *Sojourner Truth*, 202, 203.

50. Ashley, "Frances Titus," 35, 39. (The first of Truth's scrapbooks is in the University of Michigan Library, Bentley Historical Library, Bernice Bryant Lowe Papers. The other two have been lost.)

51. ST, *Narrative*, 171.

52. ST, *Narrative*, 152, 153.

53. "Sojourner Truth: Extracts from Her Lecture on Capital Punishment," 136.

54. Sojourner Truth, "Personal Reminiscences," *Chicago Inter Ocean*, August 13, 1879, 3.

55. NIP, *Sojourner Truth*, 254, 261.

56. Judith Castleberry, "Black Women's Holy Ghost Work, Then and Now," *Black Perspectives*, July 28, 2017, https://www.aaihs.org/black-womens-holy-ghost-work-then-and-now/.

Chapter 18

1. "Sojourner Truth" *Rochester (NY) Democrat and Chronicle*, December 24, 1875, 8.

2. *Reading (PA) Times*, October 14, 1876.

3. Sojourner Truth, "Personal Reminiscences," *Chicago Inter Ocean*, August 13, 1879.

4. Eric Foner, *Reconstruction: America's Unfinished Revolution, 1863–1877* (New York: Harper Perennial, 2014), 148, xxv.

5. *Detroit Free Press*, October 3, 1879, 3.

6. "A Remarkable Old Lady," *National Republican*, April 21, 1874.

7. *Reading (PA) Times*, October 14, 1876.

8. Martin Ashley, "Frances Titus: Sojourner's 'Trusted Scribe,'" *Heritage Battle Creek, a Journal of Local History* 38 (Fall 1997): 40.

9. "Some Notable Women, and the Curious Stories Told of Them," *Burlington (VT) Free Press*, August 1, 1878, 4.

10. "Sojourner Truth," *Brooklyn (NY) Times Union*, December 7, 1878, 2.

11. CM, *Sojourner Truth*, 243, 244, citing *New York World*, December 7, 1878; *Vineland (NJ) Weekly*, December 25, 1869; *Lansing (MI) Republican*, June 7, 1881; *Battle Creek (MI) Nightly Moon*, November 26, 1883; *Chicago Inter Ocean*, Nov. 27, 1883.

12. *Livingston Daily County (MI) Press and Argus*, July 10, 1879; "Sojourner Truth at Home," *Detroit Free Press*, July 4, 1879, 6.

13. Nell Irvin Painter, *Exodusters: Black Migration to Kansas after Reconstruction* (New York: Norton, 1986), 237.

14. "Views on the Recent Exodus: Lecture Last Night at the Langley Ave. M. E. Church," *Chicago Inter Ocean*, August 13, 1879, 3.

15. "Personals: Sojourner Truth," *Chicago Tribune*, March 8, 1880, 4.

16. Foner, *Reconstruction*, 600.

17. James Leiker, "Race Relations in the Sunflower State," *Kansas History*, Review Essay Series, Autumn 2002, https://kshs.org/publicat/history/2002au tumn_leiker.pdf, 222.

18. "Sojourner's Journey: What the Old Lady Hopes to Accomplish Out in Kansas," *Junction City (KS) Tribune*, August 21, 1879, 1; *Chicago Daily Inter Ocean*, August 13, 1879, 3; "Sojourner Truth," *Chicago Tribune*, August 12, 1879, 7.

19. Sojourner Truth, "Public Letter," *Chicago Inter Ocean*, April 16, 1881, 9.

20. *Topeka (KS) Daily Capital*, October 13, 1879, 4.

21. Darcy Grimaldo Grigsby, *Enduring Truths: Sojourner's Shadows and Substance* (Chicago: University of Chicago Press, 2015), 186, quoted from the *Topeka (KS) Colored Citizen*, October 11, 1879.

22. "Tidings of Sojourner Truth: A Letter from Frances Titus to Mary K. Gale," *Boston Journal*, December 3, 1879, Sojourner Truth Papers, Library of Congress.

23. "Mass Meeting at Second Baptist Church," *Topeka (KS) Daily Capital*, October 8, 1879, 4.

24. *Smith County (KS) Pioneer*, October 17, 1879, 2.

25. Unidentified newspaper clipping, Collections of the Manuscript Division, Library of Congress.

26. *Topeka (KS) State Journal*, October 15, 1879, 4.

27. "Tidings of Sojourner Truth."

28. Ashley, "Frances Titus," 41.

Chapter 19

1. "Sojourner Truth: Life and Adventures of a Very Remarkable Colored Woman," *Chicago Tribune*, November 26, 1880, 7.

2. *Christian Recorder* (African Methodist Episcopal paper), June 2, 1881.

3. "Prohibition," Kansapedia, accessed March 22, 2022, https://www.kshs.org/kansapedia/prohibition/14523.

4. Truth to *Chicago Inter Ocean*, April 16, 1881, 9, in *Sojourner Truth as Orator: Wit, Story, and Song*, ed. Suzanne Pullon Fitch and Roseann M. Mandziuk (Westport, CT: Greenwood, 1997), 203–4.

5. *Owasso (MI) Times*, November 30, 1883, 8.

6. "Sojourner Truth: Extracts from Her Lecture on Capital Punishment," *Battle Creek (MI) Nightly Moon*, June 8, 1881, in Fitch and Mandziuk, *Sojourner Truth as Orator*, 135–36.

7. Darcy Grimaldo Grigsby, *Enduring Truths: Sojourner's Shadows and Substance* (Chicago: University of Chicago Press, 2015), 186.

8. "Sojourner Truth: Extracts from Her Lecture on Capital Punishment," 135–36.

9. Crystal Toscano, "The Voice of Sojourner Truth," *From the Stacks*, New-York Historical Society Museum and Library, accessed March 22, 2022, http://blog.nyhistory.org/the-voice-of-sojourner-truth/.

10. Grigsby, *Enduring Truths*, 178, 187, 184.

11. ST, *Narrative*, 234.

12. NIP, *Sojourner Truth*, 250.

13. ST, *Narrative*, 228.

14. CM, *Sojourner Truth*, 243.

15. "Sojourner Truth Dead," *Battle Creek (MI) Nightly Moon*, November 28, 1883, Willard Library, Battle Creek.

16. NIP, *Sojourner Truth*, 254–55.

17. ST, *Narrative*, 230.

18. *Battle Creek (MI) Daily Journal*, November 30, 1883, Willard Library, Battle Creek.

19. ST, *Narrative*, 230–31.

20. Sojourner Truth, public letter, *Chicago Daily Inter Ocean*, January 1, 1881, 4, in Fitch and Mandziuk, *Sojourner Truth as Orator*, 201.

Appendix

1. *Anti-Slavery Bugle*, ed. Marius Robinson, June 21, 1851, in *Sojourner Truth as Orator: Wit, Story, and Song*, ed. Suzanne Pullon Fitch and Roseann M. Mandziuk (Westport, CT: Greenwood, 1997), 107–8.

2. Mrs. F. D. Gage, "Sojourner Truth" *National Anti-Slavery Standard*, May 2, 1863, Accessible Archives, accessed Feb. 24, 2021, https://www.accessible.com /accessible/print?AADocList=1&AADocStyle=&AAStyleFile=&AABeanName =toc1&AANextPage=/printFullDocFromXML.jsp&AACheck=2.1.1.6.1.

3. Sojourner Truth, "Ain't I a Woman?" in *Feminism: The Essential Historical Writings*, ed. Miriam Schneir (New York: Vintage Books, 1994; original 1972), 94–95.

Index

Titles published in the

LIBRARY OF RELIGIOUS BIOGRAPHY SERIES

*The Kingdom Is Always but Coming: A Life of **Walter Rauschenbusch***
by Christopher H. Evans

*Strength for the Fight: The Life and Faith of **Jackie Robinson***
by Gary Scott Smith

*A Christian and a Democrat: A Religious Life of **Franklin D. Roosevelt***
by John F. Woolverton with James D. Bratt

***Francis Schaeffer** and the Shaping of Evangelical America*
by Barry Hankins

***Harriet Beecher Stowe**: A Spiritual Life*
by Nancy Koester

***Billy Sunday** and the Redemption of Urban America*
by Lyle W. Dorsett

***Howard Thurman** and the Disinherited: A Religious Biography*
by Paul Harvey

*We Will Be Free: The Life and Faith of **Sojourner Truth***
by Nancy Koester

*Assist Me to Proclaim: The Life and Hymns of **Charles Wesley***
by John R. Tyson

*Prophetess of Health: A Study of **Ellen G. White***
by Ronald L. Numbers

***George Whitefield**: Evangelist for God and Empire*
by Peter Y. Choi

*The Divine Dramatist: **George Whitefield** and
the Rise of Modern Evangelicalism*
by Harry S. Stout

*Liberty of Conscience: **Roger Williams** in America*
by Edwin S. Gaustad